DEVOTION

TRI◎◎S

*Each TRIOS book
addresses an important
theme in critical theory,
philosophy, or cultural
studies through three
extended essays written
in close collaboration by
leading scholars.*

DEVOTION

THREE INQUIRIES IN RELIGION,
LITERATURE, AND POLITICAL
IMAGINATION

CONSTANCE M.
Furey

SARAH
Hammerschlag

AMY
Hollywood

The University of Chicago Press
Chicago and London

The University of Chicago Press, Chicago 60637
The University of Chicago Press, Ltd., London
© 2021 by The University of Chicago
Published 2021
Printed in the United States of America

30 29 28 27 26 25 24 23 22 21   1 2 3 4 5

ISBN-13: 978-0-226-81610-4 (cloth)
ISBN-13: 978-0-226-81612-8 (paper)
ISBN-13: 978-0-226-81611-1 (e-book)
DOI: https://doi.org/10.7208/chicago/9780226816111.001.0001

Library of Congress Cataloging-in-Publication Data

Names: Furey, Constance M., author. | Hammerschlag, Sarah, author. | Hollywood, Amy M., 1963– author.
Title: Devotion : three inquiries in religion, literature, and political imagination / Constance M. Furey, Sarah Hammerschlag, Amy Hollywood.
Other titles: Trios (Chicago, Ill.)
Description: Chicago : University of Chicago Press, 2021. | Series: Trios
Identifiers: LCCN 2021017541 | ISBN 9780226816104 (cloth) | ISBN 9780226816128 (paperback) | ISBN 9780226816111 (ebook)
Subjects: LCSH: Kofman, Sarah. | Religion and literature. | Devotion. | Religion and politics.
Classification: LCC PN49 .D466 2021 | DDC 809/.93382—dc23
LC record available at https://lccn.loc.gov/2021017541

♾ This paper meets the requirements of ANSI/NISO Z39.48-1992 (Permanence of Paper).

To criticise is to appreciate, to appropriate, to take intellectual possession, to establish in fine a relation with the criticised thing and make it one's own.

HENRY JAMES, preface to *What Maisie Knew* (New York edition)

CONTENTS

INTRODUCTION

Amy Hollywood, Sarah Hammerschlag,
and Constance M. Furey

> History is incomplete: when this book is read, the smallest
> schoolboy will know the outcome of the current war. At the
> moment I am writing, no one can give me the schoolboy's
> knowledge.
>
> GEORGES BATAILLE, *Guilty*

> That's why he was devouring two or three books a day—to remove
> himself every minute that he possibly could from the madness of
> this life.
>
> PHILIP ROTH, *Operation Shylock*

Writing in the midst of the Second World War, Georges Bataille
directed his words to readers living in a future he could not envision: a Europe governed by fascism, in which all the Jews were
dead, all the democracies destroyed, and all the resistors murdered, or one in which some as yet unimaginable set of forces
had been let loose by the Allies' defeat of the Axis Powers. So
often, like Bataille, we have an acute sense of imminent danger
and a much less clear understanding of what might defeat it, or
of what might rise up in its place. Again, history is always incomplete. Standing on a precipice, with war or natural disaster,
famine, plague, or economic collapse clearly in sight, we become
intensely aware of the void into which we speak. Bataille lived

one of those moments in 1939. We are living another now, in the spring of 2020, a moment of radical uncertainty; the future purport of any words we write is impossible to envision. Even the current sense of emergency might, in some future moment, seem exaggerated, might, if we are lucky—or unlucky; it depends on which crisis we are discussing—be difficult to remember. We just don't—we simply can't—know.

Each of us has written out of and to similar situations in the past, although none as acute or pressing as those facing us today. What brings the three of us together as thinkers, writers, teachers, and friends is the shared conviction that reading helps us live with and through the unknown. The questions of what reading does to us, where it takes us, who we become because of our relation to textual pasts, presents, and futures might seem far removed from the urgency of political and social crisis. The charge of escapism, to which Bataille was subject, always lurks. But we share a conviction that the nature of reading raises questions fundamental to how we think about our political futures, how we imagine modes of human relation, and how we envision alternatives to conceptions of the putatively transparent liberal subject—or, perhaps better, the subject whose eventual transparency is posited as an ideal—that undergird much current political discourse.

It matters that Philip Roth's words are those of a character in a novel, even if that character shares Roth's name and is describing the reading practices of yet another character, an Israeli soldier caught within the intractable folds of a historical-political crisis in which he is complicit but over which he has little control. It matters, too, that the relationship between the Georges Bataille of *Guilty* and Georges Bataille, the historical human being, is utterly uncertain. It might seem obvious that engaging with a fictional character alters our experience of subjectivity and of interpersonal relationships, but each of our essays suggests that fictionality is in some crucial way a feature of textuality itself. We do not intend to equate the writing of

history with that of fiction—even less so the historical with
the fictional; the intractable realities of past and present lives
and events cannot be denied. But we do insist that the literary
effects we associate with fictionality haunt language; thinking
with those texts explicitly identified as fiction helps us register
these effects and thus see them operative elsewhere. The seemingly commonsensical distinctions between the fictional and
the historical, or the fictional and the real, despite the crucial
importance particularly of the former pairing, are unable to get
at the profound effects of reading itself.[1] Our experience of identification with Bataille's and Roth's words, then, involves us in a
process in which our desire to know and determine what is the
case is both elicited and thwarted by the experience of reading
itself. If reading is an escape, it is into another form of never fully
resolvable uncertainty.

For the past couple of years, the three of us have been in-
volved in a series of overlapping conversations about religion,
literature, and the nature of reading, the results of which follow
here and in our individual essays. We have framed this conversation as one about how to enact faith in the future and fidelity
to the texts under discussion and to readers yet to come. This
has led us—to our own surprise—to characterize our interest
in reading in terms of devotion. The essays we have written are
simultaneously about devotion and perform it. Each suggests,
in its own manner and through its own particular stories, different ways to characterize the object of devotion and the stance
of the devout subject before it. We are not, however, interested
in commonplace conceptions of devotion, understood as a form
of slavish and unthinking subservience to a tradition, text, or
being; in fact, we argue this is precisely the wrong way to think
about what devotion is. To commit oneself to another, each of
us argues in different ways, is to undo the putative dichotomy
between freedom and tradition on which so many accounts of
literature and religion depend. Instead, Constance Furey writes
of vivification, energy, and artifice, Sarah Hammerschlag of

commentary, mimicry, and fetishism, Amy Hollywood of an-. archy, antinomianism, and atopia. Fictionality plays a vital role for all three of us. We make up a past, a present, perhaps a future, in which we can imagine, however briefly, living. (Imagine briefly? Live briefly? Probably both.) We are interested in literature, then, not as providing models for ethical, political, or religious life, but as creating the site in which the possible—and the impossible—transport the reader as reader, enabling new forms of thought, habits of mind, and modes of life to be enjoyed, reveled in, experimented with, thought through, deeply felt, sometimes rejected and experienced aversively (at least one of us has a very hard time reading Philip Roth, even *as* she is immersed in the vitality of his words)—in sum, at least for a period of time, inhabited.[2]

What we share is an understanding of devotion that takes the form of a pledge or a promise, a textual, temporal, and interpersonal means of engagement directed toward the future, in all its overwhelming uncertainty and unforeseeability. At the same time, devotion, both as a concept and as an affective mode, is always informed by the past; it is a bridge between past and future defined by commitment. The term *devotion* itself is irrevocably marked by its past, indeed by its religious past. In classical Latin it simply meant to dedicate by means of a vow, but during the Christian Middle Ages, the Latin word and its cognates in the romance languages were strongly associated with commitment specifically to God. Thomas Aquinas devotes a question of his *Summa Theologica* to defining *devotio*: for Thomas it is not an outwardly made and attested pledge, but instead a movement of the will, "an interior act" of religion, "nothing else than a resolve readily to give oneself to things concerning the service of God."[3] Questions about the relationship between the inner and the outer haunt the term, so that in the sixteenth century devotion often functions as a synonym for piety, and both are understood as stances toward God that can be feigned.[4] Hence Polonius's suggestion to Ophelia that with "devotion's visage and pious action we do sugar o'er the devil himself."[5]

At around the same time Shakespeare wrote these words, the term makes its way back into the realm of personal relations, referring to attachment to another, yet it never fully divests itself of the specific religious connotation it gained in the medieval context. In English, to speak of devotion to another person, text, or cause always carries a whiff of the idolatrous, a holdover from Christian usage in which commitment to anything other than God involves an overvaluation of the object. The lingering doubleness of the term is exactly the point; our essays show readers standing in a relation of devotion to texts in ways that undermine the opposition between a singular God and the multiplicity of idols. The very forms of false belief and counterfeit worship articulated and defined by Christians and Jews as idolatry (and, as Hammerschlag shows, also as fetishism) are defined as such because they threaten the naturalized hierarchies on which the monotheistic traditions rest. Christian and Jewish dismissals of idolatry are thus attempts to cover over the more complex and multiple modes of relation already present within these traditions by projecting them onto those characterized as outsiders.[6] It is in this sense that we invoke devotion: as a striving for fidelity that is always in some way unsure of, unsettled and challenged by, even if always also attached to, at home with, comforted by, its object. We are emphatic, then, in our commitment to the view that to read devoutly is *not* to engage in "uncritical reading."[7] Understood in this way, devotion links religion and literature, for, as all three of our essays reveal, historically, religious and literary modes of reading are always imbricated with each other. Those twinned concerns, moreover, are always tied, even if not reducible to, the political.

We see this in Furey's account of Sir Philip Sidney and Martin Luther on the Psalms, an analysis that focuses on the convergence of Sidney's and Luther's understanding of what it means to read faithfully. For both Sidney and Luther, Furey argues, devotional reading exceeds the content of the scriptural psalms because it is affected by and directed toward the formal features of the text, the ways in which the text vivifies itself and its readers through its use of voice, metaphor, and personification. Sidney's and Luther's emphasis on the way in which the text affects the reader, rather than the ways in which the reader interprets it, associates textual vivification with freedom *from* the natural limitations that constrain historians, philosophers, and other writers, according to Sidney, and the historical literalism Luther scathingly attributes to Jews and heretics. Crucially, for Luther and Sidney, and for Furey, this access to variable voices and multiple ways of apprehending a text's imaginative promise *is* devotion.

The politics of this devotion is apparent in the way the text locates the reader on the terrain where the real encounters the ideal. An individual reader finds what she already thinks and feels reflected in the many voices, personae, and metaphors of the psalms, Luther explains, but a new reality becomes available to those readers who receive what the text has to offer—the singular presence and promise of Christ. Sidney makes a corollary claim when he describes poetry as uniquely capable of conjuring what he calls a "golden" world *and* awakening readers' desire to inhabit it, without succumbing to the distractions of mere fantasy or the dangers of frivolous distractions. Neither writer offers a liberatory politics: Sidney maintains that poetry serves the realm by cultivating a reader's capacity for self-governance and restraint; Luther is explicit that devotion excludes any who fail to disavow interpretation, as he demands faithful readers must. Nevertheless, both writers' attention to what today we might call the emotional effect and transformative potential of literature—of writing, in other words, that refuses simply to mirror or assess the known world—together with their insistence that the texts they celebrate liberate the reader, invite us to think more deeply about the long history of Christian reading in relation to claims made today about what we read, and how, and why.

The links between religion, literature, and politics are also evident in Hammerschlag's reading of Sarah Kofman, whose

Jewish upbringing in France is both a forsaken past and the source for her seemingly inexhaustible stream of ink. Her voluminous writings are devoted to the work of commentary, not religious but philosophical and literary. Kofman works to undo the very distinction between philosophy and literature, finding in the practice of commentary a form of devotion that reveals the impulse toward sovereignty in the history of thought, while at the same time performing a divestment of her own inescapable drive toward knowledge and self-mastery. Hammerschlag, in commenting on Kofman, follows Kofman's lead, performing a mode of reading that calls into question her own aspirations for originality and truth, forcing her to recognize the ways in which these aspirations are analogous to the exercise of political dominance that can only assert power and control through the denigration of others. At the same time, in highlighting the themes of the fetish and the apotropaeon—the amulet, symbol, or act used to avert evil and misfortune—that appear across Kofman's corpus, Hammerschlag thinks with Kofman about the possibility that we can express our longing for security and protection in forms that advertise their fictionality and thus reveal these desires in ways that oscillate between expression and divestment, sometimes by employing humor, irony, or parody, sometimes through the act of repetition itself, strategies that expose Kofman's project to the charge that it is derivative. The fetish, then, a concept that has been wielded as a foil to prop up claims to spiritual purity, truth, and authenticity, emerges from this reading as a form to be reclaimed. Literature is shown to be a site in which we enact devotion while submitting it to the rule of the fetish, such that it only works as a site of investment when its truth is called into question.

Hollywood's readings of the poets H.D. and Susan Howe link religion and literature to politics in similar ways. For both H.D. and Howe the question of how to receive Christian and other religious pasts as ruin and as fragment is inseparable from the question of how to understand the task of survival in the face of world war and intense social and cultural crises. This labor not only takes poetic form but it is one for which poetic form provides a space that exceeds the fixity of place, allowing for the articulation of what Hollywood calls an atopic imaginary. In the face of contemporary critiques of dystopia as engendering political hopelessness and apathy, Hollywood explores the instability of the category itself. Bringing together work by the German jurist and political philosopher Carl Schmitt and the expatriate American H.D.'s wartime triptych, *Trilogy*, Hollywood shows that each engages in thought experiments that might be taken as dystopic, but just as easily as utopic— and hence, as refusing the sharp contrast on which these generic distinctions are made. Schmitt and H.D. also bring into play issues central to the work of the contemporary US poet Susan Howe, with which Hollywood closes her essay. Howe's poetry and essays, particularly in *The Nonconformist's Memorial*, lead Hollywood to posit the usefulness of the idea of atopia, a thinking of the past, present, and future in which the alpha privative points to a more radical kind of "no place" than that first posited by Thomas More's utopia. The alpha privative does not, as commonly misunderstood, simply negate a term or predicate, but instead asks that we try to think the term or predicate as without limitations, without the specificity that defined boundaries provide. At the center of Hollywood's argument is the idea that literature—and other works of the imagination—may be the necessary non-place, or place without the limitations of place, for thinking pasts and futures that are literally uninhabitable— and yet whose psychic, imaginative, intellectual, and affective existence is vital for human life.

All three of us share an interest in understanding the ways in which these modes of reading provide a resource for imagining forms of conduct that reject self-sovereignty as a starting point. Our readings converge around the conviction that claims to sovereignty are always illusions propped up by the violent denigration of others. We are led, through these readings, to reflect both on why it is so difficult to unsettle the liberal ideal of freedom as self-determination and to think about how the very activity of reading, with its investment in the words of another, and the accompanying practice of commentary, train us for different affective, intellectual, and embodied modes of life. There is no one political vision in these papers, but all are political: the focus on techne in Furey's sources foregrounds the question of *how* reading connects us to collective imaginaries; Hammerschlag's account of Kofman stages an encounter with the allure of authority; and Hollywood demonstrates the imagined worlds that can be built from a deep and critical devotion to historical and textual fragments called on and reimagined in the face of an unknown future.

In previous work, each of us has considered questions about devotion, faith, and mastery in relation to literature, religion, and politics. Although we work on very different archives, the diverse sources with which we engage—among them the writings of medieval Christian mystics and Renaissance poets, premodern and early modern theologians and postmodern critical theorists, Jewish philosophers and contemporary poets and novelists—all pose the challenge of how to think the relationship between religion and literature. Even as our sources and the specific topics with which we engage differ, our work has been animated by a shared interest in exploring the ways in which texts project authority, even as they unsettle any presumption of certainty or stability by requiring readers to attend to their artifice. Literature, Hammerschlag suggests, following the work of Jacques Derrida, particularly when theorized in relation to religion, "can produce a concept of freedom explicitly divorced from sovereignty."[8] She follows Derrida in defining literature as work that inherits from political and religious traditions, while divesting itself of these traditions' insistence on exclusivity and transcendent authority. With Derrida, Hammerschlag reads literature as the "imaginary" supplement to democracy. Understood in this way, she concludes that literature can reveal the opacity of the subject, without a divine guarantor assuring the subject that there is one who sees better.[9]

Yet religious texts can also perform similar work. This is true for the Jewish and Christian sources with which the three of us work, but perhaps even more so if one goes beyond these traditions to think with radically different imaginaries.[10] Religion not only places one in the world, creating an authoritative tradition in which one might live and understand oneself and one's community, but is also often disruptive, unsettling, utopic—in a word, critical.[11] It is essential that religion be thought in all of its variant modalities as we explore its relation to literature and to politics.

As Hollywood and Furey show elsewhere, opaque subjects are to be found in premodern sources, for appeals to transcendence can themselves become a site of "the undoing that enables communication."[12] This is true in the medieval mystics who have most intrigued Hollywood, and in the humanist, theological, and poetic sources Furey studies. The mode and effect of undoing varies, of course. Hollywood shows how mystic texts entwine the cataphatic with the apophatic, the naming and unnaming of the divine, variously asserting and denying claims about God and forever expanding the range of the human terms with which we necessarily think.[13] The somewhat more conventional and canonical sources Furey studies refuse the logic of sovereignty in different terms, by lingering over the nuances of spiritual discernment, insisting on the devotional value of errancy, and offering diverse and contested theories of verbal signification.[14]

It was this past work that motivated us to raise anew the question of how to think the relationship between religion and literature. While the specifically Christian version of the question of how religion and literature relate goes back, at the very least, to the moment when Augustine heard a voice telling him to "take and read," even within that very specific history the categories of religion and literature are highly unstable. We have no intention of invoking either term as though they indicate concepts that can be applied across cultures or employed univocally for different periods of history. At the same time, we recognize the necessity of working with these categories, particularly at this moment in time, given certain trends within the study both of literature and of religion.

Standing outside of literary studies proper, trained as each of is in the study of religion, we have been struck by the chorus of voices insisting that there is something unsatisfying about the way those professionally trained to engage with literature do their work. In mapping this uneasiness, many turn first to the late Eve Kosofsky Sedgwick's "Paranoid Reading and Reparative Reading, or, You're So Paranoid, You Probably Think This Essay Is about You." Sedgwick worries about the persistence of what she calls, following ideas first articulated by the philosopher Paul Ricoeur, a "hermeneutics of suspicion." Ricoeur has subsequently been taken up by a number of people in literary studies (and by scholars in other fields also weary of suspicion), yet it is not clear how fully he is read. For while Sedgwick's notion of "reparative reading" never loses hold of the important role played by critique, even internal to the act of reparation itself, subsequent scholars have been less precise in their analyses.[15]

For Ricoeur the crucial distinction is between two modes of interpretation or "two interpretations of interpretation." The first is interpretation as the "recollection of meaning," the second, as the "reduction of the illusions and lies of consciousness."[16] A host of contemporary literary critics, like Sedgwick, worry that their field has been overtaken by reduction, with no possibility for reading beyond paranoia, the symptom, or critique.[17] What this move misses, or what the appeals to Ricoeur scattered throughout this work miss, is that for Ricoeur "the recollection of meaning" must always pass through the process of critique.

In introducing his analysis of Freud as one of the three "masters of suspicion," along with Marx and Nietzsche, Ricoeur asks what stands in opposition to this interpretive stance:

> The contrary of suspicion, I will say bluntly, is faith. What faith? No longer, to be sure, the first faith of the simple soul, but rather the second faith of one who has been engaged in hermeneutics, faith that has undergone criticism, postcritical faith. Let us look for it in the series of philosophic decisions that secretly animate a phenomenology of religion and lie hidden even within its apparent neutrality. It is a rational faith, for it interprets; but it is a faith, because it seeks, through interpretation, a second naïveté. Phenomenology is its instrument of hearing, of recollection, of restoration of meaning. "Believe in order to understand, understand in order to believe"—such is its maxim; and its maxim is the "hermeneutic circle" itself of believing and understanding.[18]

Despite opening with the claim that the contrary of suspicion is faith, Ricoeur immediately claims that faith has always already been subject to criticism. This sets the stage for his account of the "masters of suspicion," who on his reading are less enemies of faith than critics who insist on the necessity of purifying it from of its mistakes, illusions, and prejudices. Hermeneutics, he argues, is marked by a double exigency, "animated by this double motivation: willingness to suspect, willingness to listen; vow of rigor, vow of obedience."[19]

Ricoeur, then, is postcritical before post-critique, yet he is also insistent that critique never ends. Oddly, we find ourselves heartened by remembering that in Ricoeur we find a thinker able to articulate the interplay between subservience and critique internal to the act of interpretation itself and, simultaneously, keenly aware of the limitations of Ricoeur's thought for helping us move forward in our projects. For Ricoeur maintains the belief that the idols must be toppled, the fetishes shown to be false gods, the sovereignty of the subject and of the religious other in their monotheistic singularity protected. He aspires to transparency, even as he knows that it is never possible this side of the grave. Our question, throughout this introduction and in the essays collected here, is what happens if we recognize that such transparency is not a good to which we should aspire? That instead, it masks a will to power destructive of those others through whose denigration (for Ricoeur, those "simple souls" with their naïve faith) we claim to know ourselves? Is there something about loving literature, the stance so many literary scholars fear has been denied them, that enables us to think critically about power even as we submit to the words of another—even as we love them, learn from them, are transported by them?[20]

One way in which we approach that question here is by considering in all three of our essays what it is for a text to exert power over us, what it is to feel the draw of its allure, sometimes even when we recognize the dangers of its vision. In reading Luther, Furey is attracted by his concept of a spiritualized text, but unsettled by its tethering to a condemnation of Jews and heretics. In reading Kofman, Hammerschlag considers not only the generosity of Kofman's method but also its perils, what she risked in allowing her body of work to be parceled out across the library's stacks, her contribution subordinated to the "great masters" about whom she writes. Hollywood reveals the ways in which Susan Howe's poetry is itself a meditation on what it means to inherit the legacy of those who murdered, raped, and stole in order to build a putatively new world, what it is to be devoted to texts that justified the killing of a king and both recorded and enabled the destruction of indigenous communities in the northeastern United States. Even the staging of our three texts together dramatizes this danger. In juxtaposing an essay on Luther that takes into account the fact that his approach to interpretation is tied to his condemnation of Jews with an essay about a writer and thinker whose work bears and lays bare the scars of Auschwitz, we aim to foreground the stark reality that texts can break faith with their readers.

The Bible, the canons of Western philosophy and theology, and much of the literature of modern Europe and America have been instruments of destruction. Reading them often means coming face to face with that violence. Now more than ever, as Americans finally begin to dismantle the monuments that glorified the history of white supremacy, we must, as readers, consider our modes of reading and our religious, literary, and philosophical canons anew. We must recognize not only how different kinds of reading foster new approaches to our collective futures but also that the notion of the canon, with its concept of "the classic"—and the aura of a particular kind of devotion that floats around that term—has caused irreparable harm. Not every reading can or should or will be a devotional one. Not every putative classic merits our love or even our sustained attention. Yet we often love texts that are also injurious to us, an experience any woman who reads knows intimately. The reckoning demanded by the present moment, most immediately by Black Lives Matter, will entail for some a refusal to read the rebarbative texts that fostered and continue to foster violence; for others it will give rise to historical and critical analyses that help us to live with and in opposition to the legacy of these texts and to find collective ways to repair the damage of colonialism, racism, and sexism. These readings will sometimes bear the marks of the kind of devotion we describe here; at other times, that will be impossible. Our gamble in these essays is that it is valuable, perhaps necessary, to work through the love we sometimes have even for texts that do harm.

We would like to think that Religious Studies is ideally suited for some of this work, particularly the subfield of Religion and Literature, in its focus on textuality and its concern for the cross-pollination across religious traditions and beyond them. Religion and Literature has long been an area of specialization within the study of religion, and it has more recently emerged as a subfield within literature departments. Similar work can be found in philosophy, where a number of thinkers have turned to literature as a way to think through ethical and political issues.[21] That the subfield exists at all is in part a relic of a particular European and American history, one in which the affective work enacted by devotional reading of the Psalms and other biblical and religious texts was self-consciously taken up by poets, fiction writers, and early literary critics. This is not to say that literature displaces religion, although for some it does. For many, however, the reading of literature and the reading of religious texts—a distinction that itself often does not stand—occur side by side, often reinforcing each other. The theorization of why and how to read literature, moreover, from at least the early modern period in England, often involves thinking about the ways in which texts elevate and educate the reader affectively; literary critics explicitly look to religious texts and the reading of religious texts as a way to understand at least some aspects of what reading literature is.[22] As Furey's essay makes clear, these early interactions are vital for us. Like Jewish and Christian commentators on the Psalms, we understand reading devoutly as the attempt to inhabit the voice of another, with all of the possibilities and dangers that entails.

Within twentieth-century religious studies, this history has often been forgotten, or is at best implicit. One extremely influential approach is that pioneered by Nathan Scott at the University of Chicago in the 1960s.[23] For Scott and his students, literature is heralded for its capacity to reveal an ontological dimension of depth, for its capacity to counter humanity's "impoverishment" in a secular world.[24] Borrowing language from Paul Tillich's theology of culture, such a view not only imports a Protestant impulse to salvage the kernel from the husk, the living word from the dead letter; it also brings with it the logic of idolatry by which certain objects of devotion are deemed false or superficial. More recent attempts to rethink the subfield have also tended to begin from a shared theological, largely although not exclusively Christian, sensibility.[25] Thus they emphasize religion's and literature's mutually edifying qualities, failing in the process to question the stability of the categories themselves or their historicity.[26] Our interest in fictionality and fetishism runs counter to these lines of thought. In fact, it is literature's fabricated form, its dalliance with deception and counterfeiture, that make it fundamental to the study of religion. For as each of us shows, albeit by very different means and with very different objects of inquiry, reading devoutly complicates the distinctions between subject and object, between form and content, between text and context, just as it demands we articulate what it means for us to say that we belief, have faith, or are devoted.

To stand in a relationship of devotion, fidelity, responsibility to the artificial, the fictional, the fetish, the atopic, is to refuse the logic of sovereignty. It is to refuse claims to mastery, either a text's over the reader or the reader's over a text. Yet it is not to eschew the demand for articulating criteria by which we judge one reading apt, another unworthy of its object—or, more pressingly, one form of life livable, another deathly. In the end, there are legions of texts not worthy of our devotion. We have focused here on texts that for us are. H.D., in the face of the Second World War, having lived through the horrors of the First and prescient about what was to come, went to Freud for help imagining how to survive, how to live, in the face of death. Writing about her time with Freud, bringing it together with her explorations of the occult and esoteric, she describes psychoanalysis as the recognition that we are all haunted houses.[27] Sarah Kofman wrote from a similar insight, even as she, like H.D., saw Freud himself as one of those figures who use the discourse of science to justify his own dominance, burying the insights that might reveal a contrary portrait of reality. For Kofman the way forward was not to depart from the "masters" but to read them again, to travesty their texts and thus reveal the instability of their representations. Luther violently denounced the Jews for turning scripture into an idol even as he claimed their language and stories essential to the right reception of Christ's message. He could neither divest Christianity of its Jewish past nor live without it. By rewriting it, he also altered the future.

But as these authors show, no amount of rewriting will ever render the past fully legible; none will make it present. The past is as uncertain, as unknowable, as the future. The present itself is never within our grasp. "Between two negations / horror of the world / Could not leave the world."[28] In reading what we love and loving what we read, we also refuse it, attempting in that place in between to honor an "obligation" to "The People / Contemporary History": "O make me / of Joy."[29]

NOTES

We are grateful to the University of Chicago Press and its staff, especially Alan Thomas, who initiated work on the volume, and Kyle Wagner, who saw us through. The two anonymous readers for the press helped us to find the final form of the book. Although we can't claim to have answered all of their insightful questions, we are tremendously thankful for the time and care they took with the manuscript and heartened by their encouragement for and excitement about the project.

1. See Catherine Gallagher's landmark essay "The Rise of Fictionality," around which much of the English-language debate about literary fictionality and the novel revolves. Undergirding her complex claims about the specificity with which the modern English novel emphasizes its own fictionality, rendering "the spirit of 'ironic' assent . . . a universal requirement," lie presumptions about what is believable and what is not, what could be real and what cannot be real, that are highly contingent. The real is equated, without much reflection, with the historical and the empirical, arguably a move made by the eighteenth-century English novel but not one, we think, that can be taken as given in quite the way that some of these novels, and Gallagher herself, do. Hence Gallagher's argument that the novel and self-conscious deployment of and reflection on fictionality depend on the production of "realist" narratives. In a curious reading of Sir Philip Sidney's criterion for poetry,

one that we argue cannot be taken as prescriptive for all pre- and early modern readers, Gallagher argues that "earlier fictions could be distinguished from lies if they were manifestly improbable." These "honest fictions" only become fictions, in Gallagher's sense, retroactively: "Fictionality that operates only in this one way, however, cannot be said to stand on its own as a separate concept from fantasy." For that, "plausible stories" are required. The question of who or what determines plausibility remains unanswered. See Catherine Gallagher, "The Rise of Fictionality," in *The Novel*, vol. 1, *History, Geography, and Culture*, ed. Franco Moretti (Princeton, NJ: Princeton University Press, 2006), 347, 338, 339. The argument begins with Catherine Gallagher, *Nobody's Story: The Vanishing Acts of Women Writers in the Marketplace, 1670–1820* (Berkeley: University of California Press, 1994), and continues, with new inflections, in Catherine Gallagher, *Telling It Like It Wasn't: The Counterfactual Imagination in History and Fiction* (Chicago: University of Chicago Press, 2018).

For an excellent account of the way in which many eighteenth-century novels, particularly the Gothic, operate in quite different ways, see Katherine Ding, "'Searching after the Splendid Nothing': Gothic Epistemology and the Rise of Fictionality," *English Literary History* 80 (2013): 543–73. Gallagher's claims have been roundly criticized by those working on medieval European texts, a set of objections usefully summarized and added to by Julie Orlemanski, "Who Has Fiction? Modernity, Fictionality, and the Middle Ages," *New Literary History* 50 (2019): 145–70. See also the forum on Orlemanski's essay, and a closely related piece by Michelle Karnes, in *New Literary History* 51 (2020): 229–73.

Finally, there is a large body of literature in German, mostly by narratologists, dealing with the question of fictionality. For the relation between this scholarship and Gallagher's essay, see Monika Fludernik, "The Fiction of the Rise of Fictionality," *Poetics Today* 39 (2018): 67–92.

2. Throughout this introduction, we speak of texts and reading, terms that suggest a primacy placed on writing and the book.

For our essays, this is in fact the case. Yet oral traditions are also, we think, read in the act of reception, and we hope that aspects of what we say here might usefully be extended to them. Moreover, in thinking about a book like the Psalms, the lines between written and oral, solitary reading and communal recitation, are much more fluid than modern conceptions of writing and the book might suggest.

3. Thomas Aquinas, *Summa Theologica*, II.2, question 82.

4. This ambivalence is confirmed by the history of the word: in seventeenth-century English, "feigning" was closely associated with fiction, and both were understood to connote deceit as well as beneficent works of imagination. See, for example, the *OED*'s first two definitions for "fiction," now both obsolete: (1) "action of fashioning or imitating" and (2) "feigning, counterfeiting; deceit, dissimulation, pretence." The third definition describes fiction as "feigning that is not necessarily deceitful" and "fiction as opposed to fact," with illustrative examples for both the positive and negative possibilities, including "poetical fiction" (opposed to fact but not deceitful) and "popish priesthood is blasphemous fiction" (deceptive). *OED Online*, s.v. "fiction, n."

5. *Hamlet*, act 3, scene 1.

6. Sarah Salih, in "Idol Theory," *Preternature: Critical and Historical Studies on the Preternatural* 4, no. 1 (2015): 13–36, argues that polemics against idolatry in the medieval period were driven not by the fact that the idol was understood to be an inanimate object, but by its uncanny status between objecthood and animacy. The destruction of idols was, she writes, "the sign of a historic rupture, of the breaking of the power of the pagan deities; in the long run . . . this ensures their survival, for the miracle [that animates them and then destroys them] gives them a place for evermore in Christian iconography" (22). See also Bruno Latour, *On the Modern Cult of the Factish Gods* (Durham, NC: Duke University Press, 2010), on which Salih herself draws. Latour argues that the Western concept of belief carries with it a stark differentiation between the animation of subjects and the inanimacy of objects; this allows "false

belief" to be attributed to "pagan" cultures, even as the distinction disguises the fact that the west does not live or practice a relation to objects that reflects such a stark distinction.

7. For the complex interplay between critical and uncritical reading, and the relative newness and undertheorization, at least within literary studies, of the former, see Michael Warner, "Uncritical," in *Polemic: Critical or Uncritical*, ed. Jane Gallop (New York: Routledge, 2004), 13–38. For attempts to forestall the assumption that religious reading is necessarily uncritical, see Amy Hollywood, "Reading as Self-Annihilation," in Gallop, *Polemic*, 39–63, reprinted with additional notes in Amy Hollywood, *Acute Melancholia and Other Essays: Mysticism, History, and the Study of Religion* (New York: Columbia University Press, 2016), 129–48.

8. Sarah Hammerschlag, *Broken Tablets: Levinas, Derrida, and the Afterlife of Religion* (New York: Columbia University Press, 2016), 144.

9. Hammerschlag, *Broken Tablets*. For this particular point see Immanuel Kant, *Religion within the Boundaries of Mere Reason*, included in Kant, *Religion within the Boundaries of Mere Reason, and Other Writings*, ed. Allen Wood and George di Giovanni (Cambridge: Cambridge University Press, 2018). It should be noted that there is a large body of philosophical material on the question of fictionality, material in which we have a strong interest but not time or space to explore fully here. Kant's account of the "as if" is crucial to many of these discussions.

10. Crucial illuminating examples can be found in recent discussions of African Diasporic Religions, but of course there are many others. See Aisha Beliso-DeJesús, *Electric Santería: Racial and Sexual Assemblages of Transnational Feminism* (New York: Columbia University Press, 2015), and Solimar Otero, *Archives of Conjure: Stories of the Dead in Afrolatinx Cultures* (New York: Columbia University Press, 2020). Writing in relation to Caribbean materials, in this case a novel by Sylvia Wynter, Mayra Rivera asks the vital question of whether more fully embodied rituals might be necessary "to cultivate affective orientations and to intentionally recreate ourselves."

"Are the humanities," Rivera asks, "equipped to guide us toward this sense of embodied counterpoetics as both imaginative discourse and transformative practice—to counter the colonial and capitalist forces that shape our being? Do we need to invent new rituals, a counter-aesthetic and a counter-ethics?" See Mayra Rivera, "Embodied Counterpoetics," in *Beyond Man: Race, Coloniality, and Philosophy of Religion*, ed. An Yountae and Eleanor Craig (Durham, NC: Duke University Press, 2021). See also, in the same volume, Amy Hollywood, "On Impassioned Claims: The Possibility of Doing Philosophy of Religion Otherwise."

Rivera's question is a very live one for us. On the one hand, we share the concern that literature is limited in the ways in which it can transform persons, communities, and worlds. On the other, at least some of us have pressing concerns about what happens when one attempts to realize imagined ideals materially and concretely, in and on human bodies. Perhaps this is a particular problem for Christianity with its literalizing tendencies, one that might be forestalled within other religious traditions. Yet the value of literature and other realms of the imagination, including religious worlds that exist precisely as imagined, is that they provide grounds for working out complex affective and intellectual truths often too dangerous to embody fully. At the same time, we recognize the particular privilege on which this emphasis on the freedom of imagined worlds rests, the rootedness of these ideas, as we encounter them at least, within western traditions of thought, and the colonizing use to which these western conceptions of literature have been put. Hence, for us, the value of understanding religion and literature as speaking to each other and performing similar tasks, while at the same time maintaining the analytic distinction between them, at least within and on the edges of the traditions with which we work. On the specific problems raised by Christian tendencies to demand its truth be literalized and rendered historical, and for signs of resistance to this move from within the tradition itself, see Hollywood, "Reading as Self-Annihilation." For the role western literature plays in colonial and imperialist projects, see Gauri Viswanathan, *Masks of Conquest: Literary Studies and British Rule in India* (New York: Columbia University Press, 1989); Michael Allen, *In the Shadow of World Literature: Sites of Reading in Colonial Egypt* (Princeton, NJ: Princeton University Press, 2016); and the response to Allen's book by Siraj Ahmed, "Criticism and Catastrophe," https://tif.ssrc.org/2017/08/15/criticism-and -catastrophe/.

11. See Tyler Roberts, *Encountering Religion: Responsibility and Criticism after Secularism* (New York: Columbia University Press, 2013), esp. 23–48, and for an extension and elaboration of Roberts's argument, Hollywood, *Acute Melancholia*, 9–18. Roberts derives his account from reading across the corpus of Jonathan Z. Smith.

12. Furey uses this phrase in "The Hermeneutics of Intersubjectivity" (lecture, American Academy of Religion annual meeting, San Diego, CA, November 25, 2014), glossing Amy Hollywood, *Sensible Ecstasy: Mysticism, Sexual History, and the Demands of History* (Chicago: University of Chicago Press, 2002), in relation to Judith Butler, *Undoing Gender* (New York: Routledge, 2004). Butler's observation that "we are undone by each other" (19) can be specified by what Hollywood explains about the medieval mystics, who imagined and experienced divine love as a transcendent force with immanent effects. Mystical experience allows one to "transcend one's own particular body and opens one to the other" (222). Love then works in the way that suffering and self-laceration do for Bataille, Furey concludes, as the undoing that enables communication.

13. See especially the essays collected in Hollywood, *Acute Melancholia*.

14. See especially Constance M. Furey, "Body, Society, and Subjectivity in Religious Studies," *Journal of the American Academy of Religion* 80, no. 1 (2011): 7–33; Constance M. Furey, "Discernment as Critique in Teresa of Avila and Erasmus of Rotterdam," *Exemplaria* 26, nos. 2–3 (2014): 254–72; and Constance M. Furey, *Poetic Relations: Intimacy and Faith in the English Reformation* (Chicago: University of Chicago Press, 2017).

15. See Eve Kosofsky Sedgwick, "Paranoid Reading and Repara-

tive Reading, or, You're So Paranoid, You Probably Think This Essay Is about You," in *Touching Feeling: Affect, Pedagogy, Performativity* (Durham, NC: Duke University Press, 2003), 123–51. The essay first appeared as the introduction to *Novel Gazing: Queer Readings in Fiction*, ed. Eve Kosofsky Sedgwick (Durham, NC: Duke University Press, 1997), 1–37. Note that Elizabeth Weed gets Sedgwick exactly right in her acute analysis of the difference between Sedgwick's call for reparative reading and Sharon Marcus and Stephen Best's call for "surface reading." See Elizabeth Weed, "Gender and the Lure of the Postcritical," *Differences* 27, no. 2 (2016): 153–77.

16. Paul Ricoeur, *Freud and Philosophy: An Exercise on Interpretation*, trans. Denis Savage (New Haven, CT: Yale University Press, 1970), 32. For the refusal of what they call "symptomatic reading," associated largely with the work of Fredric Jameson, see Stephen Best and Sharon Marcus, "Surface Reading: An Introduction," in "The Way We Read Now," special issue, *Representations* 108, no. 1 (2009): 1–21. On the desire for a postcritical literary studies, see Rita Felski, *Uses of Literature* (Oxford: Blackwell, 2008), and Rita Felski, *The Limits of Critique* (Chicago: University of Chicago Press, 2015).

Elizabeth Weed, as noted earlier, does an excellent job demonstrating the problems with Best and Marcus's argument, in particular its confusion of the Althusserian symptom, so vital to Jameson's work, and Ricoeur's account of the "masters of suspicion." Weed does not explicitly address Felski, who like Sedgwick, makes direct appeals to Ricoeur. Yet the same problem is visible within Felski's work as within Best and Marcus's; there is a persistent refusal of critique, which leads to a banishment of the political as of central concern to literary studies (despite some assertions to the contrary). Although Felski eschews Best and Marcus's language of surface and depths, and points to a wide range of interesting affective aspects of reading, she is persistently unclear about what precisely she understands critique to be and why, therefore, it is a problem. What bothers her, as she puts it, is a certain tone and style of thought within literary studies, one we think might be best captured by the language of "debunking." We under-

stand her impatience and her desire yet think that a model of reading as devotional allows critique and affective attachment to work
together rather than antipodally to each other. See Weed, "Gender
and the Lure of the Postcritical"; Felski, *Uses of Literature*.

Joseph North argues that the problem with literary studies is
not with critique or symptomatic modes of reading, but instead
with the loss of literary criticism as a distinct part of the work
of literature departments. He therefore argues for a distinction
between what he calls literary criticism and literary scholarship,
which he argues coexisted uneasily for a time. Since the 1970s at
least, he claims, literary criticism has been displaced by literary
scholarship—knowledge production on the model of the sciences
and "hard" social sciences—that is largely contextualist and historicist in approach. As a result, there is no real place for a literary
criticism that works toward the project of aesthetic education or
the cultivation of sensibility. North does not want the latter to be
what he calls idealist, Kantian, and conservative. (He is clear that a
return to the Leavisites or to the New Criticism is not the answer,
although he does revisit what precedes them in the person of I. A.
Richards, who, North argues, gives accounts of close reading and
criticism that, while inadequate, are linked to the form of criticism
for which he argues.) North proposes, without fully describing, a
materialist literary criticism, grounded in close reading and the
cultivation of sensibility. He asserts that Richards's aesthetics was
materialist, if inadequately theorized.

We are much more convinced by North's distinction between
literary criticism and literary scholarship than by those posited
between critical and uncritical or symptomatic and surface reading. The problem is that North does not tell us or show us quite
enough about what he takes close reading and literary criticism
to be, and he gives little indication of what a materialist aesthetics
might look like, other than that it will be of necessity political and
leftist. The other problem with North's book is the rather cava-
lier way in which he reduces much excellent literary scholarship,
scholarship we believe often includes literary criticism of the sort

that interests North, to its historicist and contextualist framings. In addition, he overlooks vital works of African American literary criticism that perform precisely the kind of engaged reading North describes, looking to literature as sources to think with and be transformed by rather than as solely in need of historicization and contextualization for their proper understanding. (And of course, the two projects are significantly less distinct than North sometimes suggests.) See Joseph North, *Literary Criticism: A Concise Literary History* (Cambridge, MA: Harvard University Press, 2017). For powerful examples of the kind of literary (and visual cultural) criticism we are describing, undertaken by scholars in literary studies and in religion, see Christina Sharpe, *In the Wake: On Blackness and Being* (Durham, NC: Duke University Press, 2016); Joseph Winters, *Hope Draped in Black: Race, Melancholy, and the Agony of Progress* (Durham, NC: Duke University Press, 2016); J. Kameron Carter and Sarah Jane Cervenak, "Black Ether," *CR: New Centennial Review* 16, no. 2 (2016): 203–24; and J. Kameron Carter, "Black Malpractice (A Poetics of the Sacred)," *Social Text* 37, no. 2 (2019): 67–107.

Despite these caveats, and North's complete disinterest in religion, his project parallels certain aspects of our own. We share his conviction of the importance of close reading, and also wonder whether there might be a materialist conception of religion that would stand alongside and with a materialist aesthetics.

17. Not all of this work, only a small portion of which is cited above, makes explicit reference to Ricoeur.

18. Ricoeur, *Freud and Philosophy*, 28.

19. Ricoeur, *Freud and Philosophy*, 27.

20. For a particularly moving and insightful articulation of the problem in just this way, see Deidre Shauna Lynch, *Loving Literature: A Cultural History* (Chicago: University of Chicago Press, 2015).

21. The problem here, as with much of Religion and Literature, is the tendency to focus on content over form and to take literary texts as exempla for already articulated philosophical (or theological) views. For one prominent example of this tendency, see Martha Nussbaum, *Love's Knowledge: Essays on Philosophy and Literature*

(Oxford: Oxford University Press, 1990). The problem with Nussbaum's mode of reading is rendered dramatically in her interpretation of the young David Copperfield, orphaned, subject to the cruelty of his stepfather and his stepfather's sister, sitting in his bed "reading as if for life." For Nussbaum, David is engaged in the work of developing a moral sensibility. Yet the text belies that description. David Copperfield, as the narrator of his own story, recalls and justifies his childhood reading despite its often immoral content. The characters that filled the novels he read, novels left behind by his dead father, were a "glorious host," who kept him company: "They kept alive my fancy, and my hope of something beyond that place and time, —they, and the Arabian Nights, and the Tales of the Genii, —and did me no harm; for whatever harm was in some of them was not there for me; I knew nothing of it." Although David Copperfield is intent on maintaining his innocence as a child, the primary force of the passage lies in his rapturous recollection of the ability, through reading literature, to occupy another space and another time in the midst of intense mourning and trauma. This is what matters to him, not moral exemplarity. Charles Dickens, *The Personal History of David Copperfield* (Oxford: Oxford University Press, 1989), 55.

Toril Moi makes the case for the usefulness of ordinary language philosophy to the study of literature, and in particular attends carefully to Stanley Cavell's work on literature and film. While Moi's faith in ordinary language is bracing and might prove to be useful for a host of literary critical projects, Cavell seems subject to the same pitfalls we see in Nussbaum's and Moi's work, and at times, to those we see in Felski. See Toril Moi, *Revolution of the Ordinary: Literary Studies after Wittgenstein, Austin, and Cavell* (Chicago: University of Chicago Press, 2017).

22. A great deal of interesting work has been done on the interplay between the reading of religious texts and the development of English literary criticism. Given the importance of the study of divine poetry to the articulation of an English literary tradition, and the enormous shadow cast by Spenser and Milton on that tradition,

it is not surprising that criticism emerges at the site on which literature and religion converge. The broader history, one that gives
detailed attention to the role of the Psalms and Hebrew biblical
poetry, has yet to be written, but intriguing pieces of the story are
laid out in Clement Hawes, *Mania and Literary Style: The Rhetoric
of Enthusiasm from the Ranters to Christopher Smart* (Cambridge:
Cambridge University Press, 1996); Debora Shuger, *The Renaissance
Bible: Scholarship, Sacrifice, and Subjectivity* (Waco, TX: Baylor University Press, 1998); Shaun Irlam, *Elations: The Poetics of Enthusiasm
in Eighteenth-Century Britain* (Stanford, CA: Stanford University
Press, 1999); Jon Mee, "Anxieties of Enthusiasm: Coleridge, Proph-
ecy, and Popular Politics in the 1790s," in *Enthusiasm and Enlight-
enment in Europe, 1650–1850,* ed. Lawrence E. Klein and Anthony
J. La Vopa (San Marino, CA: Huntington Library, 1998), 179–203;
Jon Mee, *Romanticism, Enthusiasm and Regulation: Poetics and the
Policing of Culture in the Romantic Period* (Oxford: Oxford University
Press, 2003); Lori Branch, *Rituals of Spontaneity: Sentiment and Sec-
ularism from Free Prayer to Wordsworth* (Waco, TX: Baylor University
Press, 2006); and William R. McKelvy, *The English Cult of Literature:
Devoted Readers, 1774–1880* (Charlottesville: University of Virginia
Press, 2007).

23. See Nathan Scott, *The Broken Center: Studies in the Theological
Horizon of Modern Literature* (New Haven, CT: Yale University Press,
1966).

24. Scott's Tillichian language, while not identical to Matthew
Arnold's faith in culture as "the disinterested endeavor after man's
[sic] perfection," shares with it a belief in literature's capacity to
edify and sustain. This puts him squarely within the tradition of
F. R. Leavis as it is discussed by North. See North, *Literary Criticism,*
46–55. For Arnold's importance to the field of Religion and Literature, see Joshua King, "The Inward Turn: The Role of Matthew
Arnold," in *The Routledge Companion to Literature and Religion,* ed.
Mark Knight (New York: Routledge, 2016), 1–26. T. S. Eliot's importance in the development of the subfield, as well as that of the New
Criticism, also requires sustained attention. For an early articula-

tion of these debts, see Giles Gunn, "Introduction: Literature and Its Relationship to Religion," in *Literature and Religion*, ed. Giles Gunn (London: SCM Press, 1971), 1–33.

25. Although there have been persistent attempts to think Religion and Literature beyond the West and beyond Christianity, Christianity continues to play a commanding role in the field. For an early articulation of the desire for a broader scope, one in which the term literature may be too capacious to remain useful, see Anthony Yu (1987) and Larry D. Bouchard (2005), "Literature: Literature and Religion," in *Encyclopedia of Religion*, 2nd ed., ed. Lindsay Jones (Detroit: Macmillan, 2005), 5466–76. For a recent attempt to include a wide range of religious traditions within the field, see *The Cambridge Companion to Literature and Religion*, ed. Susan M. Felch (Cambridge: Cambridge University Press, 2016).

26. See, for example, the journal *Religion & Literature*, particularly the issue devoted to the outcome of a Mellon Working Group on Religion and Literature hosted by the University of Notre Dame, *Religion & Literature* 14, nos. 2/3 (Summer/Autumn 2014). Something that recurs across this work is an emphasis on content. There is something curious about the tendency given the centrality of genre to the development of Religion and Literature as a subfield, at least at the University of Chicago. On this history, see Larry D. Bouchard, "Religion and Literature: Four Theses and More," *Religion & Literature* 41, no. 2 (2009): 12–19.

An overlapping group of scholars engages with Rita Felski's work, bringing together the postcritical and what some of them term the "postsecular." (Lori Branch's work is particularly important on this topic.) Our concern with this move, in addition to the eschewal of critique we have already discussed, is the ways in which the postsecular is appropriated from a figure like Talal Asad to do very different work than that performed by his anthropology of the secular. Asad is intent, across his scholarship, on demonstrating that the secular, secularism, and secularity are always articulated in relation to—arguably even as a form of—Christianity. He does not embrace this historical, sociological, philosophical, theological phenomenon, however, but asks who it renders illegible. It is not at all clear that there can be a postsecular within Asad's terms. To embrace the postsecular as a way to think and read undeterred by the critical legacies of Marx, Nietzsche, Freud, DuBois, de Beauvoir, and many others, is to perform the very act of appropriation and othering Asad's work analyzes. It is very hard to see how returning to symbolic anthropology and the work of Clifford Geertz, as Tracy Fessenden suggests, is possible without careful attention to Asad's blistering critique of that work. See Talal Asad, *Genealogies of Religion: Discipline and Reasons of Power in Christianity and Islam* (Baltimore, MD: Johns Hopkins University Press, 1993), and Talal Asad, *Formations of the Secular: Christianity, Islam, Modernity* (Palo Alto, CA: Stanford University Press, 2003). For the strong claim that Christianity is secularism and secularism Christianity, see Gil Anidjar, *Blood: A Critique of Christianity* (New York: Columbia University Press, 2016); for a forum on Anidjar's book, see *Marginalia/ LA Review of Books* (March 2015). Finally, see the cluster of essays on Felski's book, particularly the pieces by Branch and Fessenden, together with Felski's response, in *Religion & Literature* 48, no. 2 (2016).

It should be added that there is much wonderful criticism being written that thinks about religion and literature together. Our questions are with the theoretical framing of the field.

27. H.D., *Tribute to Freud* (New York: New Directions, 2009), 146.

28. Susan Howe, *The Nonconformist's Memorial* (New York: New Directions, 1993), 111.

29. Howe, *Nonconformist's Memorial*, 56, 57.

VIVIFYING POETRY

SIDNEY, LUTHER, AND THE PSALMS

Constance M. Furey

1. SCRIPTURALIZATION

I came late to the Psalms. They were not part of the soundscape of my childhood, as they are for Jews and Christians who grow up praying and chanting or singing these scriptural prayer poems. To me the Psalms seemed, like Shakespeare, something every educated person should read, but all I knew of either was a few famous lines. In a college course on the Hebrew Bible, the Book of Psalms was overshadowed by the unexpected sexiness of the Song of Songs. And when I enrolled in a graduate seminar on Martin Luther, I was entirely unprepared to understand what the Psalms meant to this monastic professor of biblical studies better known as an iconoclastic Christian theologian.

The syllabus of that Luther seminar revealed that a whole week would be spent reading Luther's early lectures on the Psalms, delivered several years before the Augustinian monk penned his 95 Theses, called Pope Leo X a whore of Babylon, renounced the priesthood, persuaded legions of monks and nuns to leave their enclosures, and declared that Christians are saved by faith, not works.[1] If ever proof were needed that graduate seminars are thorough, this was it: what could we possibly learn from the *Dictata super Psalterium* (1513–1515), Luther's long lectures on a single book of the Bible, a book of prayer poems, no less, far removed from the Pauline letters and other well-known scriptural sources of Luther's controversial theology?[2] The professor made clear that Luther should be read as a late medieval thinker rather than a revolutionary innovator. Nevertheless, we approached the Psalms as we would a treasure hunt, searching for clues that inspired the monk to challenge Rome and reconceive salvation. This is how most Luther scholars treat the *Dictata*, assessing the relationship between that early commentary, medieval theology, and the reformer's later teachings.[3] The Psalms might be biblical poems, but neither Luther scholars nor we the students, following in their wake, considered Luther a reader of lyric poetry.

Then a poet's psalms took me back to Luther's. Sir Philip Sidney, a courtier poet of the English Renaissance and author of the sonnet sequence *Astrophel and Stella*, gave the psalmist a cameo role in *The Defence of Poesy*, one of the era's most influential works of literary criticism, still read in English lit survey courses.[4] This was likely around the same time Sidney began translating and poeticizing the entire Book of Psalms—a project completed by his sister, Mary Sidney Herbert, and hailed by no less than John Donne as an inspiring source for all subsequent English poets.[5]

Sidney's psalms are unquestionably poetic. And yet the significance of the Psalms to his argument in *The Defence of Poesy* is disputed. This disagreement among scholars exposes entrenched and often unacknowledged assumptions about how religion differs from literature. It is tempting to conclude that Sidney redirects sacred energy from scriptural to secular poetry. What he actually does is more interesting: Sidney finds in scriptural poetics the energy characteristic of all poetry he deems worthy of the name. Rereading Luther on the Psalms with Sidney in mind primed me to wonder about Luther's interest in the psalmist's poetics, and to notice an intriguing parallel: just as Sidney celebrates the force and energy of David's use of voice and personification, Luther hails the vivifying effect of the psalmist's Word. I should not have been surprised by this shared interest in how particular kinds of texts alter readers. Sidney and Luther both express what devout Christians (and Jews) had been experiencing and saying about the Psalms for centuries, that these biblical poems are unique in their capacity to affect readers because they give voice to all feeling, ranging from anger and despair to hope and wonder, and teach the faithful to speak to God.[6] In this scriptural culture, a culture that singled out the Psalms as the most important devotional book in the Bible, both Luther and Sidney elaborated claims about how particular kinds of writing can reorient readers toward a world that can as yet only be imagined.

Luther, the theologian and biblical scholar, concentrates his commentary on the promissory power of the Word of Christ, thereby conflating divine presence with a poetics of communication. Sidney, the courtier poet, often described as more interested in secular than biblical poetry, reveals the irrelevance of this distinction in his theory and practice of poesis. Luther insists that reception must supersede interpretation (and denies his own interpretive work by condemning it as a form of idolatry characteristic of Jews and heretics). Like Sidney, who proclaims that poetry names the sort of writing effective not because of how readers understand the content but because of how they are moved by the language, Luther privileges textual energy.

Sidney and Luther are thus both engaged in what Vincent Wimbush calls "scripturalization." Wimbush, whose early work on African American biblical hermeneutics inspired a transhistorical theory, frames the fundamental question this way: "What is the work 'humans' make 'scriptures' do?" The effects of this work are not preordained. We can use scriptures to conscript ourselves, reinforcing regnant constructions of the human in service to dominant powers such as nation-states. Or we can scripturalize alternatives. Underscoring scripturalizing's active suffix, Wimbush describes it as a dynamic and interactive process that represents "possibilities for making liquid, more complex, and unstable . . . the established relationships and occupation of spaces that define the regime." What we do to regimes we can also do to ourselves, for here too are "possibilities for the unmaking or alternate shaping of the human."[7]

To ask what work humans make scriptures do is to ask a host of related questions: what ways of knowing are deemed legitimate? What are the phenomena, dynamics, forms of expression, and sets of relations for which scripture might be shorthand? What expressive forms are invoked? What psychological needs are met? What do inventors understand themselves to be doing? How is the difference from other activities to be explained? What does this distinction mean for ongoing human claims about knowledge, cognition, communication, and relationships? Finally, and crucially, what does scripturalization mean for the construction, the reconstruction, and the deconstruction of the human?[8]

Wimbush's questions are akin to those posed by Luther and Sidney. They are the queries, too, animating this book's broader project and our investigations of devotion in H.D. and Susan Howe and Jacques Derrida and Sarah Kofman, just as in Sidney and Luther and the Psalms. Wimbush's scripturalization names not only those texts that a given group nominates as sacred but the kinds of writing or inscribing invested with the authority to constitute or complicate—to make, unmake, or remake— the human. Our term "devotion" connotes the intensities as well as the uncertainties of this constellated process. We begin here, with two premodern writers, biblical psalms, and devotions conjoined to canonical scriptures, in order to demonstrate two things. First, how works oriented to and by the Bible anticipate and participate in questions we are still asking today about the politics of reading and devotion to literature. Second, the ways premodern sources can challenge and perhaps even change assumptions we have about how appeals to divine inspiration curtail and enable human possibilities, and the ways we imagine literature and its politics.

Certainly there are important boundaries to be drawn between official scriptures—texts whose authoritative status is established and policed by religious institutions—and the sources explored in the next two essays, works by modern writers beholden to publishing houses, readers, or their own vision of authorial integrity. So too, when discussing divinity, it matters whether our sources understand themselves as subjects of a sovereign monotheistic god, devotees of many gods, plagued or aided by spirits, or denizens of a world devoid of supernatural forces. But it does not always matter in the way we might expect, with monotheism on one end of a sliding scale, facilitating forms of subjection that serve oppressive regimes, and secularism on the other end, fostering an independence that encourages liberatory politics. Moreover, the political stakes of imaginative writing are set into relief by the definition of the political Wimbush invokes, citing the French philosopher Jacques Rancière, who defines the political as the "terrain" on which "the verification of equality confronts the established order of identification and classification."[9] Setting aside Rancière's valorization of equality as the highest ideal—a claim that emerges out of a specific tradition spanning from the Greek *demos* to the modern French state—we amend his definition to articulate a key premise of our own work: the political is the space where social realities confront aspirational ideals.[10]

Sidney and Luther work in this topography of the political, both writing from positions of relative social privilege, both invoking and creating socially authoritative sources that also celebrate unfulfilled ideals.[11] What they say about the animating, motivating power of psalms and poetry more generally (in Sidney's case), and the Book of Psalms specifically (in Luther's), presents itself as vital to ongoing discussions about the making and remaking of human beings. Following Wimbush, we might ask the following questions of Sidney as well as Luther: What sort of knowledge was he claiming? What sort of person was he cultivating? And what sort of textual relationship was he envisioning, for himself and his auditors and readers? Here, however, the work in question requires us to redirect the query, for Luther and Sidney both shift the locus of agency from author to text. Sidney's theory, substantially derived from the Psalms, focused less on the poet than the poesis, or the art and craft of imaginative writing. What sort of knowledge did poesis convey? What sort of person did poesis cultivate? And what sort of relationships, between authors and texts and readers?

Luther was likewise averse to formulations that suggest the writer or reader takes precedence over the text. It was not he but the Word claiming knowledge, cultivating a person, and establishing a relationship with readers. For Sidney as well as Luther, then, the knowledge sought was vitally dependent on specific features not unique to poetry but essential to what we call poetic writing: delight in metaphor and play of voices (including comfort in switching among grammatical voices and the imputation of voice to nonhuman objects and creatures). Their psalm-inspired work directs us to attend to the way textual voices conjure and communicate persons and stage interactive dynamics.

These Renaissance and Reformation poetics have enlivened my sense of scripture's as well as literature's political possibilities. They have also alerted me to some of the dangers that poetics might incline us to ignore. Sidney aligns imaginative texts with a polity's need to keep people in check. In Sidney's work, poetry proves its political value by cultivating measured restraint and moderation in its readers. Luther's interest in the spiritualized text motivates his condemnation of Jews and heretics. There is no neutral position, in Luther's account: those who seek to interpret the text are deadened by the effort and dangerous to anyone who comes in contact with them. Luther's celebration of the life-giving text depends on his often erroneous—and, for that reason, all the more revealing—condemnation of those who resist its animating power. These accounts of textual liveliness also necessitate disciplinary practices, socially as well as individually. For Sidney, the Psalms model what he claims for poetry more generally: that its decorum and mode of self-governance effectively serves an imperial regime.[12] In Luther's view, the Psalms facilitate and even demand that Christianity supersede Judaism. For both men, this same scriptural book encourages a mode of textual engagement that decenters the self by displacing power from readers to words.

These are notable insights and problems, and collectively they confirm the value of thinking religion and literature together. I came late to the Psalms, but what I learned about them from Sidney and what Sidney, in turn, enabled me to learn from Luther, reveals what we lose when we imagine historical influence as separable from theological insight and treat both as apolitical. Historically, Christian devotion to the Psalms was shaped by classical rhetoric's concern with how words, both oral and written, communicate persons and evoke emotions in listeners and readers. Theologically, the pious were taught that the multiplicity of voices and personae in the Psalms made it possible for each individual reader to experience the psalmist's words as her own *and* to facilitate the transition from sinful self-centeredness to a God-centered salvation. Politically, the Psalms confirmed that truth was to be found in and through words, that these words had to be savored to be understood, and that words could remake a human by teaching them that receptivity to the voice of another (poetically enacted in the Psalms as the voice of multiple others, not all human but all vivid and present as speaking persons) was more important than self-assertion and self-definition. In the comparison that follows, then, I try to illuminate all this through an appreciative reading of two canonical sources: Sidney, who is still a cultural touchstone in literary studies,[13] and Luther, who remains a central Christian *and* cultural figure (the latter because of the manifold ways Protestantism has shaped perceptions of what religion "should" be, even for non-Christians, throughout the globe).[14] My mode of appreciative reading also conceals and displaces ambivalence I feel about the sorts of dangers noted in the previous paragraph. This too has political significance—the difficulty, as I am tempted to describe it, of extolling ideals without losing sight of material reality.

2. SIR PHILIP SIDNEY ON THE PSALMS

Philip Sidney's famous work of literary criticism first appeared in 1595, under two different titles. Publisher William Ponsonby, of London, printed it as *The defence of poesie*. The title page of Henry Olney's edition, printed in the same city, declared Sidney's work *An apologie for poetrie*. Although the initial descriptors— *defence* and *apologie*—are essentially synonymous, the difference between *poesie* (the writerly craft) and *poetrie* (the product of that craft) is the primary subject of Sidney's work: how does *poesie* turn black ink into living words? And what effect does poetry have on, and in, the world? Notice also that neither title of Sidney's famous work refers to poets. "I speak of the art, and not of the artificer," Sidney says.[15] We should heed this self-description. Sidney's concern is not the poet's inspiration but the inspirational effect of the poetry.[16]

The complexity of Sidney's claim about poetic inspiration— and the way his account elides distinctions between religious and secular poetry—is often overlooked, however, by those who debate the political implications of his argument. Consider, for example, Catherine Bates's argument that Sidney's *Defence* should be read as a subversive work, as a treatise that ultimately exposes the *indefensibility* of poetry. Standard readings maintain that Sidney argues poetry is socially and politically profitable because it is pedagogically effective: poetry moves hearts as well as minds and inspires virtuous action.[17] Bates counters this by demonstrating that the treatise contests every element of its own argument. The *Defence*, she concludes, upsets the logocentric, patristic, and patriarchal order by superseding the Protestant humanist pedagogic view of the poet.[18] Notably, Bates's framework presumes what Sidney's treatise refuses: a clear distinction between religious poets (authorized by divine inspiration) and secular poets (defined by modern interpreters as those who claim creative inspiration for themselves). For Bates, the question is whether Sidney subverts the role of the Protestant poet by claiming for the "right" poet what he attributes to the "divine" poet. Does he claim godlike powers for the secular poet? she asks. The question instead should be whether we have rightly understood Sidney's categories.

The "right poet," Sidney says, is "lifted up with the vigour of his own invention."[19] In Greek and classical Latin, the "invention" that Sidney attributes to the right poet was primarily an oratorical and rhetorical term, meaning the discovery of apt arguments with the aim of persuasion.[20] In Christianity, the devotional significance of invention's connotation of discovery is confirmed by the Feast of the Invention of the Cross, celebrating the discovery of the Cross in Jerusalem by Constantine's mother, St. Helena.[21] Sidney may appear to be cleaving devotional from rhetorical invention when he says that divine poets "did imitate the inconceivable excellencies of God," while right poets are those who "borrow nothing of what is, hath been, or shall be."[22] The distinction, however, is not self-evident.

Indeed, as Daniel Lochman explains, in Sidney's work "scriptural and right poets share—more or less fully—a single 'inspiration,' that 'sacred force of divine breath." Sidney's description of heavenly "poesy"—a word which appears for the first time in the treatise in reference to David's work—converges in all important respects with his account of the inspirational effects of the right poet's craft. Moreover, Sidney notably rejects claims of divine inspiration and heroic fury in detailing the prophetic powers of the *vates*, or divine poet.[23] Rather, for the divine poet as for the right poet, the power of their *poesie* inheres in the various ways they find to create living voices on the page. Through metaphor, personification, direct address, and the interplay of first- and third-person voices, the poets discover something new, and move beyond mere copying into a realm beyond Nature, beyond the "bare was" of the historian and the dry abstraction of the philosopher to the consolations and inspirations of the poetry's "never-leaving goodness," which awakens the reader's desire for the possibilities it depicts.[24]

Sidney was politically pragmatic and in favor of religious uniformity. He was a moderate Protestant acutely aware of the vagaries of royal whims, the dangers of religious extremism, and the profits awaiting those who participated in England's settler colonialism.[25] Sidney was not a rebel. Yet Sidney's own argument demonstrates that works of imagination do more than mirror their author's conscious commitments. Sidney's *Defence* deserves our attention even though it does not subvert logocentric patriarchy, because it demonstrates how the confluence of religion and literature might pose alternatives to the binary options of conformity or subversion. In Sidney's *Defence*, the locus of divine power is not a transcendent God but a poetic voice. Poetry's political effects are variable because this voice is multiple, characterized as it is by the fluid interchange of first-, second-, and third-person voices and the capacity to create speaking figures. While Sidney offers some predictable claims about poetry's usefulness and profitability—the sort of observations that align scripturalization with regnant powers—he also accentuates the *un*predictability of poetry's politics by describing poetry as untethered to the historian's "bare *was*," influenced instead by the "divine consideration of what may be and should be," and capable of changing how readers think, and feel, and act.[26]

POETRY'S ENERGY

Evocative descriptions of linguistic force and animation appear on nearly every page of Sidney's *Defence*. Poetry purifies, enables, and enlarges, Sidney explains. Poetry inspires and energizes: it can "lift up the mind," cure the sick soul, move men to goodness and "make them know that goodness whereunto they are moved."[27] The "peerless poet," Sidney says, knows how to "strike, pierce," and possess the "sight of the soul." Poetry awakens a "true and lively knowledge."[28] Sidney insists that language can thereby claim the agency usually associated with people, for poetry has "that same forcibleness or *energia*, as the Greeks call it, of the writer."[29] In fact, in one of those etymological details that confirms what a nuanced reading of an entire text might suggest, the *OED* reports that definitions of the English word *energy* include the now obsolete "ability or capacity to produce an effect." The word was applied from the outset to faith (defined in a 1556 treatise as "a certain living and a continuall working power and energie, that sitteth not idle in mennes consciences") even as the same period saw "energy" used to describe rhetorical effect (a 1549 treatise on the Ten Commandments praises the superior energy of a Hebrew word, while a 1565 work praises the phrase "he begat us again to a lively hope" as imbued with a "greater energy" than an awkwardly phrased version of the same idea).[30] Sidney's claims about poetry's energy, force, and liveliness incorporate both definitions, as he considers how the feigning and representing characteristic of this kind of writing moves the reader.

Sidney's concern with how poetry engages a reader's desires can be detected in the first substantial section of the treatise, even though his explicit aim is to confirm poetry's prestige by hailing practitioners from the past and from other cultures, to prove poetry is both venerable and universal. The Psalms make their most prominent appearance in this section, entering a scene already crowded with examples from Greece, Rome, Italy, England, Turkey, Ireland, Wales, and the Americas. Capitalized names and places flash by in Sidney's whirlwind tour of humanist sources, making it easy to miss the fact that the tour guide says little about the poets but much about the energizing qualities and transformative effect of their poetry.

Homer, Hesiod, and other poets of ancient Greece deserve to

be called "fathers of learning," for they drew the "wild untamed wits" of their compatriots to "an admiration of knowledge" with a "charming sweetness." Herodotus deserves to be listed alongside these other Greek writers, for although he was a historian, not a poet, he enlivened history with his "passionate describing of passions." Dante, Boccaccio, and Petrarch prepared Italy to be a "treasure-house of science." In England, Gower and Chaucer "encouraged and delighted" others to "beautify our mother tongue." And Plato, too, joins this list of exemplary poets, despite his criticism of poetry. Plato's subject was philosophy, Sidney concedes, but his writings were poetic, for in his dialogues Plato "feigneth many honest burgesses of Athens to speak" as they never could have done for themselves, and sets them in motion with the "well ordering of a banquet," the "delicacy of a walk."[31]

This attention to the quality and effect of the writing rather than the inspired status of the writer is true also as Sidney universalizes his claim beyond the Greco-Roman canon, declaring poetry a "great passport" to "the gates of popular judgements," and an art practiced even in "nations . . . where learning flourisheth not."[32] Underscoring the calculations of social status obviously in play here, the *OED* cites Sidney's use of "passport" as the first time this word was used to mean a quality or attribute that gives access to status or privilege. Passport also meant then what it means today: a license to pass from one country to another. Both meanings—poetry's claim to supersede political as well as social boundaries—converge in Sidney's text. He quotes Cicero's old dictum that "even barbarians do not dishonor the name of poet," but where Cicero's universality traded on a linguistic criterion, with "barbarian" as a catch-all category for those whose speech sounded like incomprehensible babble to speakers of Greek and Latin, Sidney signals his own immersion in the geopolitics of the day by choosing examples from English colonies and military rivals.[33] In Turkey—where Muslims were poised to threaten Christian domination in Europe—there were not only "law-giving divines," or muftis, but also poets. On the Irish island, Sidney said, learning "goeth very bare," yet poets are held in "devout reverence." (Ireland was suffering under the English crown's newly oppressive efforts to extend colonial dominion, an effort Sidney's father aided and critiqued as a governor of the colonized island, and Sidney himself endorsed in his "Discourse on Irish Affairs" [1577]). Revealing his close reading of Peter Martyr's account of American culture, included in a 1555 compendium, Sidney refers to ceremonies known as "*areytos*" in order to explain how the "hard dull wits" of the "most barbarous and simple Indians" are "softened and sharpened" with the "sweet delights of poetry."[34] Finally, countering the classical genealogy with one that is more specifically English, Sidney refers to Wales as home to the "true remnant of the ancient Britons." Poets there, he observes proudly, survive still today, despite the Romans, Saxons, Danes, and Normans, whose invasions threatened to wipe all learning from the land.

Amid these descriptions of readerly pleasure and teacherly skill are hints of Sidney's reluctance to affirm traditional claims, newly popular in the sixteenth century, about poetry's esoteric power. Sidney recalls the legend of Amphion, whose verse moved the stones used to build Thebes. Music issuing from Orpheus's lute tamed a "stony and beastly people." These and other stories of transformation explain, according to Sidney, why Romans called a poet *vates*, meaning diviner, foreseer, or prophet, a "heavenly title" that signifies "heart-ravishing knowledge."[35]

"Heart-ravishing knowledge" is not the same as the "divine fury" invoked by many of Sidney's poetic peers, particularly those influenced by theories of the occult. Sidney's idiosyncratic description identifies the prophet as a figure who feels what he knows, based on a false etymology that derived *vates* (diviner) from *vi mentis* (with violence of mind). By linking poetry's prophetic power to heart-ravishing knowledge, Sidney foreshadows what later sections of the treatise assume, that poetry names a concern with emotional change and the question of how language can both affect and reflect what is felt.

In the immediate context, however, this epithet elides the transition from linguistic virtues to the power of prophecy, from the charming sweetness, feigned conversations, and delicate movements Sidney highlights in his descriptions of exemplary poets and poetry to the intensities of the *vates*.[36]

To illustrate these intensities, Sidney includes even uses of poetry he deems superstitious, as with the Roman practice of imputing talismanic power to verses from Virgil. Sidney gives this practice an English genealogy, narrating how Albinus, a second-century governor of Britain, selected at random a line from the *Aeneid*, "arma amens capio nec sat rationis in armis" (with frenzy seized, I take up arms though there is no reason in it), and quoted the Roman poet's line whenever he launched into frenzied action in defense of the British Isles. Sidney acknowledges that Albinus lost control with frightening frequency, but he withholds political or moral judgment. Is this an example of poetry empowering good governors or bad? Does Virgil's verse encourage virtue or vice? Sidney draws no conclusions about the activity that poetry inspires, choosing instead to focus on the way poetry inspires action. Although it is "a very vain and godless superstition" to think that "spirits were commanded by such verses," Albinus's appeal to the word is exemplary. And however mistaken its account of causality, the practice of quoting Virgil rightly shows "great reverence" for his potent poem.[37]

This veneration of poetry is likewise justified by the fact that the oracles of Delphos and Sibylla delivered their prophecies in verse form, displaying an "exquisite observing of number and measure in the words" that appropriately expressed the "high flying liberty of conceit proper to the poet." Number and measure had occult connotations for many thinkers in the sixteenth century. "High flying liberty" could conjure images of esoteric knowledge. Sidney, however, stays low to the ground, observing instead that poesy "does seem to have some divine force in it."[38]

Sidney's equivocating language cues the reader to wonder what a divine force might entail. What could it be, if not couched in mystery or experienced as frenzied or supernatural?

Here Sidney summons David, known by tradition as author of the Psalms, for an appearance that is as vivid as it is brief. David is an example of a *vates*—a prophet, foreseer, or diviner, as Sidney defines it. "And may not I . . . say that the holy David's Psalms are a divine poem?" he asks. Immediately after the passage about David, Sidney introduces other types of poets, seemingly distinct but all creators of what Sidney calls "fiction."[39] He invokes the Greek work *poiein* to define the poet as "a maker" and compares the poet's fictions to Nature's depth, and then lists three different kinds of fiction-makers—the divine poets, the historical or philosophical writers, and the "right poets"— seemingly in order to leave the first behind as he focuses on the difference between the second and third.[40]

Many readers understandably conclude that "right" or secular poets are the primary subject of Sidney's *Defence*, because other than this short, albeit memorable, account of David's craft, the work contains only glancing references to the "poetical part" of Scripture. A few, observing that David's appearance is more significant than its brevity would indicate, argue that it betrays confusion or indecision on Sidney's part. Bates says Sidney wants to claim divine status for right poets but dares not do so directly. Anne-Marie Miller-Blaise says Sidney partially presents David as a right poet but does not go all the way.[41] Anne Lake Prescott, who demonstrates the many ways that Psalms influenced Sidney's view of poetry, pronounces herself puzzled by the way Sidney presents David as an inspired model only to then deny the role of inspiration in the work of the right poet. "It was, I think, precisely the peculiar status of the Psalms, so like 'right poetry' and yet beyond emulation," Prescott conjectures, that explains why Sidney alternatively hails and sequesters David.[42] The appeal to David betrays Sidney's ambivalence, Ramie Targoff observes, for he cannot decide where biblical prayer poems stand in relation to his primary subject, the right poet who is "monarch" of all human sciences and knowledge "according to the human conceit." Targoff consequently concludes that Sidney's invocation of the Psalms betray a "nervous and self-conscious attempt to reconcile poetry and prayer."[43]

Yet there is nothing nervous about Sidney's rendition of David's achievement. In hailing the Psalms, Sidney speaks as a confident biblicist *and* rhetorician, offering a bravado celebration of biblical poetics. The work of King David is rightly described as divine, he explains, for the following reasons: because his songs are free, changing and musical, entertaining and magical; because the Psalms evoke joyful animals and leaping hills, and set the stage for the entrance of a majestic god. All this in a few memorable lines:

> And may I not presume a little further, to show the reasonableness of this word *vates*, and say that the holy David's Psalms are a divine poem? If I do, I shall not do it without the testimony of great learned men, both ancient and modern. But even the name of psalms will speak for me, which being interpreted, is nothing but songs; then, that it is fully written in metre, as all learned hebricians agree, although the rules be not yet fully found; lastly and principally, his handling his prophecy, which is merely poetical. For what else is the awaking his musical instruments, the often and free changing of persons, his notable *prosopopoeias*, when he maketh you, as it were, see God coming in His majesty, his telling of the beasts' joyfulness and hills leaping, but a heavenly poesy, wherein almost he showeth himself a passionate lover of that unspeakable and everlasting beauty to be seen by the eyes of the mind, only cleared by faith?[44]

Were it not for the tongue-twisting *prosopopoeia*, set apart in italics, a reader might lose sight of the technical rhetorical points ensconced in the lively scene. David does everything a poetical prophet should do. Prophecy must be communicated, and this prophet, a passionate lover of everlasting beauty, is adept at poesy, the "skill or crafte of making."[45]

This enumeration of heavenly craft assumes the reader's knowledge of the Psalms and classical rhetoric alike. The awaking of musical instruments evokes the rhetorical strategy of invocation, as in the psalmist's line "I will sing unto Thee [O Lord] among the nations" (Psalm 57:9). The "often and free changing of persons" signals the interchange of voices, difficult to describe but on display throughout the entire Book of Psalms, where the grammatical voice readily switches from first to second to third person, and the speaker alternates and even merges divine and human: "I have set my King upon Zion," David declares in Psalm 2:6, ventriloquizing God, before speaking for himself in the next line: "I will declare the decree, The Lord hath said unto me, Thou art my son." The voice switches again in the final lines. "Serve the Lord in fear," the psalmist concludes, in words that may be his or God's: "Kiss the Son, lest he be angry" (Psalm 2:11–12).[46]

With prosopopoeia, the next rhetorical strategy listed, Sidney uses the technical term for personifying speakers—a term known from rhetorical handbooks filled with examples from Greek and Roman literature, and readily illustrated with Psalm 50's line about the heavens declaring divine righteousness. The final item on Sidney's list, the psalmist's capacity to "maketh you see," refers to rhetorical animation, demonstrated by Psalm 29's description of how the "voice of the Lord" "breaketh cedars," "divideth the flames of fire," and "maketh the wilderness to tremble." The destruction wrought by divine speech is itself enacted on the page, as words bring this chaotic scene of linguistic destruction to life. Adjoining lines evoke quieter scenes of delivery and discovery, for God's words also "maketh the hinds to calve, and discovereth the forests" (Psalm 29:5, 7–9). Implicit in these lines is a twofold claim: God is the great practitioner of rhetorical animation, and rhetorical animation enacts what God proclaims.

Sidney's excursus on the linguistic liveliness of the Psalms begins with a deferential question and predictable answers, before introducing something more surprising. "May not I presume a little further," he asks, "to show the reasonableness of this word *vates*, and say that the holy David's Psalms are a divine poem?" It is entirely reasonable to describe the Psalms as both divine and poetic, his first three points confirm. On this, external authorities and conventional definitions agree. Learned men, past and present, regularly refer to the Psalms as sacred songs, Sidney observes first. His second and third point appeal to the most basic definition of poetry. The very word "psalm" connotes song, he reminds his readers—a point that confirms that the biblical Psalms are rightly understood as lyrical. Moreover, "all learned hebricians agree" that they are written in meter, though the metrical rules are not yet fully known. Although this last point, about meter, is contested by modern scholarship, Sidney's description of why the Psalms are poetic otherwise accords with what scholars today know about these biblical texts. Many, although by no means all, Psalms were composed to be sung in the temple cult, likely with orchestral accompaniment. Indeed, the Hebrew term for "psalm" is *mizmor*, which means "something sung," and this is what the word connoted from its earliest appearance in vernacular English, as in a 1510 text, referring to reports from Portuguese explorers, about non-European "hymns and psalmes and other orasouns." This meaning holds in Puttenham's contemporary *Arte of English Poesie* (1589), describing musicians who greeted an audience with "a Psalme of new applausions."[47] Hebrew prosody continues to confound those who associate poetry with regular metrics of the kind manifested in Greek and Latin poetry, and Sidney's confidence that "learned hebricians" would discover "metrical rules" was unfounded.[48] Still, Sidney's observation that the title of this biblical book underscores its poetic nature can be amplified by comparison with the name used in the Hebrew Bible, where the Psalms are referred to collectively as *Tehilim*, "Praises," an alternative title that emphasizes content.

Sidney's predictable points make it easy to overlook the un-predictable aspect of what follows. After three conventional ob-servations confirming the reasonableness of his claim that the Psalms are rightly described as divine poems, Sidney strikes out on his own, becoming more lyrical himself as he insists that di-vinity inheres in the poetry itself. "Lastly and principally," he explains, the focus will be on "his handling his prophecy, which is merely poetical." Prophecy is poetic. Sidney goes on to per-form what he proclaims here, by evoking a landscape enlivened by a sacred power.[49]

Why? If Sidney's goal was simply to enlist scripture to his cause, it would have sufficed to remind readers that the Bible contains poetry and poetry is therefore endorsed by the Bible. Alternatively, if Sidney's aim was to cover poetry in a patina of holiness, he might have just reiterated that David's Psalms are rightly considered holy because David himself was a bibli-cal prophet. Or Sidney could have gone the esoteric route, for example by invoking calculations of number and measure that preoccupied many of his contemporaries, especially in France but in Tudor England as well, who pursued quantitative and musical experiments with the Psalms.[50] Why associate proph-ecy with the most obvious and basic features of poetic language?

John Guillory speculates that this failure to affirm that a transcendent deity is the source of David's prophetic power re-flects Sidney's inchoate desire to replace God with the imagina-tion. Sidney's *Defence* represents a moment in European litera-ture when the idea of imagination began to "wander," Guillory contends. Well aware that imagination was not a new term or a novel concern, Guillory nevertheless detects a significant shift in Sidney's work, suggesting that the *Defence* works in the gap that had opened up between theories of *furor poeticus* (related to inspiration of the prophets) and new notions of creativity. The *Defence* does not fully develop what would become a notion of autonomous artistic creativity, Guillory observes, but it moves in that direction by detaching imagination from its traditional association with images and perception.[51] Quoting Sidney's claim that Plato divinized poetry in a way he himself did not, Guillory says that Sidney avoids attributions of divine inspiration when talking about the Psalms for the same reason he eschews claims of godly intervention in talking about nonbiblical poetry: because Sidney does not believe an external force is the source of poetry's power. "The originality of Sidney's *Apology* perhaps lies in just this intuition," Guillory conjectures. Sidney "must redeem poetry from its fallen state, its secularity, without returning, as Tasso did, to the mystified notion of the inspired poet."[52]

Guillory rightly recognizes that Sidney abjured mystified notions of the inspired poet. Sidney redeems poetry *without* appeal to an inspired poet. And yet even Guillory's subtle account of imagination presumes a static distinction between secular and divine poetry. "The imagination enters upon the English scene," Guillory concludes, "uneasily allied to a view of poetry emptied of divinity."[53] Here Guillory presumes the very idea that needs to be explored. To empty poetry of divine *inspiration* is not necessarily the same as emptying it of *divinity*. Although Guillory acknowledges that Sidney does not sequester the Psalms by simply listing them as a scriptural antecedent and warrant for secular poetry, he seems unprepared to learn from Sidney's own account of what makes David's poetry divine. Put simply, Sidney rejects divine force, not divinity. Indeed, there has yet been no satisfactory answer to the question Guillory raises: why does Sidney's defense of poetry, divine and otherwise, eschew claims of divine fury and esoteric forces?

Most scholars, seeking to answer this question, appeal to the version of Sidney as a moderate Protestant concerned with social order, first detailed in the biography by his friend Sir Fulke Greville: "He made the Religion he professed, the firm Basis of his life; For this was his judgement (as he often told me) that our true-heartedness to the Reformed Religion in the beginning brought Peace, Safetie, and Freedom to us."[54] Guillory himself assumes this when he argues that Sidney viewed poetry as a kind of "moral mimesis," and wanted especially to "moralize" the imagination.[55] Decorum is Sidney's highest value, Nandra Perry argues, and understandably so, given his searing experience of seeing dismembered bodies and mass killings during the St. Bartholomew Day's Massacre, and the less dramatic but equally influential everyday experiences he had of the unruliness of corporate bodies. Sidney was, after all the son of a courtier father who was in and out of favor, and a courtier himself subject to the whims of more than one monarch.[56] Robert Stillman offers a theological explanation for Sidney's refusal to implicate God in his arguments about poetry's social value, explaining that it can be attributed to what he learned from reformed theologians, especially Melanchthon, about the importance of differentiating human and divine nature.[57] Leaving aside any attempt at explanation, two editors of a modern critical edition of Sidney's *Defence* nevertheless confirm the premise: although many contemporary defenses of poetry, particularly on the continent, claimed "divine fury" as the source of poetry's power, Sidney eschewed esotericism.[58]

The answer on display in Sidney's own work differs, however, in the following way: for Sidney, the divinity of the Psalm inheres not in an external source or in a hidden content but in textual features, including the interchange of voices, personification, and rhetorical animation. This inspired form is not exterior *to* the words. Form is the energy *of* the words, the energy here attributed to the psalmist's poetics—the capacity to have an effect associated, as described above, with both faith and rhetoric.

David may be sequestered in the early pages of the treatise. But his poesy—the rhetorical skill inscribed on the page— persists. Sidney's first use of the word *poesy* is in reference to David, describing the way his changing voices and personifications bring God, the beasts, and the hills to life as "heavenly poesy." The word next appears in Sidney's "more ordinary opening," with the standard rhetorician's reference to Aristotle's notion of *mimesis*: "Poesy therefore is an art of imitation," Sidney explains, "which is to say, a representing, counterfeiting, or figuring forth," like a speaking picture.[59] Heavenly poesy is like all other poesy in this respect: its liveliness and efficacy depends on linguistic artifice. Crucially, the passages linking David's poesy to poesy aligned with Aristotle's notion of mimesis are primarily concerned to differentiate both from Nature. David's poesy, like the other poesy Sidney defends, imitates *and* invents. All poesy, biblical and otherwise, is imaginative in this sense: it is a form of imitation free of slavish replication. Poetry's feigning and counterfeiting is different than copying, Sidney insists. By figuring forth, divine poets and right poets alike create the linguistic equivalent of a speaking picture, using words to bring their worlds to life.

All this suggests that for Sidney the important distinction is not between divine poets and right poets but between imitation and copying.[60] All poetry worthy of the name, according to his definition, differs from slavish copying because it transforms the reality it reflects. "There is no art delivered to mankind that hath not the works of Nature for his principal object," Sidney observes, *except* poetry. Astronomers and musicians and lawyers and grammarians and rhetoricians and logicians and physicians are all "actors and players, as it were, of what Nature will have set forth." This is true even of the metaphysician, for although he deals in abstractions that should be counted supernatural, even so he too "doth . . . build upon the depth of Nature." Poetry stands alone in this respect. "Only the poet, disdaining to be tied to any such subjection, lifted up with the vigour of his own invention, doth grow in effect into another nature." This sentence introduces Sidney's most expansive vision of poetry. The poet, he says, makes "things either better than Nature bringeth forth, or, quite anew." Uniquely among all practitioners of human arts, poets are not bound to take Nature as the object of inquiry; poets are not "actors and players" performing at Nature's behest. A poet, uniquely, goes "hand in hand with Nature" *and* beyond, "not enclosed within the narrow warrant of [Nature's] gifts, but freely ranging only within the zodiac of his own wit." This passage concludes with Sidney's strongest contrast between poetry's power and natural creation: "Nature never set forth the earth in so rich tapestry as divers poets have done; neither with pleasant rivers, fruitful trees, sweet-smelling flowers, nor whatsoever else may make the too much loved earth more lovely." Nature's world is "brazen," Sidney says in one of the *Defence*'s most memorable contrasts, while the poets deliver a world that is "golden." Mere copyists are bound to nature, while poetry's art of imitation, properly practiced, creates something that expands beyond the materials used in the creation.[61]

Reading this exalted vision of poetic creativity—freely drawing on the wit or mind to conjure golden worlds—some conclude that Sidney subverts the hierarchy that places God above humans. Others detect ambivalence or hesitation. Sidney himself, however, takes this opportunity to remind readers that poetry's world is golden insofar as its words bring people to life. The question you should be asking yourself, Sidney says, is whether poetry has brought forth so true a lover as Theagenes—a hero and lover in *Aethiopica*, a Greek prose romance by a fourth-century Christian bishop, and a model for Sidney's *Arcadia*. Can poesy conjure so "constant a friend" as Pylades, so "valiant a man" as Orlando, hero of Ariosto's *Orlando Furioso*, "so right a prince" as Cyrus (hailed by English humanists as a model for monarchs because of his "gentleness, prowesse, liberalities, wisedome, and memorie")? Do the lines of a poem convey the all-around excellence of Virgil's Aeneas (also a favorite exemplar for English humanists)?[62]

Poetry surpasses Nature not because it can create worlds, but because of *how* it creates worlds. The artifice that some take as reason to demean poetry is in fact poetry's point of pride, Sidney insists. Nature can make a Cyrus, but only poetry can reveal the workings of that creation, the "why and how that maker made him." The power of God, in other words, is the capacity for artifice. Humans confirm they are made in the image of the "heavenly Maker" when, "with the force of divine breath," they bring forth things surpassing nature.[63] Understood in context, the force of divine breath echoes the claims made about David a few paragraphs earlier and the definition of poetry as the art of imitation in the very next passage. Otherwise it would seem to be in direct contradiction to a later caveat, that Plato "attributeth unto Poesy more than myself do, namely, to be a very inspiring of a divine force, far above man's wit."[64] Sidney does not privilege access to a force beyond human powers. Neither is he intent on claiming godlike status for human writers. His point is to illuminate what godlike powers entail, for right poets as for David: "neither let it be deemed too saucy a comparison to balance the highest point of man's wit with the efficacy of nature; but rather give right honour to the heavenly Maker of that maker, who having made man to His own likeness, set him beyond and over all the works of that second nature."[65] The inescapable ambiguity of this sentence, suggesting simultaneously that humans are mere copies of God *and* equally free to create, is the ambiguity also of poetry, according to Sidney: a type of writing characterized by use of specific techniques to represent, counterfeit, and figure forth worlds that surpass what Nature has on offer. Sidney thereby does away with any meaningful distinction between divine and right poets. Both imitate and invent (which is to say, discover). In the process, both transform what they've copied.

POETIC DEVOTION

We can see Sidney's attempts to practice what he preaches not only in the lively writing that fills the pages of the *Defence* but also in the forty-three psalm poems he completed before his death. Here Sidney's *imitatio* of the psalmist's voice is indeed *inventio*, locating the reader in the textual present, the psalmist's past, and the salvific future simultaneously—using words to declare the success of what the psalmist's voice aspires to achieve: "To him my voice I spread / From holy hill hee heard mee" (Psalm 3, ll. 14–15). The colorful effect of this juxtaposition can be better understood in comparison to the Geneva Bible's blanched description: "I did call unto the Lord with my voice, and he did hear me from his holy mountain" (Psalm 3:4). The immediacy of this scene might be also be compared to the Sternhold Psalter's more relaxed sense of time: "Then with my voyce upon the Lorde I did bothe call and cry: And he out of his holy hill: did heare me by and by."⁶⁶ In Sidney's version, the interaction is immediate and localized: a small figure at the foot of a mountain calls out, and the mountain, itself conflated with the person of God, somehow conveys that the call has been heard. Active listening personified!

Vivid also is Sidney's description in Psalm 5, when both the speaker's heart and his enemies' tongues are moving figures, albeit to different ends: "And in thy fear, knees of my hart will fold, / Towards the temple of thy hollinesse . . . Their throate it is an open swallowing grave. Whereto their tongue is a flattring instrument" (Psalm 5, ll. 27–28). For this passage, too, the Geneva Bible has a more anodyne description—"& in thy feare will I worship towards thine holie Temple"—while the Sternhold renders the lines as a simple confirmation of obedience: "Therefore will I come to thy house, /trusting upon thy grace: And reverently will worship thee, toward thy holy place" (Psalm 5:7). Moreover, the decision, in both Geneva and Sternhold, to describe the tomb simply as an "open sepulcher" sharpens by contrast the vividness of Sidney's swallowing grave.

In Psalm 6, Sidney directly poses the central question of *energeia*: "Can, of thy praise, the tongues entombed make / A heav'nly story?" (Psalm 6, ll. 15–16). His question greatly expands what is available in either the Geneva Bible or Sternhold Psalter, reconfiguring the former's question—"in the grave who shalt praise thee?"—into the more urgent matter of whether Sidney's poetry can give mortal voices the capacity to tell immortal tales. Sidney's framing excludes the possibility of divine intervention or revelation: the question instead is whether human speech, subject to the swallowing grave, might nevertheless have an energetic effect on the reader—the effect associated with faith and rhetoric alike.

Notably, in this poetic context, Sidney's reference to a "heaven'ly story" does not carry the connotation so much of narrative as of the interest in time, place, person, and setting associated with the Greek rhetorical notion of *energeia*. In his study of *enargeia* (or vividness, which, in the Renaissance, was often conflated with *energeia*'s connotation of vitality), as a rhetoric of experience, Gerard Sharpling observes that dialogue was an optimal format for Renaissance writers seeking to move people with their writing, because of the presumption inherited from classical rhetoric that transformation was an interactive process.[67] Sidney wonders, "how long (O Lord) shall I forgotten be? / What? ever?" (Psalm 13, ll. 1–2). The question presumes a hearer, even as it expresses fear of not being heard. "There is no speach, nor language, which/ Is soe of skill bereaved," he goes on, "But of the skies the teaching cries, / They have heard and conceaved" (Psalm 19, ll. 9–12). Speaking and being heard creates a reciprocal dynamic that overrides questions of skill: "there be no eye, but read the line / from some fair booke proceeding: / Their words be sett in letters great / For ev'ry bodies reading" (Psalm 19, ll. 13–16). Terrence Cave says that this effusive use of language, the bounty of *copia*, elides distinctions between true and false language and renders moot any distinction between words and what they represent.[68] "Therefore my tongue shall never lack / Thy endless praise: O God, my king, / I will thee thanks for ever sing," Sidney writes in Psalm 19 (ll. 37–39), confirming an effusive trust in language undaunted by uncertainties about how words relate to reality.

In *De Copia*, the rhetorical handbook he published in 1512, Desiderius Erasmus illustrates his understanding of *energeia* by referencing passages from Quintilian, as when Quintilian talks about how a phrase like "a city taken by storm" (*expugnatam*

civitatem) can be vivified by moving beyond descriptive detail
to convey a sense of speed and breathlessness.

> Some people fleeing, not knowing where they are going, others
> locked in a last embrace of their loved ones, the wails of babies
> and women, and old men cruelly preserved by fate to see this day;
> then we shall see the inevitable plundering of secular and sacred,
> the running to and fro of men carrying off loot or looking for
> more, prisoners in chains, each in charge of his personal robber.[69]

Here, Sharpling observes, the "sense impressions created by
the scene of destruction in the first part of the passage lead to
a precipitous exploration of the effect of calamity at a personal
level."[70] Sidney does something very like this in his poetic rendering of Psalm 32:

> Thus I, press down with weight of paine,
> Whether I silent did remaine
> Or roar'd, my boanes still waste.
> For some both day and night did stand
> On wretched me, thy heavy hand,
> My life hott tormentes tasted.
>
> Till, my self, did my faults confesse,
> and opened mine one wickedness
> Whereto my hart did give me:
> So I my self accused to God,
> And his sweet grace streight eas'd the rodd,
> and did due paine forgive me. (ll. 7–18)

Here the self who speaks to God, in words derived from texts
written originally in another language—texts made available to
Sidney by Latin, French, and English translators and changed,
in turn, by him into yet another poetic English version—claims
what the words convey for himself, speaking in the first person,

but not for himself alone. According to the speaker, what he experiences is altered because the words are heard by another.

THE PSALMIST'S SUBJECT

In short, Sidney's psalm poems manifest the energy his *Defence* identifies as poetry's greatest virtue. Nevertheless, even for those who recognize that biblical poetry is key to Sidney's case for "right" poetry, it is easy to minimize his interest in biblical *poetics*. Two examples illustrate this point. Kimberly Coles, who memorably describes Sidney's Psalter as the laboratory for his poetic principles, argues that Sidney is unable to reconcile the contradiction between his Calvinist belief in the hobbled will and his humanist confidence in the erected wit. According to Coles, in other words, the primary issue is not poetic but theological.[71] Roland Greene likewise recognizes that Sidney's English versions of the Psalms represent the English poet's attempt to put his principles into practice. But Greene's argument, that Sidney aspired to create a Psalter that "in delivering its fiction, struggles free of ritual uses at nearly every hand," concludes that Sidney ultimately failed to subsume ritual poetry's communal voice into fictional poetry's singular poetic "I." For Greene, in other words, the primary issue is not the language itself but what language reveals about the state of the subject.[72]

These readings, sophisticated though they are, reflect the common impulse to steer attention away from the poetics to the poet. But Sidney's case for the power of poetry is consistent in this one respect, from start to finish: poetry's power is internal rather than external to its language. Poetic energy arises from the interplay of voices, personification, and metaphor, and thus the effect these linguistic forms have on the reader. This is true in Sidney's description of the Psalms as "merely poetical" just as it is when he declares "right" poetry superior to historical or philosophical writing: divinity *is*, in short, the energy of the poetic voice.

Sidney imbibed this understanding of poetic energy from a long tradition of Christian psalmic devotion and commentary. The language of the Psalms gives voice to all possible feelings, Athanasius of Alexandria explained in the fourth century, so that each person can find a Psalm that fits her mood, amplifies it, and directs it toward God.[73] In the words of Athanasius's sixteen-century English translator, the "alterations of every mans hart" can be found in the Psalms. More than that, the Psalms make these alterations or feelings more intense, for in the Psalms what is in the reader's heart is "lively paynted to his owne sight."[74] This does not mean the Psalms reinforced a solipsistic devotional interiority, according to this commentarial tradition, for the assumption was that these distinctive feelings, experienced within, were also shared feelings, which enabled each reader to identify and even merge with a different personage. "We know, love, and experience God," Cassian said, also in the fourth century, in a book *The Rule of St. Benedict* directs monks to read, "when our experience and the Psalmist's experience converge." This experiential convergence makes it possible to truly know and love God, transforming the one who sings and reads and prays the words of the Psalms into the author of the Psalms, traditionally identified as the biblical King David and theologically associated with the Holy Spirit, as well as Christ: "When we have the same disposition [*affectum*] in our heart with which each psalm was sung or written down," Cassian explains, "then we shall become like the Holy Spirit, the author of the Psalms."[75] This same commentarial tradition offered a rhetorical or stylistic explanation for the distinctiveness of the Psalms (here encapsulated by a sixteenth-century English translator of John Calvin's commentary on the Psalms): "whereas other partes of holy writ . . . do commonly set down their treatises in open and plaine declarations: this parte [the Psalms] consisting of them all, wrappeth up things in types & figures, describing them under borrowed personages."[76]

In his work on the Psalms, Sidney—like Luther—demonstrates how the "borrowed personages" of the text serve as the locus of devotional reading. This is a crucial context for understanding the final line of Sidney's Psalm paragraph, where he concludes that the everlasting beauty revealed by the passionate psalmist can be "seen by the eyes of the mind" only if the mind's eye is "cleared by faith."[77] Scholars of Christian history may know the "eye of faith" motif from early Christian writers such as Jerome or Augustine of Hippo.[78] Yet Sidney's reference to how the beauty inscribed in the Psalms can be seen by the eyes of the mind links to an account, just two paragraphs later, of how poetry manifests the "*Idea*" of the work. Just as the eyes of the mind can see only if cleared by faith, so too the "skill of the artificer standeth in that *Idea* or fore-conceit of the work, and not in the work itself." In both cases, he seems to be invoking something external to the words in order to explain how the words become revelatory. For each instance, this notion that an external force is required is belied by the emphasis on how the medium enables perception. "That the poet hath that *Idea* is manifest," Sidney explains, "by delivering them forth in such excellency as he hath imagined them."[79]

What Sidney offers here is not a philosophically rigorous account of the relationship between words and ideas but instead his own foray into his own era's vexed questions about the reliability of perception. In early modern England, as Elizabeth Swann has shown, Augustine's concerns about how the corporeality of the eye impedes its access to self-knowledge became the basis of a general skepticism about the eye's capacity to see. Taking Sir John Davies's *Nosce Teipsum* (1622) as her example, Swann shows how Davies follows Augustine in trying out, and then rejecting, the eye analogy.

> Is it because the minde is like the eye [. . .]
> Not seeing it selfe, when other things it sees?
> No doubtless, for the minde can backward cast
> Vpon her selfe, her vnderstanding light;
> But she is so corrupt, and so defac't,
> As her own image doth her selfe affright.[80]

Davies then departs from Augustine in suggesting that it is possible to make a mirror of one's mind—to know, in other words, not directly but through mediated self-representation.[81] In Davies, as in Sidney, this mediation is the poem itself. As Swann puts it, "Davies poeticises the soul in order to discern it."[82] This brief excursus underscores the perils of simply assuming that Sidney invokes faith as a commonplace or an external guarantor, to ensure what rhetoric alone cannot achieve. Sidney instead affirms that poetry is a source of faith's clarifying knowledge.

3. MARTIN LUTHER

There are no obvious reasons to compare Sidney, an English poet, and Luther, a German theologian who died eight years before Sidney's birth. Perhaps it is even stranger to do so without any claims of direct influence, and in a sequence that ignores Luther's historical precedence.[83] My choice to pursue this comparison, and its ordering, can be attributed to a combination of scholarly and personal idiosyncracies. The immediate impetus was a paper I heard at a conference panel on Sidney, suggesting that Luther could be counted a poetic rival, for Luther's successive revisions of his German Psalm translations reveal a poet's mind at work.[84] Was the poetic Luther there to be found even in his early Psalm commentaries, I wondered? Could my newfound appreciation of the Psalms, and of the long commentarial tradition's reliance on the classical rhetorical tradition, change the way I approached a text I remembered as a graduate school slog?

My previously published work on Luther was about his use of invectives—a topic inspired by the way students recoiled from his rhetoric.[85] I wrote it in the early years of teaching Luther, wanting my students to have ways of thinking beyond their first reactions, to appreciate that Luther, like his message, was multifaceted, and to learn something of what my own teachers had taught me: that the vile is often entwined with the virtuous, that the attempt to separate good religon from bad religion has a long and damaging history, and that the power of language is multifaceted. In the article I argued that Luther's rhetoric was fierce because he believed sinful self-deception was so insidious and entrenched. He railed against everything he deemed misguided—including the greedy trade in indulgences, a metaphorical understanding of the Lord's Supper, and Erasmus's attempt to keep the peace by agreeing to disagree about free will—with equal ferocity, believing any and all of these mistakes served the devil's aim: to blind people to the gospel's good news of salvation through Christ. Luther wanted to clear the way and shock people into recognition of a truth that convention, custom, and self-absorption—whether prideful or despairing—prepared them to deny. This same worldview motivated Luther's attacks against peasants seeking relief from their overlords and his increasingly harsh condemnation of Judaism in the abstract and actual Jews in sixteenth-century Europe.[86]

Satisfied with my own explanation for Luther's reliance on invective, I continued teaching but not writing about him for years, preferring instead to work on poetry and other less polemical forms of theology. And so it was with some surprise, leavened with a researcher's excitement about the possibility of new insights or interpretations (and, in this case, a bit of self-satisfaction about my own willingness to revisit a source I had once disdained), that I returned to the section of the library filled with row upon row of works by and about Luther and, for the first time in twenty years, picked up the *Dictata*.

Poetry paved the way for a newly sympathetic reading. What had been a long, boring commentary became a captivating work of poetic theory. Luther confirmed what I had learned from Sidney and other commentators about the vivifying power of the Psalms. Luther also intensified traditional claims about the Psalms' "unique virtue" by insisting with characteristic vehemence that their efficacy depended on the text itself, not the reader. The Luther I encountered in the *Dictata* was not entirely unfamiliar. I already knew him as a sometimes didactic and

abrasive teacher who was also psychologically astute, pasto-
rally sensitive, and very often willing to speculate as he spoke.
But I had not known him as a poet, and that is what he became
in my reading—not because he was crafting lines of poetry but
because he was a perceptive theorist of poetics, easily related
to the translator who created ever more poetic Psalms and the
skilled composer that musicologists refer to admiringly as the
songbird of Wittenberg.

My single-minded focus on Luther's poetics made it possible
to minimize or ignore aspects of his work that were alienating.
Luther's doctrinal statements about Christ suggest a simple
faith I have never had or aspired to. Reading poetically, however, I could subsume his insistence that every correct reading
depends on Christ into an account of textual vivification. Reading poetically also shielded me from Luther's anti-Judaism by
giving me license to assess his attacks on Jews as illustrative of
his efforts to differentiate deadening interpretation from enlivening reception. In one way my reading clearly violates Luther: I draw attention to some aspects of his thought and ignore
others; I marginalize ideas and beliefs he deemed essential; and
I could fairly be described as misrepresenting his aims. In another
way, however, my reading is entirely faithful to Luther, for in its
single-mindedness it mirrors his approach to Jewish sources.

Just as I consider everything in light of a single primary topic,
so too Luther steals from Judaism to make something of his own,
exploiting Jewish scholarship and distorting Jewish interpretations in the process. Interpreting Luther in this way, I am not
directly encouraging violence, as Luther's readings and writings
certainly did, both in his own day and subsequently. Rather, as
the first half of this essay confirms, I am looking where Sidney
has taught me to look. My readings of Sidney (and by extension, Luther), like Sidney's own poetics, are thereby situated at
a remove from the urge to conquest and dehumanization pervasive in Sidney's society, as in our own. These readings (Sidney's of poetry, mine of Sidney, and mine of Luther) might

thereby be complicit in the perpetuation of a destructive status quo. But the way I read, like the readings I teach, is motivated by the conviction that learning to recognize and assess the way we are all speaking in the voices of others is essential to politics experienced as the collective process of navigating the terrain where the real confronts the ideal and the possibility of creating a world that does not default to violence. To consider the analogy between myself and Luther is thus to bring to the fore questions about how devotional reading breaks faith *and* keeps faith with its sources and its readers. To notice my own ambivalence about Luther, and the ways that he himself would not recognize the poetic figure I depict, is to learn from Luther and also— I hope—to expose the dynamics not only of my own devotional reading, but of his.

"THE VIRTUE OF THE BOOK OF PSALMS IS UNIQUE"

Martin Luther was devoted to the Psalms throughout his career. As a monk, he prayed them daily. He had the entire book memorized long before he became a doctor of theology, at the University of Wittenburg, in 1512. Two years after concluding the *Dictata*, his first university lectures, Luther wrote a book on the seven "penitential" psalms, *Die Sieben Bußpsalmen*, which became the first book published under his name, in the spring of 1517.[87] He lectured on the Psalms between 1518 and 1521, during three of the most eventful years of a life that never lacked intensity. While debating papal representatives, living under the threat of excommunication, and penning the three famous works of 1520 that spread his message far beyond theological circles, Luther composed an incomplete commentary on the Psalms. The first volume of this work, carefully revised and printed in fascicles with the title *Operationes in Psalmos*, was published in 1519 and the last in 1521.[88] Seven years later, in 1528, Luther completed his first German translation of the Psalms. In 1530 he published a pastoral guide to the Psalms. A year later, when he revised his translation, he provided an exposition of the first twenty-five psalms. To defend this revision of the Psalter, Luther offered a systematic account of the right use of the Psalter, dividing prophetic, instructive, consoling, prayer, and thanksgiving Psalms in 1533.[89] The Psalms also play a prominent role in Luther's 1545 account of how he, a miserably scrupulous monk, found relief. There, he tells us he was preparing his second lecture on the Psalms while rereading Romans when a new interpretation of Romans 1:17 made him feel as if he was "altogether born again," and a "totally other face of the entire Scripture showed itself."[90]

In one important respect, however, "this totally other face of the entire Scripture" was the same visage Luther had seen years earlier in the Psalms. What he encountered in the Psalms from first to last was the clarion voice of Christ, promising salvation. Printed at the head of the Psalm texts provided to each of Luther's students, with room to write down the words of his lecture, was the voice of Christ: "I am the door; if anyone enters by Me, he will be saved, and will go in and out and find pasture" (John 10:9).[91] Christ is the subject and object of all of the Psalms, Luther declared in tandem with Christian exegetical tradition, and he echoed Augustine specifically—whose *Ennerationes in Psalmos* were cited 250 times in the *Dictata*—when he reminded his auditors that the literal meaning of each Psalm refers to Christ.[92] What he rejected was not so much allegory, for over the centuries allegorical interpretations, such as the notion that the Song of Songs is a love song between God and the soul, had come to be read literally. Rather, Luther set his interpretation over against the historical, declaring that the literal meaning is prophetic. "We have the mind of Christ" (1 Cor. 2:16), Luther assured his readers in an early lecture. "Every prophecy and every prophet must be understood as referring to Christ the Lord, except where it is clear from plain words that someone else is spoken of."[93]

Over the course of the lectures, Luther's emphasis on the prophetic and the words of promise becomes even more pronounced. This shift culminates, or is easiest to see in its most concentrated form, in his lectures on Psalm 119, for reasons discussed below. In studies of the *Dictata*, scholars have singled out Luther's interpretation of this later Psalm because his claim that it is prophetic anticipates his gospel hermeneutic— the principle that the whole of the Bible preaches the good news that Christians are saved by Christ, through faith.[94] I have come to understand that the true intrigue of Luther's early lectures is how he merged a traditional emphasis on the way the Psalms convey the person of Christ with sacramental immediacy with his characteristically dogged insistence that readers should receive rather than interpret, and that the singular message to be received was Christ's prophetic promise of salvation.

A long succession of Christian commentators on the Psalms argued that these biblical prayer poems speak directly to the heart because of the way they use metaphors and voices to conjure sensory and emotional experiences. Luther, too, delighted in the capacity of words to communicate feeling. In this book of the Bible he found what pious readers before and after him had found: the whole range of human emotions, crucially dependent on the words that give expression to these feelings. The "virtue of the Book of Psalms is unique," Luther explained in the preface to his 1528 German translation, for it contains "in the briefest and most beautiful form" everything that is to be found in the Bible. It is "easy," Luther observed, "to understand why the Book of Psalms is the favorite book of all the saints. For every man on every occasion can find in it Psalms which fit his needs, which he feels to be as appropriate as if they had been set there just for his sake."[95]

Luther agreed with his commentarial predecessors that the Psalms are exceptionally effective because our primary needs are emotional. "The human heart is like a ship on a stormy sea driven about by winds blowing from all four corners of heaven," Luther writes with poetic sympathy. "In one man," he explains, "there is fear and anxiety about impending disaster; another groans and moans at all the surrounding evil. One man mingles hope and presumption out of the good fortune to which he is looking forward; and another is puffed up with a confidence and pleasure in his present possessions." These storms teach us to speak "sincerely and frankly," to "make a clean breast." But although this lesson comes from experience, one which we each must feel for ourselves, one person alone cannot give voice to those things that lie in the "bottom of [our] hearts." Speech is the "most powerful and exalted of human faculties," Luther affirms. However, this does not mean that each person already has the words and craft needed to give voice to their experience. To "lay bare" the heart, to see the "deepest treasures hidden in [the] soul," and to understand the nature and causes of human action, we need the "noble utterances" recorded in the Psalms.[96]

"Where can one find nobler words to express joy than in the Psalms of praise or gratitude?" Luther asked. "Or where can one find more profound, more penitent, more sorrowful words in which to express grief than in the Psalms of lamentation?" Emotion relies on speech, and speech gains power from its capacity to express emotion. For him, above all, the Psalms exemplify the height of poetic power. "So, too, when the Psalms speak of fear or hope, they depict fear and hope more vividly than any painter could do, and with more eloquence than that possessed by Cicero or the greatest of the orators."[97] Employing the words of the Psalms, one can talk to God and sing with the saints. In the Psalms, the church itself is "depicted in living colors, and given a living form."[98] "You want to know yourself?" Luther asks of his reader. The Book of Psalms is a "beautiful, bright, polished mirror." In it you can see yourself, but not only that—also the church, and "God Himself." The liveliness of Luther's language mirrors the vividness he attributes to the words of the Psalms. The Psalter's words, he insists, are potent and powerful, unparalleled in their vitality.[99]

What Luther encountered in the Psalms is abundantly clear

in his earliest Psalm lectures: first, the enlivening power of the Word, uniquely concentrated in this biblical book because of the way the voice of the psalmist gives voice to the believer; second, his insistence that Christ is the Word, and the Word is the source of salvation; and, finally, his conviction that the right understanding of salvation depends on a perspectival shift. In *Freedom of a Christian* and in other works from 1520, Luther would say clearly that the focus must be on faith, not works, not on what sinners do to merit salvation but on how salvation is received as a free gift of divine grace. So too, years earlier, in the *Dictata*, he emphasizes a corollary point that is foundational to all the rest: a right and true apprehension of oneself and of God, and indeed of reality, depends not on how readers interpret the Word but on how the Word affects readers.

"REVIVE ME ACCORDING TO YOUR WORD"

Thus in the earliest lectures in the *Dictata*, as throughout the entire series, Luther relished the fecund imagery, seldom missing an opportunity to praise the Word's generative power. "Happy are those who . . . delight in the law of the Lord, and on his law they meditate day and night," Psalm 1 declares, for "they are like trees, planted by streams of water, which yield their fruit in its season, and their leaves do not wither" (Psalm 1:1–3). What the Psalm says about the righteous, Luther applies to the words they reflect upon: "The very rock of Scripture gushes forth abundant streams and flowing waters of knowledge and wisdom, and grace and sweetness besides." It is a subtle but important shift in emphasis, from crediting meditation with insight to reminding readers that the source of this insight is the Word. "Knowledge of Scripture is water in a very special way," Luther continues, "in that it washes, irrigates, and makes fertile . . . for 'grace is poured upon your lips'" (Psalm 45:2). The intertextual citation, between the first and the forty-fifth Psalms, underscores that this fruitful knowledge is received, drunk like water but also, as the reference to lips indicates, conveyed linguistically, by the Word. Quoting again from John, Luther reminds his readers, "The words which [Christ] speaks are life and spirit" (John 6:63). The words of the Psalms are the words of Christ, "worthy to be written not on stones and in dead books but in living hearts." What in Psalm 45 seems more obviously to be a description of how the reader's meditation brings benefits "whose leaves will not wither" becomes a reminder, in Luther's account, that this good comes from Christ. For the "leaves are words," Luther says, and from these words, from Christ the Word, comes all that we need.

Following the Christian commentarial tradition, Luther affirms that meditation transforms what is otherwise inert, fixed, and inaccessible into a generative source of goodness, a plethora of meanings and "an abundance of understanding burst forth." "Therefore, whoever desires to be richly educated and, as it were, be flooded with the flowing waters of knowledge," Luther advises, "let him surrender himself to meditate on the law of the Lord day and night."[100] In Psalm 119, these tender descriptions of traditional meditation give way to a singular focus on testimony and promise. "Your testimonies are my meditation," the psalmist declares in verse 24. To meditate on the testimony or promise of Scripture is now Luther's vital message. He cannot find a single previous commentator who has interpreted this Psalm in a prophetic sense, he tells his auditors, astonished by the blindness. Nevertheless, he declares unconditionally: Psalm 119 is prophetic! Here Luther equates the prophetic with the literal, explaining that the literal-prophetic is the "foundation of the rest." Promise, testimony, prophecy—these are synonymous at this point in Luther's analysis. "For this reason we rejoice, because we believe the divine promises, and we hope for and love the things which He promises."[101]

The modern editors of the Jewish Study Bible point out that Psalm 119 has often been devalued because of its monotonous emphasis on "law," readily—if wrongly—interpreted by Christians as a rigid set of divinely mandated rules. Indeed, the

Psalm uses eight words for "torah," corresponding to its eight-fold acrostic, and nearly all of the 176 verses of the Psalm offer a distinctive synonym for law or torah. Yet this proliferation is the key to Psalm 119's distinctive devotional emphasis, the JSB editors observe, for this Psalm is remarkable in making torah rather than God the focus of devotion.[102] Luther was certainly not the first to perceive that this thematic concentration focused readers' attention on communication, but he thought he was.[103] Christ is known through Christ's Word, Luther says again and again. The result is a sustained commentary on the need to receive rather than interpret the Word. Faith, too, is received rather than cultivated. Elaborated as they are together in Luther's commentary on Psalm 119, faith and words attain a kind of synchronicity. Luther glancingly reminds readers to invest their faith in what the words describe. While his commentary stresses the need to deepen or focus faith on the correct meaning of the divine Word, Luther does not, on the whole, present faith as dependent on the correct meaning or interpretation of scriptural words. Instead, he equates faith with the vivifying *power* of the Word. Christ *is* the Word. The efficacy of the Word, as Luther sees it vividly, is in its capacity to transmit the life-force it signifies: Christ's promise of salvation.

Luther's preferred word to describe the efficacy of words is *vivificare*, to vivify or bring to life. Rare in classical Latin, *vivificare* was often used in ecclesial Latin to describe the action of the Holy Spirit. Explaining verse 25 of Psalm 119, for example, rendered as "Revive me according to your word" in the NRSV and "Vivifica me secundum verbum tuum," in the Vulgate, Luther declares that this "vivificatio" is "of the Spirit itself" (*est ipsius spiritus*). In this early instance, he loops the work of the spirit back around to the action of one worked on by the Spirit. The *vivificatio* that is "of the Spirit itself," he clarifies, is "of the spiritual will" (*voluntatis*). Here he echoes what in medieval Christian theology had become a standard account of the relationship between faith and love: "No matter how learned and enlightened in faith a person may be, unless he also wants and does it with the heart, he does not yet live."[104] As the commentary unspools, however, Luther largely abandons pastoral admonitions about the heart and spiritual will, concentrating instead on the enlivening power of the Word in itself.

Noting that *vivifica* "occurs often in this whole Psalm" (verses 25, 37, 40, etc.), Luther tells his readers he has heard of commentators who would link the first seven verses (Psalm 119:33–39) of the stanza with the seven gifts of the Holy Spirit (*sapientia, intellectus, consilium, fortitudo, scientia, pietas, timor*). He is not sure exactly how these unknown commentators drew the links, or whether those he draws align with any previously provided. Taken with the possibility nevertheless, Luther offers his own version. The primary message, he concludes, therefore "'set a law before me,' that is 'instruct me,' namely, anew" (*scilicet a novo*).[105] Quite right, then, that this set of verses is read in the third canonical hour, when the Holy Spirit was given, for this is the work of the Holy Spirit, Luther observes with satisfaction, transforming the law from stricture into rejuvenating instruction.[106]

Commenting on Psalm 119's reference to a slumbering soul, Luther observes that the Word of God rectifies this shortcoming, for it alone "has motive power" (*vim motivam*). The Word is both sufficient in itself—like a fire that "not only gives light but that also produces heat"—and the source of all that is needed.[107] "Run back to the Word," Luther says, "and you will be strengthened in your purpose."[108] This, he insists, is the Word's answer to the psalmist's recurring plea: "in your ways enliven me" (*In via tua vivifica me*).[109] The Psalms transmit the person of Christ by communicating the *promise* of Christ, and readers find Christ by reading the Psalms, "because faith has to do with things that do not appear, things that cannot be taught, shown, and pointed out—except by the Word."[110] Christ is the prophetic voice and, literally, the words of promised salvation.[111]

Luther signals the priority of words over works by insist-

ing that when the Psalm's speaker refers to being "exercised
[*exerceri*] in wondrous works," he is referring only to the activity of the Word. "Words cannot be exercised in any other way
than with the tongue," Luther says, "it is certainly something
else for works to be exercised." For him, to be active in "wondrous works" means "to discuss, speak, and debate the words of
Christ and 'chirp' them to each other sweetly and swiftly [*invicem
garrire cum suavitate et alacritate*], like the little birds in May."[112]
Smoothly aligning human speech with avian song, Luther suggests that the words of Christ are as sensual as they are sensible,
redolent with feeling as well as meaning. To work with the words
of Christ is to participate in sweet and swift exchanges.[113] "I have
trusted in Thy words," Luther resolves, quoting a later line from
the same Psalm, for words are the source of "grace manifested
and the glory promised."[114] He understands the subject of this
Psalm to be precisely that: the grace-manifesting and glory-
promising word. In lieu of the speaker who demonstrates his
fidelity by imitating divine speech and trying to follow God's
judgments, Luther's psalmist gives us the Word alone.[115]

"INVENTORS OF JEWISH VANITIES"

We need the guidance of the Word, Luther says, because we
would otherwise have to rely on our own thought and will. To
seek with the "whole heart," he explains, means "there is nothing
of one's own will present." Luther accuses "heretics and Jews" of
misunderstanding this line, for when they worship "with a great
heart," it is "according to their own will." Psalm 119, however,
conveys that those who seek need "the mind of Christ,"[116] which
is to say, "the mind or understanding in the Scriptures.[117] To see
Christ in these Old Testament words thus requires repudiating
what Luther deemed the mistake of *historical* interpretation.
"Certain Hebrew rabbis" read the Psalms this way, Luther maintains, but they should be understood as "falsifiers and inventors of Jewish vanities." The historical reading is not just false

but dangerously inventive, for it betrays the reader's attempt to draw knowledge and use from the text, to make the Psalms a resource for "Jewish vanities."[118]

This link between Jews, hazardous exegesis, and human depravity was just one version of Luther's anti-Jewish attacks, which ranged from condemning Jews in the abstract, as figures in the Bible or imagined interpreters of Scripture, to politically potent arguments that Jews should be expelled from the areas where he hoped the true Gospel was taking hold. The Jews "have at all times been Christ's greatest enemies," Luther wrote in a 1521 commentary on Psalm 68. In his 1544 Lenten lectures on Isaiah 53, the "suffering servant" passage, he offered this expansive version of the centuries-old blood libel accusation: "The Jews still kill Christ daily, not in the sense that they merely desire to do so, but rather in fact. For they slaughter many Christian infants and children. In short, they are killers forever."[119] Outraged and incredulous that the faithful people of the Old Testament still said no to Christ, Luther fulminated throughout his life against those who represented what he viewed as the greatest threat to the Gospel: a rejection of Christ as subject and object of all divine communication and action.[120] The "certain rabbis" invoked at the outset of the *Dictata*, in 1513, hereby personify what Luther believed was a common and lethal impulse for readers to claim God's Word for themselves, to make their own interpretations, rather than Christ, the subject and object of the text.

When Luther insists that the Jews cannot be among those who "walk in the law of the Lord" (Psalm 119:1), that Christ gave the "synagog" a "bill of divorce" because of her "uncleanness," his claim is characteristic of a long history of Christian supersessionism.[121] This need to distort and dismiss a Jewish interpretative tradition betrays Luther's apocalyptic urgency and conviction that what he perceived as the contemporary problem of increasing Jewish intransigence signified the devil's frightful power.[122] When Luther details the problem by noting that the Jews defiled the law because they "did not take the Law as signifying, but as fulfilling and sufficient," he demonstrates how this anti-Judaism entwines with a concern about *how* words signify.[123] The Jews "isolated and put aside the spirit" of faith, according to Luther, because they settled for words rather than meaning. This is the dead letter, "like the flesh of Christ without the divinity." By recycling and embellishing this familiar Christian trope, Luther can exaggerate the distinctiveness of the metaphorical power he claims for the Psalms: "the true meaning and theological significance" of the psalmist's words "is like the divinity in the flesh of Christ, the spirit in the letter, the soul in the body, the life in things and the honey in the honeycomb, the kernel in the shell, the wine in the vessel, the oil in the lamps."[124] According to Luther, the clarity and impact of the psalmist's message derives from metaphorical language rather than historical interpretation: this is how the words of the Psalms convey "the life in things."

Throughout his commentary, Luther personifies his contrast between the spirit and the letter by aligning the former with Christians and the latter with Jews, frequently culminating in a claim of contrast about the stifling effect of the law and the vivifying power of the word. Jews, in Luther's eyes, are those who subject themselves to death by failing to understand this relationship between law and word. In one version of this argument, he appeals to etymology, noting correctly that the Hebrew noun "law" has the same root as the word for "teach," "because in fact Torah, which is the word for law, etymologically denotes instruction, document, or doctrine." This demonstrates, of course, that what Luther claims for the law is already clear to anyone who knows Hebrew. The Mosaic law has been given, but when the Vulgate says, "set before me for a law the way of Thy statutes," Luther notes that in Hebrew it means simply "teach me Lord" (*instrue mihi domine*). Rather than acknowledging that basing his claim on the Hebrew betrays his proximity to Jewish interpreters, Luther adamantly insists on a break as absolute as life versus death: when Moses requests the law, Luther explains, "it becomes clear that he is seeking another law, namely, an evangelical and spiritual one."[125]

Luther's anxiety about his proximity to Jewish interpreters is palpable when he glosses the psalmist's reference to the "law of Thy mouth" (*lex oris tui*) by noting that the psalmist is not content to just say "law." "Law of Thy mouth" specifies that it is the law of God, not of Moses, and therefore a word that has life-giving energy in and of itself. The "law of Thy mouth" is "the living and spiritual Word." This energy is denied to those who prioritize their own interpretation and focus on the content of the law and the actions it requires, for "all things live for it, whether words or deeds."[126] For the people of Israel, Luther observes, words are like a wineskin hardened by frost or dried up by smoke: the focus on interpretation, the fruitless quest to understand and adhere to the meaning of the words, renders them unable to contain or convey an enlivening spirit. The "Word of promise," by contrast, is like a flexible and capacious vessel, from which those who focus on receiving rather than interpreting the word might "receive the Gospel wine in the coming Christ."[127] Luther's anti-Judaism is thereby essential to his claim that reception must supersede interpretation. Rejecting rival claimants to the words, Luther attributes to them an idolatry he disavows in himself—a fixity Luther himself does not acknowledge or seem to recognize, but that is all too apparent in his absolutist insistence that the words be interpreted as a message of comfort and promise.

CONFORMING TO THE TESTIMONIES OF SCRIPTURE

Explaining what it means to prioritize scripture over our own thoughts, Luther says testimonies should not enter our meditation but our meditation should enter the testimonies "and be shut up in them and savor them." He appeals here, for the first time in this commentary on Psalm 119, to patristic writers, for whom "nothing was to be done unless it conformed to the testimonies of the Scriptures and to the holy teachers." We should receive, ponder, and savor the meaning of the testimonies. Luther supplements this with a fragmentary marginal reference to Hilary of Poitiers's *De Trinitate* II.3, which says that when scripture is distorted, the fault lies with the interpreter, not the text. Luther invokes this to confirm that people want to "impose their meaning on Scripture and do not permit its sense to be imposed on them." He thereby seeks to sustain the claim that Scripture applies to each individual while denying that Scripture is subject to individual interpretations. Luther characterizes what he opposes as idolatry, concealing the logical fallacy of his own position (his dismissal of interpretation is, of course, an interpretative move) as all accusers do, by condemning in others what they fear in themselves. Accusations of idolatry often inspire memorable metaphors, and Luther's is no exception. "And so they make idols out of the gold of divine Scripture," he says, evoking the glint of a precious metal to describe the dangerous allure of scriptural interpretation: "they do not meditate on the statutes of God but they want the statutes of God to meditate on theirs, that is, become their meditations."[128]

Luther's directives to attend to the promise of Christ are not thereby opposed to traditional meditation: the primary shift is one of perspective, a shift he believes the Psalms prompt and foster by showing readers that the words they need are provided for them, that interpretation is a form of idolatry (a dangerous problem precisely because it so closely resembles true devotion), and that what they find in the Psalms resonates with experiences past and present while simultaneously shifting one's orientation to the future, to a promised ideal, already realized in Christ and apprehensible to the reader, who thereby experiences the comfort and joy of feeling what she does not yet possess.

4. CONCLUSION

Heiko Oberman writes that Luther's reformation breakthrough was a "matter of life, not of thought, study, reflection, or meditation, but of life in the most complete sense of the word."[129]

Luther's "life" was inseparable from "thought, study, and re-flection," Brian Cummings counters, in a study arguing that Lu-ther's theology depended on his "habits of reading."[130] Accord-ing to Cummings, these habits are semantic, discoverable by tracking Luther's attention to passive and active forms of verbs, for example.[131] Yet Oberman and Cummings, invaluable though their studies are, hereby elide something crucial about the rela-tionship of the Psalms to Luther's evangelical theology—an atti-tude and emphasis pervasive in the *Dictata*, as in all of Luther's later writings on the Psalms.[132] Even as Luther's interpretations of specific Psalms varied, even as he worried over diverse gram-matical and linguistic issues, even as his project of translating the Psalms into German strove for accuracy and clarity and—increasingly—poetic elegance,[133] he was, always, shaped by the long tradition of reading, praying, and reciting the Psalms and by commentators who hailed the enlivening power of the Psalms, often attributing it to the psalmist's lyric voice.

"Nothing forced is permanent, and what is held without love and delight is not held for long," Luther wrote near the outset of the *Dictata*, in his commentary on Psalm 1: "Christ does not want His rule to rest on force and violence, because then it would not stand firm, but He wants to be served willingly and with the heart and the affections."[134] Luther wrote this at a time when, according to his retrospective account, his primary feeling was hostility toward the merciless God whose judgment he could never satisfy. That may have been Luther's frustration as he approached the confessional, but it was not his experience of the Psalms. Rather than just passive and active verb construc-tions, or exegetical comparisons, or knotty issues confronted in the translation of Hebrew into Latin and German, what Lu-ther imbibed and taught was a poetics of voice and metaphor essential—or so he insists—to the Psalms' distinctive capacity to give voice to feelings *and* to alter the feelings we give voice to.

This is the Luther I am moved by, whose writings seem to me more inspiring and immediate than his life, the Luther that Sidney and the Psalms prepared me to appreciate. My own reading of Luther, a reading I think can fairly be called devotional, keeps faith with my sources in some ways while betraying them in others. There are no innocent readings (though our desire to believe that there could be is itself an important question, well worth some attention). There are, as this comparison of Sidney and Luther underscores, far different consequences for some betrayals than others. To poeticize Luther is rightly to recognize how important Psalm poetics were to him, and his poetics to those he influenced, past and present (and those Luther's ideas and music and translations influenced, and continue to influence, are legion). It is also to obscure the ongoing violence of those many forms of Christianity which, whether tacitly or explicitly, make exclusivist claims to Scripture and truth, with what history confirms are often deadly results for those deemed illiterate, or idolatrous, or recalcitrant—all accusations grounded in Christianity's relationship to Judaism but never only targeted against Jews.

With the vast history of Christian cruelty in mind, Sidney seems a far safer object of devotion and source for those interested in the literary legacy of the Psalms. Sidney's infidelities are minor compared to Luther's, just as—even in Sidney's day—literature's standards for inclusion and mechanisms of exclusion are less obviously disciplinary, mystified, and institutional than theology's. But the point of this study, juxtaposing Sidney and Luther (canonical sources of Christianity's hegemonic traditions of theology and literature) with Sarah Kofman (a Jewish commentator whose fidelity to philosophical masters models an alternative to philosophical mastery), as well as H.D. and Susan Howe (poets who craft atopias from the shards of religious pasts), is that devotion is always political, even if never *only* political.

"What is the work 'humans' make 'scriptures' do?" Vincent Wimbush asks. What sort of authority is claimed, what expressive forms are privileged, and what sort of human is made, unmade, or remade in the process? For Sidney, poetry's knowledge is resonant—depicting ideas and feelings that the reader recognizes as their own but also, reading them in words written by another, as not *only* their own. The poetics of voice and personification are, according to Sidney, crucial to this process, thereby perpetuating the claim inherited from Greek thought and classical rhetoric, that person and voice are nearly synonymous, while contributing to a form of cultivation that deems the ability and opportunity to speak in multiple voices essential to the experience of being a singular person. For Luther, knowledge is poetic in the sense that it is conveyed by Christ the Word through metaphors and testimonials voiced by multiple personae. The poetics of the Psalms, according to Luther, prompt a remaking of the human by transmitting the comforting message of a future salvation in words forceful and applicable in the here and now. It may seem that Sidney's focus is on the poet's craft while Luther emphasizes reception, but this is a false dichotomy, because for both it is about the medium of the word. Literature does not rely on the power of excommunication, the consensus of councils, or the creedal uniformity deemed essential in most of Christianity's versions of religion. Literature nevertheless shares with religion the emphasis on identifying with and speaking with other voices. Literature and religion are, in my view, thus both political, and crucial to the cultivation of political sensibilities. It is in this sense that the inventive site of poetry is the terrain also of politics and religion: where words and emotions and images and voices culled from the everyday are recast in sequences and forms that delight and intrigue and surprise the reader, the human, who might thereby become—or so Sidney, Luther, and the psalmist each in their own way maintain—a devotional subject rather than a sovereign self.

NOTES

I first imagined this book during a conversation with Alan Thomas, who launched the TRIOS series in order to do just that—turn conversations into books. Conference panels organized by Jason

Kerr and Daniel Lochman, where I presented versions of the Sidney material, gave me the opportunity to learn from them as well as Richard Strier, Robert Stillman, and Kimberly Johnson. Kris Trujillo and Eleanor Craig, visionary collaborators, created many opportunities to think it through in relation to devotion. This essay was improved by suggestions by graduate student and faculty colleagues at Indiana University, as well as David Marno and Rebecca Schorsch, and would be unthinkable without Amy Hollywood and Sarah Hammerschlag. Special thanks also to Kyle Wagner for his sustained enthusiasm for the project; Joel Score for his keen eye; Margaret Slaughter for research help and hunting down sources rendered nearly inaccessible by the pandemic; and to Jason Fickel, who knows more about devotion than I ever will.

1. Of many good biographies of Luther, Heiko Oberman's *Luther: Man Between God and the Devil* (New Haven, CT: Yale University Press, 1989), remains invaluable. The five hundredth anniversary of the 95 Theses, in 2017, encouraged the publication of several new ones. Among these, see especially Lyndal Roper, *Martin Luther: Renegade and Prophet* (New York: Random House, 2016).

2. Martin Luther, *Dictata super Psalterium* (1513–1515), in *D. Martin Luthers Werke*, vols. 3 and 4 (Weimar: Herman Böhlau, 1885, 1966). I have relied on the translations in *Luther's Works*, vols. 10 and 11, ed. J. Pelikan and H. T. Lehmann (Philadelphia: Fortress, 1955–1986); hereafter cited as *LW*.

3. For an account distinctive in focusing as much on form and context as on the content of these Psalm lectures, see Gerhard Ebeling, *Lutherstudien*, 3 vols, (Tübingen: J. C. B. Mohr, 1971–1989), vol. 1. See also Brian Cummings, *The Literary Culture of the Reformation: Grammar and Grace* (Oxford: Oxford University Press, 2002), 68–79. Important works in English that comb the *Dictata* for theological insights include Scott Hendrix, *Ecclesia in Via: Ecclesiological Developments in the Medieval Psalms Exegesis and the Dictata Super Psalterium (1513–1515)* (Leiden: E. J. Brill, 1974); Samuel J. Preus, *From Shadow to Promise: Old Testament Interpretation from Augustine*

to Luther (Cambridge, MA: Harvard University Press, 1969); and G. Sujin Pak, *The Judaizing Calvin: Sixteenth Century Debates on the Messianic Psalms* (Oxford: Oxford University Press, 2010).

4. A lively overview of Sidney's life appears in Alan Stewart, *Philip Sidney: A Double Life* (London: Chatto & Windus, 2000).

5. *The Psalms of Sir Philip Sidney and the Countess of Pembroke*, ed. J. C. A. Rathmell (New York: New York University Press, 1963). This Psalter can also be found online at http://www.luminarium .org/renascence-editions/sidpsalms.html. John Donne, "Upon the Translation of the Psalmes by Sir Philip Sydney, and the Countesse of Pembroke his Sister," line 20, in *The Divine Poems*, 2nd ed., ed. Helen Gardner (Oxford: Clarendon Press, 1978), 33–35.

6. See for example, Mary J. Carruthers, *The Craft of Thought: Meditation, Rhetoric, and the Making of Images, 400–1200* (New York: Cambridge University Press, 1998); Jean Leclercq, *The Love of Learning and the Desire for God: A Study of Monastic Culture* (New York: Fordham University Press, 1974); and Amy Hollywood, "Song, Experience, and the Book in Benedictine Monasticism," in *The Cambridge Companion to Christian Mysticism* (Cambridge: Cambridge University Press, 2012), 59–80.

7. Vincent L. Wimbush, "Scripturalizing: Analytical Wedge for a Critical History of the Human," in *Scripturalizing the Human: The Written as the Political*, ed. Vincent L. Wimbush (New York: Taylor & Francis, 2015), ii.

8. Wimbush, "Scripturalizing," 12–13.

9. Jacques Rancière, *The Politics of Aesthetics*, ed. and trans. Gabriel Rockhill (New York: Bloomsbury, 2013), 89.

10. Much work has been done on the political import of the history of reading and of literature. For a survey of the scholarship as well as an important argument about modern liberalism's reliance on literature, see Michael Allen, *In the Shadow of World Literature: Sites of Reading in Colonial Egypt* (Princeton, NJ: Princeton University Press, 2016), and the response by Siraj Ahmed, "Criticism and Catastrophe," https://tif.ssrc.org/2017/08/15/criticism-and -catastrophe/. A challenge to the current consensus, arguing that

the literature's capacity to cultivate sensibilities can and should be understood as essential to progressive politics, is provided by Joseph North, *Literary Criticism: A Concise Political History* (Cambridge, MA: Harvard University Press, 2017). See the discussion of North in relation to the debate about critique, in the introduction to this volume.

11. This security was only relative, as Sidney well knew, as part of a family subject to the vagaries of royal power and as witness to the carnage of the St. Bartholomew's Day Massacre in Paris, in 1572, when visiting on a diplomatic mission; Sidney was still in his teens at the time. One of the people he met, the great Protestant logician Petrus Ramus, was thrown from a window and disemboweled during the carnage. Sidney himself was a victim of violence: he died in his early thirties, from a wound suffered during a battle between Dutch and Spanish forces while he was the English governor of Flushing, in the Netherlands. Luther's family had less money and social power, and while writing his early commentaries on the Psalms, he was still safely ensconced within his Augustinian order. Luther's firsthand experiences of social vulnerability came later, when his attacks on papal power put his life in danger and led to his excommunication.

12. On the politics of Sidney's poetry, see Blair Worden, *Philip Sidney's* Arcadia *and Elizabethan Politics* (New Haven, CT: Yale University Press, 1996), and Robert Stillman and Nandra Perry, "Sacred and Scandalous: Philip and Mary Sidney's Reforming Poetics," in *Oxford Handbook of Early Modern Literature and Religion*, ed. Andrew Hiscock and Helen Wilcox (Oxford: Oxford University Press, 2017), 324–44. For the argument that moderation became a powerful ideological tool in Elizabethan England, see Ethan Shagan, *The Rule of Moderation: Violence, Religion, and the Politics of Restraint in Early Modern England* (Cambridge: Cambridge University Press, 2011).

13. Evidence of this is provided by Catherine Gallagher's reference to Sidney in "The Rise of Fictionality," in *The Novel*, vol. 1, *History, Geography, and Culture*, ed. Franco Moretti (Princeton, NJ:

Princeton University Press, 2006), as discussed in the first note in our introduction.

14. Tomoko Masuzawa, *The Invention of World Religions; or, How European Universalism Was Perceived as the Language of Pluralism* (Chicago: University of Chicago Press, 2005); David Chidester, *Savage Systems: Colonialism and Comparative Religion in Southern Africa* (Charlottesville: University of Virginia Press, 1996).

15. Philip Sidney, *An Apology for Poetry; or, The Defence of Poesy*, 3rd ed., ed. Geoffrey Shepherd and Robert W. Maslen (Manchester: Manchester University Press, 2002), 93. All citations are to this edition.

16. For related arguments about the Sidney material discussed here see Constance M. Furey, "Impersonating Devotion," *Representations* 153 (2021): 11–28, and "Making New Persons: Literary Conversion in Sidney, Erasmus, and George Herbert's 'The H. Communion,'" *Sidney Journal* 38, no. 2 (2020): 127–52.

17. On the use of literature, considered by many anachronistic when applied to premodern (and, it should be noted, often assumed to be inapplicable also to non-Western) writings, see Brian Cummings, "Literature, Theology, and Hermeneutics: Erasmus on Literature and Knowledge," in *Literature, Belief and Knowledge in Early Modern England: Knowing Faith*, ed. Subha Mukherji and Tim Stuart-Buttle (London: Palgrave Macmillan, 2018).

18. Catherine Bates, *On Not Defending Poetry: Defense and Indefensibility in Sidney's Defence of Poesy* (Oxford: Oxford University Press, 2017), 14.

19. Sidney, *Apology*, 85.

20. For a fuller discussion of Sidney's relationship to this tradition, see Volkhard Wels, "Imaginatio oder Inventio: Das Dichterische Schaffen und sein Gegenstand bei Puttenham, Sidney und Temple," *Poetica* 37, nos. 1/2 (2005): 65–91.

21. "Invention of the Cross," in *The Concise Oxford Dictionary of the Christian Church*, ed. E. A. Livingstone (Oxford: Oxford University Press, 2013); Louis Van Tongeren, *Exaltation of the Cross: Towards the Origins of the Feast of the Cross and the Meaning of the*

Cross in Early Medieval Liturgy (Liturgia condenda 11) (Leuven: Peeters, 2000); see also John H. Corbett "Relics," in *Encyclopedia of Early Christianity*, ed. Everett Ferguson, Fredrick W. Norris, and Lawrence Wolfson (New York: Routledge, 2010).

22. Sidney, *Apology*, 86, 87.

23. The quote from Lochman appears in Daniel T. Lochman, "'The *Countess of Pembroke's Arcadia* is for the body . . .' and soul: *Energeia* and Enaction in Sidney's *Apology* and *Arcadia*," *Sidney Journal* 38, no. 2 (2020): 5–28, 15. On the point that Sidney equates divine inspiration with poetic creativity, see also Robert Stillman, "'I am not I': Philip Sidney and the Energy of Fiction," *Sidney Journal* 30, no. 1 (2012): 1–26. Sidney's disinterest in prophecy and esotericism is discussed by Katherine Duncan-Jones and J. A. van Dorsten, eds., *Miscellaneous Prose of Sir Philip Sidney* (Oxford: Clarendon Press, 1973).

24. Sidney, *Apology*, 86.

25. See Stillman and Perry, "Sacred and Scandalous."

26. Sidney, *Apology*, 93, 102.

27. Sidney, *Apology*, 88, 87.

28. Sidney, *Apology*, 90. Compare to the discussion of memory in Mary J. Carruthers, *The Book of Memory: A Study of Memory in Medieval Culture*, 2nd ed. (Cambridge: Cambridge University Press, 2008).

29. Sidney, *Apology*, 113.

30. *OED Online*, s.v. "energy, n." For essential work on Sidney's notion of *energeia*, see the special issue, "Energeia," *Sidney Journal* 38, no. 2 (2020), ed. Daniel Lochman, which includes articles, listed above, by Lochman, Stillman, and myself.

31. Sidney, *Apology*, 82–83

32. Sidney, *Apology*, 83.

33. Sidney, *Apology*, 83. For reference to Cicero, see Shepherd and Maslen, in Sidney, *Apology*, 128, citing Cicero, *Pro Archia poeta*, 9.18–19. For analogous references see George Puttenham, *The Arte of English Poesy: A Critical Edition*, ed. Frank Whigham and Wayne A. Rebhorn (Kent, OH: Kent State University Press,

1970). Puttenham notes the cultivating of poetry even among "the American, the Perusine & the very Cannibal" (10).

34. Sidney, *Apology*, 83. Martyr's work was translated and included in Richard Eden's *The Decades of the Newe Worlde* (1555). Shepherd and Maslen also note that a fuller account of the *areyto*, described as a ceremonial ring-dance accompanied by song, was given by the Spaniard G. F. de Oviedo (1535) in *Natural History of the West Indies*, trans. and ed. Sterling A. Stoudemire (Chapel Hill: University of North Carolina, 1959), 38. The etymology is from D. G. Brinton, "from Arawack *aririn*, "rehearse," "repeat" (Shepherd and Maslen, in Sidney, *Apology*, 129).

35. Sidney, *Apology*, 83. On esoteric traditions, see Frances Yates, *The Art of Memory* (1966; Chicago: University of Chicago Press, 2001), 254–65, and D. P. Walker, "Orpheus the Theologian and the Renaissance Platonists, *Journal of the Warburg and Courtauld Institute* 16 (1953): 100–120. Thomas Elyot's *The Boke Named the Governour. Edited from the 1st ed. of 1531 by Stephen Croft* (New York: B. Franklin, 1967), 120, refers to poetry as "the first philosophy that ever was knowen"; a good way to teach children "nat onely maners and naturall affections, but also the wonderfull werkes of nature"; and a "science misticall and inspired, and therfore in latine they were called *Vates*, which worde signifyeth as moche as prophetes." Compare Puttenham, *Arte*, chap. 8, 16–23; Minturno, *De poeta*; Richard Willes, *De Re Poetica* (Oxford: Luttrell Society/B. Blackwell, 1958). On the *Pléïade*, see Robert J. Clements, *Critical Theory and Practice of the Pléïade* (Cambridge, MA: Harvard University Press, 1942), 51–77, and Frances Yates, *The French Academies of the Sixteenth Century* (Nendeln, Liechtenstein: Kraus Reprint, 1968).

36. Sidney, *Apology*, 83; the source of this false etymology is given in Shepherd and Maslen, in Sidney, *Apology*, 130.

37. Sidney, *Apology*, 84, quoting Virgil's *Aeneid* 2.314.

38. Sidney, *Apology*, 84

39. Sidney, *Apology*, 85. For the definition of fiction in Sidney's day, first and foremost "the action of fashioning or imitating," but with connotations of deceit as well as a crafting capable of enhanc-

ing apprehension of truth, see the introduction to this volume. The question of fiction's relationship to truth could plausibly be described as the central issue in the *Defence*. Basically, Sidney thinks poetry (i.e., "feigning" or "fiction") can be true or false, depending. Contra Puttenham, who explains that poetic creations are "fictitious" by clarifying that this means they are "well-known by all but believed by none," Sidney says poetry has the greatest claim to truth because it can bring ideas to life and make them believable or true in the mind of the reader. He brings up the arguments, from Augustine, among others, that poets lie and deceive, and works out his claims for fictional truth by comparing poetry to history and philosophy. History, which he refers to as the account of the "bare was," has "some advantage to the gross conceit" or trivially aesthetic use of language, and it can claim to offer "true" examples where poetry's are "feigned" (see Sidney, *Apology*, 93; cf. 96). In this sense, he acknowledges the distinction between true and fictional *but also* denies the significance of the distinction, concluding that poetry's "feigned example hath as much force to teach as a true example" (93). Likewise, he says, philosophy can claim the accuracy of a "purely methodical proceeding" but ultimately falls short because it's unconcerned with pleasure. For this reason—because historical and philosophical writing does not move or delight the reader— their truth "lies dark before the imaginative and judging power" unless "illumined or figured forth by the speaking picture of poesy" (90).

40. Sidney, *Apology*, 85, 86–87.

41. Anne-Marie Miller-Blaise, "'The Name of Psalmes Will Speak for Me': Le rôle des Psaumes dans la conception Sidnéienne de la musique de la poésie," *Etudes Epistémè* 18 (2010): 34–50.

42. Anne Lake Prescott, "King David as a 'Right Poet': Sidney and the Psalmist," *English Literary History* 19 (1989): 131–51, quote on 147.

43. Ramie Targoff, *Common Prayer: The Language of Public Devotion in Early Modern England* (Chicago: University of Chicago Press, 2001), 145n57.

44. Sidney, *Apology*, 84.

45. See Shepherd and Maslen, in Sidney, *Apology*, 133, citing Ben Jonson's definition in *Discoveries* (1641) and Sidney's corresponding use of poesy as carefully distinguished from poetry defined as the *product* of the art.

46. From the 1599 Geneva Bible. See Rivkah Zim, *English Metrical Psalms: Poetry as Praise and Prayer, 1535–1601* (Cambridge: Cambridge University Press, 1987), 35.

47. Robert Alter, *The Book of Psalms: A Translation with Commentary* (New York: W. W. Norton, 2007), xx. For the English references, see *OED Online*, s.v. "psalm, n."

48. Alter commends the concise article by Benjamin Hrushovski, "Prosody, Hebrew," in *Encyclopedia Judaica*, vol. 13 (2007): 1195–1240. For the argument that biblical poetry is characterized by parallelism rather than meter, see James Kugel, *The Idea of Biblical Poetry: Parallelism and Its History* (Baltimore: Johns Hopkins University Press, 1998).

49. Sidney, *Apology*, 85.

50. See Yates, *Art of Memory* and *French Academies*; J. A. van Dorsten, *The Radical Arts: First Decade of an Elizabethan Renaissance* (London: Oxford University Press, 1970), chap. 8.

51. Sidney was not alone in this, according to John Guillory in *Poetic Authority: Spenser, Milton, and Literary History* (New York: Columbia University Press, 1983): Boccaccio, he explains, believed that "the pagan poets could not have been inspired but rather generated their verse out of a *vi mentis* [energy of the mind]" (5). Surveying the controversy sparked by Dante, about whether a poetic text might be "sacred," Guillory concludes that it was as though the entire debate "were meant to give a name to this anonymous 'energy of the mind.'" To illustrate this controversy's conclusion, Guillory cites Jacopo Mazzoni: "phantasy is the true power over poetic fables, since she alone is capable of those fictions which we of ourselves are able to feign and put together. . . . It follows that poetry is made up of things feigned and imagined." Mazzoni, *Della difesa della "Commedia" di Dante* (Cesena, 1688), translated in

Allan H. Gilbert, *Literary Criticism: Plato to Dryden* (Detroit: Wayne State University Press, 1962), 386–87. See also Michelle Karnes, *Imagination, Meditation, and Cognition in the Middle Ages* (Chicago: University of Chicago Press, 2011), and Richard Kearney, *Wake of Imagination: Toward a Postmodern Culture* (London: Routledge, 1994): "Kant, Fichte, and Schelling have the honor of 'releas[ing] imagination from its long philosophical imprisonment,'" thereby allowing "man" to "declare his autonomy from all given being" (Karnes, 1, quoting Kearney, 131–32).

52. Guillory, *Poetic Authority*, 11.

53. Guillory, *Poetic Authority*, 11. According to Guillory's genealogy, this process of naturalizing the supernatural remains submerged in Jacopo Mazzoni and Sidney and is confronted directly by Tasso, who returns to *vates*.

54. Sir Fulke Greville, *The Life of the Renowned Sir Philip Sidney*, ed. N. Smith (Oxford, 1907), 35.

55. Guillory, *Poetic Authority*, 10–11.

56. Nandra Perry, *Imitatio Christi: The Poetics of Piety in Early Modern England* (Notre Dame, IN: University of Notre Dame Press, 2014), 68–69.

57. Robert Stillman, *Philip Sidney and the Poetics of Cosmopolitanism* (Burlington, VT: Ashgate, 2008). See also notes 25 and 29, above.

58. Duncan-Jones and van Dorsten, *Miscellaneous Prose*, 188–89; see also 192, on the lack of any evidence of an occult, "Brunist," attitude toward memory.

59. Sidney, *Apology*, 86.

60. This explanation has the virtue of explaining another seeming incongruity in Sidney's text, between the Roman *vates*, or poet-prophet, and the Greek *poiein*, or poet-maker, with "maker" being the word, not incidentally, used by Chaucer to describe the author of imaginative writing. On medieval notions of poetry, invention, fiction, and feigning, see the excellent article by Leah Schwebel, "The Legend of Themes and Literary Patricide in Chaucer, Boccaccio, and Statius," *Studies in the Age of Chaucer* 36 (2014): 139–68.

61. Sidney, *Apology*, 84–85.

62. Sidney, *Apology*, 85.

63. Sidney, *Apology*, 85–86.

64. Sidney, *Apology*, 107.

65. Sidney, *Apology*, 85–86.

66. Thomas Sternhold, *The Whole Booke of Psalmes Collected into Englysh Metre* (Day, 1562), https://archive.org/details/wholebooke ofpsal1584ster.

67. Gerald Sharpling, "Towards a Rhetoric of Experience: The Role of Enargeia in Essays of Montaigne," *History of Rhetoric* 20 (2002): 173–92. A deft account of the relationship between *energeia* and *enargeia* is provided in Ilona Bell, "'Drunk with Delight of Change': The Play of *Energeia* in Wroth's 'Pamphilia to Amphilanthus,'" *Sidney Journal* 38, no. 2 (2020): 101–26.

68. Terence Cave, *The Cornucopian Text: The Problem of Writing in the French Renaissance* (Oxford: Oxford University Press, 1979), 21.

69. Quintilian, 8.3.67–70, cited in *de Copia*, 577–78.

70. Sharpling, "Rhetoric of Experience," 176.

71. Kimberly Anne Coles, *Religion, Reform, and Women's Writing* (Cambridge: Cambridge University Press, 2008), 76–77, 102.

72. See Roland Greene, "Sir Philip Sidney's Psalms, the Sixteenth-Century Psalter, and the Nature of Lyric," *Studies in English Literature* 30 (1990): 19–40. Greene's argument about subjectivity is especially notable in a reading that is dazzling in its formal assessment. See especially his reading of Psalm 7: as "exposure of an inner life becomes more acute and differentiated, a reader looks somewhat less to his or her own experience and devotional outlook, somewhat more to the totality of the Psalter, to provide a context for what he or she confronts in the poem" (30). This is set against the backdrop of an argument that defines lyric as a dialectic between ritual and fictional modes. English Psalters put this into relief, offering "theoretical statements about the nature of lyric" (22). Fiction, according to Greene, is linear, alternative, impeding identification and inviting interpretation; ritual, by contrast, is cyclical, familiar, inviting identification and impeding interpretation,

re-experience, collective unity. Psalms are clearly ritual, for they "require the reading voice to assume the identity of their represented speaker" and bring everyone together under the "convenient unity of an 'I'" (23). Greene observes that the placement of the famous passage on the Psalms is inserted between and framed by two contexts that locate the ancient Western origins of the ritualist and fictionalist premises in Roman and Greek poetic theory. But "set against this 'vaine and godles' superstition of poetry's worldly efficacy is the Greek idea of the poem as a golden world, an 'imitation or fiction' that stands as an epistemological alternative to nature" (27). Consequently, Greene argues, Sidney's translations of the Psalter attempt to create fiction by creating a kind of character and a continuity of emotional experience. Was he aspiring to "a Psalter that, in delivering its fiction, struggles free of ritual uses at nearly every turn" (27)? Note Greene's appeal to three prophecies of scattering and his conclusion that what is suggested is the speaker's stake in coherence, his dread of personal *spargimento*. The "fictional unity" is subjective, Greene maintains—a response to the recurring question: "will the speaker consist"? (36). On equity and consistence, see Kathy Eden, *Poetic and Legal Fiction in the Aristotelian Tradition* (Princeton, NJ: Princeton University Press, 1986), 48.

73. Zim, *English Metrical Psalms*, 33. For an explanation of the tradition of mental painting in medieval education, see Carruthers, *Book of Memory*, 127, 226–42.

74. Zim, *English Metrical Psalms*, 27.

75. This section relies on Hollywood, "Song, Experience, and the Book," and sources cited therein.

76. This passage appears in a dedicatory letter, included in *The Psalmes of David and Others: With M. John Calvins Commentaries*, trans. Arthur Golding (London, 1571). On the *fictio* or "as if" quality of religious texts in a Christian culture shaped by this tradition of engaging with the Psalms, see Rachel Smith, "'As Often as His Heart Beat, the Name Moved': Devotion and the 'As if' in *The Life of the Servant*," *Representations* 153 (2021): 51–67, elaborating what M. B. Pranger calls the "artificiality" of Christianity, a way of life in which "authenticity could not be distinguished from form" (*The Artificial-*

ity of Christianity: An Essay in the Poetics of Monastic Culture [Stanford, CA: Stanford University Press, 2003], 244). On the importance of prosopopoeial figures, specifically, in monastic devotion, see Julie Orelmanski, "Literary Persons and Medieval Fiction in Bernard of Clairvaux's *Sermons on the Song of Songs,*" *Representations* 153 (2021): 29–50.

77. Notably, this reference to eyes of the mind is not biblical, although for many it will call to mind Paul's statement in 1 Corinthians 12 that those who see "through a glass darkly now" will in the future see "face to face."

78. Georgia Frank, *The Memory of the Eyes: Pilgrims to Living Saints in Christian Antiquity* (Berkeley: University of California Press, 2000), surveys the "eye of faith" motif in early Christianity, linking it to monastic rather than biblical sources. She notes that Paul prioritized sound in describing how he learned things "that are not to be told" (2 Cor 12:4), and that the link between eyes of faith and Paul comes not from canonical scripture but from the late fourth-century work *Visio Pauli*, which was widely translated (93). This suggests that "eyes of faith" may be less a familiar piety and more a recurring question: from early Christianity, sources repeatedly privilege the faculty of sight in order to participate in a form of "biblical realism." Deployed most often in the context of pilgrimage, the eye of faith motif argued that "one gazed *at* external features in order to gaze *through* them" (169). See also chapter 4, e.g., Paulinus describing Helena entering Jerusalem.

79. Sidney, *Apology*, 85.

80. Davies, John, *Nosce Teipsum This Oracle Expounded* (London, 1599), B2v, B3r, H4r.

81. Elizabeth L. Swann, "*Nosce Teipsum*: The Senses of Self-Knowledge in Early Modern England," in *Literature, Belief, and Knowledge in Early Modern England: Knowing Faith*, ed. Subha Mukherji and Tim Stuart-Buttle (London: Palgrave, 2018), 206. See also the discussion in our introduction, above, about literature and the opacity of the subject and absence of a divine guarantor of meaning.

82. Swann explains that "self-knowledge is predicated on a

re-presenting of the soul to itself as something which can be seen because it is made extraordinary, untethered by metaphor from its own illusory over-familiarity" ("*Nosce Teipsum*," 207).

83. Luther was born in 1483, some seventy years before Sidney (1554–1586), and they come from different backgrounds and cultural contexts. Luther, son of a town councilor who made his money from mines, entered an Augustinian monastery in 1505; became a doctor of theology in 1512; was excommunicated in 1521; and then wrote, composed, translated, and preached, prolifically and seemingly tirelessly, as a church leader until his death in 1546. Sidney was an English courtier, diplomat, and creative writer who learned from a Calvinist catechism as a child and was strongly influenced by Melanchthon as an adult, but there is no evidence that he spent time with Luther's writings or was otherwise influenced directly by the reformer whose translations, ministry, and polemical writings altered the landscape of Europe. See, as previously cited, Oberman's and Roper's biographies of Luther; Cummings, *Literary Culture*, on Luther as a creator of modern Christian Europe's literary culture; Stewart's biography of Sidney; and Stillman, *Philip Sidney and the Poetics of Cosmopolitanism*. Berndt Hamm's work on Luther is equally important; many key essays are collected in Hamm, *The Reformation of Faith in the Context of Late Medieval Theology and Piety*, ed. Robert J. Bast (Leiden: Brill, 2004).

84. Elisabeth Chaghafi, "Luther vs. the Sidneys: Psalm Translation as Poetic Paraphrase," conference paper, Sixteenth Century Society conference, Milwaukee, October 2017. Chaghafi argues that Luther reworked the Psalms, always attentive to textual accuracy and accessible language, but with an eye as well to making them more poetic; she tracks changes in his translation of Psalm 23, for example, between editions of 1524 and 1531.

85. Constance M. Furey, "Invective and Discernment in Luther, Erasmus, and More," *Harvard Theological Review* 98, no. 4 (2005): 469–88.

86. On peasants, see "Against the Robbing and Murdering Hordes of Peasants," in *Luther: Selected Political Writings*, ed. J. M.

Porter (Philadelphia: Fortress Press, 1974). For an assessment of
Luther's anti-Judaism, and how his attacks on Jews in the Bible were
both distinct from and related to his view of Jews in society, see
Brooks Schramm and Kirsi Irmeli Stejrna, eds., *Martin Luther, the
Bible, and the Jewish People* (Minneapolis: Augsburg, 2012).

87. Clare King'oo, *Miserere Mei: The Penitential Psalms in Late
Medieval and Early Modern England* (Notre Dame, IN: University of
Notre Dame Press, 2012). For the German text of the 1517 edition,
see D. *Martin Luthers Werke* (Weimarer Ausgabe; hereafter cited as
WA), 1:158–220. There is a partial English translation in *LW*, vol. 14.
See also Süß, "Über Luthers *Sieben Bußpsalmen*," in *Vierhundert-
fünfzig Jahre lutherische Reformation, 1517-1967*, 367-83 (Göttingen:
Vandenhoeck und Ruprecht, 1967) and Jared Wicks, *Man Yearning
for Grace* (Wiesbaden: F. Steiner, 1969).

88. Cummings, *Literary Culture*, 73–74.

89. Gotthelf Wiedermann, "Alexander Alexius' Lectures on
the Psalms at Cambridge, 1536," *Journal of Ecclesiastical History* 37
(1986): 15–41.

90. Rom 1:17: "Iusticia enim dei in eo revelatur ex fide in fidem
sicut scriptum est: Iustus autem ex fide vivit." "For in it the righteousness of God is revealed through faith for faith, as it is written: 'The one who is just will live by faith'" (NRSV). For the 1545
account, see John Dillenberger, *Martin Luther: Selections from His
Writings* (New York: Anchor, 1962), 11. Luther's self-described
discovery was that the "justice of God" signals divine mercy rather
than wrath, that humans are not required to make themselves
worthy of salvation but instead receive this as a gift of grace, received through faith. This was the gospel, the good news, the message of Christian freedom that Luther hailed in his most famous
works. Justification by faith is rightly identified as the core conviction animating his evangelical movement.

91. The *Dictata super Psalterium* were a classroom affair, a multi-
year course that Luther himself thought unfit for publication.
Luther began preparations almost immediately after the degree
ceremony, on October 22, 1512, by printing a suitable text of the

Vulgate, with wide margins and linear spaces, complete with headings and summaries. In the lectures themselves, this new professor proceeded in the customary fashion, offering first grammatical and philological glosses and then scholia, or wider interpretations, intended to summarize what key commentators had already said. The course ran for two years, from August 16, 1513, until October 20, 1515. For details and interpretation of Luther's christological approach, see Erich Vogelsang, *Die anfänge von Luthers Christologie* (Berlin: de Gruyter, 1929).

92. Cummings, *Literary Culture*, 99.

93. *LW* 10:7.

94. Dillenberger, "Preface to the Complete Edition of Luther's Latin Writings, 1545," in *Selections*, 3–12.

95. Dillenberger, *Selections*, 38.

96. Dillenberger, *Selections*, 39.

97. Dillenberger, *Selections*, 39.

98. Dillenberger, *Selections*, 39–41.

99. Hollywood, "Song, Experience, and the Book."

100. *LW* 11: 20

101. What readers encounter in Psalm 119, according to Luther, is not the person of Christ symbolized by the words, but the promising Word itself. The future is no longer under figures but openly conveyed and present in the text. This divide between law and promise is already in the Old Testament. See *LW* 11:195–200.

102. *LW* 11: 518. *The Jewish Study Bible*, ed. Adele Berlin and Mark Zvi Brettler (Oxford: Oxford University Press, 2004).

103. This goes to his claim that he is the first to interpret the Psalm prophetically.

104. *LW* 11:436.

105. *LW* 11:446

106. *LW* 11:446; *WA* 4:328. On the third hour, see also Acts 2: 15–18.

107. *LW* 12:437.

108. *LW* 12:438

109. The NRSV translates the line as "give me life in your ways,"

while the Jewish Bible translates it as "by Your ways preserve me." *Tanakh: The Holy Scriptures* (Philadelphia: Jewish Publication Society, 1985)

110. "Fides enim est causa, quare non possumus aliter quam verbo ostendere bona nostra, eo quod fides est non apparentium, que non nisi verbo possunt doceri, ostendi et indicari." *WA* 4:272; *LW* 11:407.

111. Preus, *From Shadow to Promise*, 181–82. Examples from *WA* 4:305, 298.

112. Both quotes from *LW* 11:437.

113. *LW* 11:436; *WA* 4:284. The Weimar editor points out that Jerome's *Psalterium iuxta Hebraeos* translates the Hebrew word that means "muse," "complain," "talk," and "sing" with *loqui* in verse 27 but otherwise with *meditari* (as in verses 15, 23): *D. Martin Luthers Werke: Kritische Gesamtausgabe* (Weimar: Hermann Böhlau, 1883). *Psalterium vetus*, in Faber's *Quincuplex Psalterium*, translates verse 15 "In mandatis tuis garriam".

114. *LW* 11:421.

115. In this fourth grouping of verses in Psalm 119, Luther encountered a condensed series of words that simultaneously request and convey action. All that "His Word" teaches is imparted by the words of the Psalm, Luther concludes. The Spirit's gifts of fear (*timor*) and strength (*fortitudo*) and knowledge (*scientia*) and godliness (*pietas*) and counsel (*consilium*) and wisdom (*sapientia*) and understanding (*intellectus*) all come to this: "not the things themselves but only the testimonies of the things are possessed." This is why it is right and good that these words are prayed daily, according to Luther, because the words are themselves the testimony, the promise. This promise is possessed not by those who can say what the words mean, but by those who have shifted their attention from their own words to the psalmist's words.

116. Note that the section explaining the link between heart and mind appears to be missing from the manuscript, although the pagination does not indicate a loss (*LW* 11:417).

117. Here Luther appeals to the Greek νοµυ rather than Latin

sensus, observing that this is the word for the "mind or understanding in the Scriptures."

118. *LW* 11:7.

119. Schramm and Stjerna, *Luther, the Jews, and the Bible*, 6.

120. Commentary on Psalm 68 (May 1521), *LW* 13:23, cited in Schramm and Stjerna, *Luther, the Jews, and the Bible*, 10.

121. *LW* 11:415.

122. Oberman, *Luther*.

123. *LW* 11:415.

124. *LW* 11:416.

125. *LW* 11:439.

126. *LW* 11:465.

127. *LW* 11:472.

128. All quotes in this paragraph from *LW* 11:431–32.

129. Oberman, *Luther*, 154.

130. Cummings, *Literary Culture*, 57. For Cummings, the claim that Luther's theology is inseparable from his exegesis means, as he says in assessing the connection between the *Dictata*'s account of Psalm 31 and Romans 1:17, "he constructs a theological argument by excavating the semantic structure of the biblical text." As an example of what Cummings means by semantic, it was in the *Dictata*, he says, that Luther recognized the importance of the passive structure of the Hebrew text. By the time of the lectures on Romans he does not reference it because it had "become embedded in his thinking as theological shorthand" (85).

131. See, e.g., Cummings's discussion of the Vulgate's use of the participle *remissae* for what in Hebrew is a passive verb, translated in Reuchlin's literal translation as *fiens levatus* ("being removed") (*Literary Culture*, 84).

132. This devotional attitude and emphasis is fairly consistent, even as Luther's interpretation of specific Psalms varies. See my account of Luther's differing interpretations of Psalm 8: https://tif.ssrc.org/2020/03/13/human-furey/.

133. Chaghafi, "Luther vs. the Sidneys."

134. *LW* 11:14.

A POOR SUBSTITUTE FOR PRAYER

SARAH KOFMAN AND THE FETISH OF WRITING

Sarah Hammerschlag

> The Fetishist is the one who says if I have to choose between the thing itself and the substitute I'll let go of the thing itself.
>
> JACQUES DERRIDA[1]

> Derrida's umbrella thus protects us from all dogmatism.
>
> SARAH KOFMAN, "Baubo: Theological Perversion and Fetishism"

1. READING HER

AT THE LIBRARY

It is a strange thing to stand before the B2430 section looking for books by Sarah Kofman. The section itself is a monument to the strength of Twentieth-Century French Philosophy, each shelf a testament to the philosophical dominance of its great thinkers: nearly five thousand books running from Althusser, past Bachelard, Bataille, de Beauvoir, Bergson, Deleuze, and Derrida to Merleau-Ponty, Mounier, Ricouer, Sartre, Wahl, and Weil. Other than a volume of selected writings, there are no books, however, by Kofman. To find the bulk of Kofman's corpus you must go elsewhere. You must look under BF to find her work on Freud and under B3318 for her books on Nietzsche, and travel even farther afield to ND and PN for those on visual art and literature. Her last book, *Rue Ordener, Rue Labat*, an autobiographical text about her childhood in Paris during World War II is shelved in the tiny section of historical works and memoirs about and by French Jews. It is on the same shelf as *A Bag of Marbles* and the life of Zalkind Hourwitz—"A Jew in the French Revolution." This division in her library placement, as out of line as it is with the cataloguing of works by her peers and teachers— Derrida, Deleuze, Nancy have entire shelves, columns of shelves even, devoted to their work and the secondary literature on them—nonetheless represents something about both her legacy and her method. Despite a prolific output—nearly thirty books in twenty-four years—her philosophical legacy is often overshadowed by her suicide in 1994 and its possible relation to the publication, months earlier, of *Rue Ordener, Rue Labat*. She is thus read as a Holocaust survivor who, like Paul Celan or Primo Levi, ultimately succumbed to the overwhelming burden of survival. As a philosopher she has been called derivative, a mere commentator, at best an excellent reader of others. She knew Freud and Nietzsche better than anyone else in the twentieth century, Jacques Derrida said in his eulogy for her.

All of the criteria by which we evaluate and choose our subjects as scholars would suggest we should dismiss Kofman as a footnote, either to her contemporaries or to the story of postwar European Jewish survival. Shouldn't we instead pay attention to the original thinkers, the revolutionaries, the true masters of their disciplines?

Kofman, however, might be able to help us think otherwise. Her corpus can be read as an inquiry into the nature of these categories, enacted through the questions that she poses as she reads the great masters—Aristotle, Plato, Marx, Nietzsche, Freud—but also through her style, which sometimes mimics her sources but in the process calls their authors' motivations, and sometimes her own, into question. In an essay for the edition of *Les Cahiers du Grif* devoted to Kofman's work two years after her death, Jean-Luc Nancy describes fidelity as "the course of her life. Not truth . . . but fidelity, the truth of fidelity, which doesn't have a final meaning, but the meaning of the course itself. The truth that returns to life and not the inverse."

Kofman said something similar in one of her epistolary exchanges with Jacques Derrida, in relation to whom she is most often situated as footnote, disciple, derivative. Derrida, with whom she worked closely and maintained a correspondence for twenty-four years, had written a long letter to Kofman in 1977, counseling her to go more slowly, not to give in to the desire to divest herself of her thoughts so quickly, to let go of a need to produce with urgency, a need he suggests they shared. She responds that in addition to this need, which she admits they share, she writes out of love for others, for those she esteems, that she writes *to exist* for those others. Without her writing, she confesses, she fears that she would no longer be of interest, would disappear.[2] It is a profound admission of vulnerability, of the human need for connection and recognition, one which one might suppose should be subordinated to the drive toward truth.

After all, we are not trained as scholars or even as casual readers to exchange our desire for truth or meaning for anything else. Fidelity as a scholarly virtue is of only instrumental value, a means to an end. We seek out truth like a prize, the thing to be harvested when everything else has been consumed or thrown away. Kofman was, as Nancy suggested, motivated to read and think differently, but she was also interested in *why*, why the quest for truth is so powerful, interested in the drives that animate it. She was interested in how the pursuit of truth protects and distracts us from confronting what perhaps motivates us even more, if only negatively, that is to say, from what terrifies us.

The last essay Kofman wrote before her suicide, published only posthumously, was an analysis of the Rembrandt painting *The Anatomy Lesson of Dr. Nicholaes Tulp*. The painting is of an autopsy, in which the body itself appears almost forgotten, for the attention of all the men is on the anatomy book at the foot

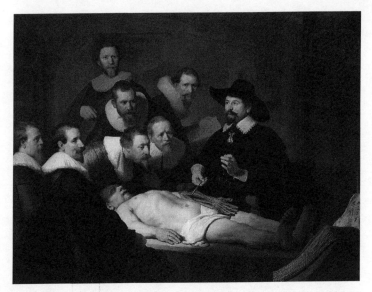

FIGURE 2.1. Rembrandt, *The Anatomy Lesson of Dr. Nicolaes Tulp*, 1632. Mauritshuis, The Hague.

of the bed. The scientific gaze, Kofman suggests in the essay, replaces the corpse with a specimen, allowing us to forget that this decaying body was only days earlier walking around, trying, like the doctors themselves, to forget his own entrails. "They do not seem to identify with the cadaver stretched out there," she writes. They do not see in it the image of what they themselves will one day be, of what, unbeknownst to them, they are in the process of becoming."

Whether or not Kofman knew that this essay would be the last thing she would write, it poses a challenge to her readers: to read her without making of her an object to be mastered, dissected, thus, without denying *our* own entrails; that is to say, with the knowledge that we too will soon be a corpse on a table.

This is an essay, then, about whether we can read with a different set of criteria. It is, on the one hand, a question that is tinged with politics, for it concerns the fact that the ideals of originality, of scholarly acuity, textual mastery even, are shot through with violence, regularly wielded to reduce others to silence. On the other hand, the question of what we're looking for when we read is so intimate and ubiquitous that it resurfaces with every sentence. For me, at least, any attempt to thwart those ideals feels indistinguishable from defeat, both because they return to the fore as the criteria by which I've been trained to evaluate my own work and everything else I read, and because anything that I produce that does not achieve these ideals feels by definition unsuccessful. In writing about Kofman here I am writing with her as my guide to this oscillation between overcoming the drive toward mastery and the acknowledgment of its inevitable return, even if only as the fear of failure. She is an exemplar of what that struggle entails, because it is evident throughout her work, her reception, and her reflections on her reception. It gives the work a startling emotional impact, and a multiplicity of registers. But at the same time, consider what she gave up—the body of her work, parceled out into pieces, hidden across the library's meandering stacks.

She was a philosopher who vigilantly asked what it is to read faithfully, devotedly, which, for her, did not mean uncritically but rather with an unrelenting commitment both to credit her sources for insights where she found them, and to be honest about locating in her textual subjects the scar tissue that serves as evidence of their authors' desires—including her own—to pursue truth, to forestall death, to be whole.

Throughout her work Kofman reminds us, sometimes through the analysis of a word, sometimes a metaphor, that there is no purity to the life of the mind once one grants the existence of the unconscious. Even in the Platonic dialogues with their language of ascent and transcendence, she recovers an equally crucial web of metaphors that connect philosophy to the fear of drowning, a search for the *poros*, the way out, a means of overcoming *aporia*, an escape from *la mer*, the sea, which cannot be separated either from the mother, *la mère*, or the *mar* of the *cauchemar*.[3] In so doing, she does not spare herself, including bits from her own nightmares, remnants from a traumatic past that she sprinkles through her work but saves for the telling until the very end of her life. The irony is that in so doing, she makes her own work a specimen that invites dissection, makes it indeed difficult to resist.[4]

This is also an essay about religion and literature. Kofman wrote about a myriad of sources, both literary and philosophical. Beyond those I highlight here, she wrote about Kant, Kierkegaard, Moliere, Rousseau, Diderot, Sartre, among others, as well as artists such as Goya, Rembrandt, Da Vinci, Magritte. Her sources range across genre, medium, and time period. References to Jewish canonical texts are sprinkled through her corpus, but never as a primary focus. When she does write about Jewish texts or Jewish themes, it is always mediated by other sources.[5] She does write about her Jewish upbringing in *Rue Ordener, Rue Labat*, and she references her Jewish background in almost every autobiographical episode in her work.[6] To say, however, that she worked as a thinker or theorist on the Jewish tradition would be a misrepresentation. One could say that there is something Jewish in her method. At the very least, she understood her own work as an inheritance from her father, Berek Kofman, a rabbi who perished at Auschwitz. Her choice of commentary, the procedure of making other authorities act as the mouthpieces for her ideas, suggests a midrashic method.[7] While that might be an avenue to reclaim her for the tradition, what interests me here is not the possibility that this would connect her back to the fold, but rather the stakes of the displacement of that method in her readings of the philosophical and literary tradition of the West.[8]

In the rabbinic tradition the attribution of an interpretation to an earlier authority strengthens the chain of transmission and its continuity while making room for interpretive discord. At the same time, it magnifies the authority of the great masters and prioritizes proximity to the source.[9] There are features of the French academic tradition, the training for the *agrégation*, which similarly support the authority of the great masters and promote the establishment of schools of thought.[10] There are resonances of both these systems in Kofman's work, reminding us of the ways in which the secular university has replicated its religious predecessors even when the ethos of freedom of thought replaces the ideal of religious devotion.[11] Kofman's work, in its pairing of the performance of fidelity with subtle procedures of resistance, manages to denaturalize systems of authority by revealing the dark chambers of force that resonate through claims to light and knowledge across the philosophical tradition. Kofman turns to literature for its capacity to parody both the philosophical and religious idioms and for a model of textual resistance that operates by thwarting the drive to analytic mastery.

In *Broken Tablets* I proposed that Derrida offers us a theory of modern literature as the inheritor of our religious traditions, mimicking its theological dynamics by means of the notion of the author and the promise of the secret of his or her intent.[12] I proposed that literature can help those of us working within religious studies, and particularly on philosophy of religion, to consider the difficulty we have in telling our story without theological placeholders. Insofar as those placeholders have the status of the imaginary, they help us see the *as if*—Kant's *als ob*—that is equally operative within the theological and philosophical spheres of inquiry. Here I follow this line of inquiry, but take it up through the themes of the fetish and the apotropaeon—the amulet, symbol, or act used to avert evil and misfortune—which appear across Kofman's corpus, sometimes explicitly tied to literature's relation to philosophy, sometimes implicitly to Kofman's conception of how her own writing relates both to the loss of her father, to the paternal law, to the Jewish law, as a correlate to this "as if."[13] What ties all of this together is Kofman's conception of her writing as the space of the "bad substitute," as Derrida dubs the fetish in *Glas*. Kofman's relationship to her Judaism appears in this light not as an abandonment but as a form of fidelity, one that can only be glimpsed through the black light of betrayal. In her own commitment to unearth the memories and traumas that guided her interests, Judaism emerges as a force of gravity, but it is always already marked by its displacement. If this makes her a modern Jewish thinker, her relation to the tradition implies a concept of reception and inheritance that blurs the distinction between religion and literature, and forces us to revisit and reorient our sense of what it means to be devoted.

AT THE ARCHIVE

In the midst of my research for this essay, after having written and presented on Kofman for some months, I made the trip to Caen to see what she'd left behind in her archive. By this point, the project had me in knots. I was, I had to admit, anxious that I had nothing new to say, that I was going over old ground, repeating ideas that had been in vogue twenty-five years ago, but also acutely aware that these doubts were only a reminder that I was playing the game that Kofman herself had fought to thwart. What did I think I'd find in the archive, some undiscovered, heretofore unseen truth? Some key to assembling her corpus otherwise?

I have always found archives thrilling, the acuteness of the concentration as I read, heightened by the sense that my time and access are severely limited and that I've gone to extraordinary efforts just to get there, proven my credentials and been granted authorization.

L'Institut mémoires de l'édition contemporaine sits at the outskirts of the small mostly modern port city of Caen, the capital of Calvados in the Abbaye d'Ardenne. To say that the city is modern is only to acknowledge that it was one of the hardest hit by Allied bombing during the Battle of Normandy and thus faced a lengthy reconstruction effort, lasting until 1962. It is against the backdrop of this mostly postwar utilitarian scene that the Abbaye d'Ardenne stands out. Built originally in the twelfth century for the Premonstratensian order, the abbey has a long history, which reflects that of the nation. Multiple times destroyed and rebuilt, it was occupied by Charles VII during the Hundred Years War, sold as a national property to private owners during the French Revolution, resurrected briefly as a Protestant church, then classified as a historical monument in 1918. It served as a resistance enclave during World War II until overtaken by German forces at the end of the war. In June 1944, following the D-Day landings, as many as 156 Canadian prisoners of war were murdered by the 12th SS Panzer (Hitler Youth) on and in the vicinity of its grounds, their bodies only discovered piecemeal in the following years. Between the 1970s and the 1990s, multiple proposals were considered and plans pursued for the historic site's restoration; all failed, until in 1995 a satisfactory solution was found and the abbey became the depository for IMEC, the nation's modern publishing archive.

Protected by an ancient exterior wall, the compound is a collection of white stone buildings of various styles dating from the thirteenth to the eighteenth century. It has been restored and updated with glass and wood details, which echo its former function as a monastery yet create a set of clean modern spaces to house the finely tuned bureaucratic system that serves the contemporary scholar of literature and philosophy. Inside the compound's walls the courtyard is maintained as a series of gardens and small orchards amid which are scattered a couple dozen green metal park chairs, similar to those found at the Jardin du Luxembourg or the Tuileries. The place is pervaded by a kind of quiet — windy skies and the occasional bird song — rarely found outside of the modern context of the "retreat center." Inside, the cathedral has been converted into the archive reading room, the side chapels lined with book stacks and the center occupied by a single column of reading tables. There is room for twenty-some researchers. The files of author correspondences, manuscript pages, scribbled notes, and press cuttings are treated with heightened reverence: weighed by the staff when they are borrowed for use, and examined only with the accompaniment of designated yellow pencils and blue paper. The files are then weighed again upon their return lest a scrap of paper slip out or a researcher become enticed by the possibility of a souvenir.

It was difficult to resist, in proximity to these objects, the archive fever that I have experienced many times before, but never in a setting that so clearly reminds one of the religious legacy that surrounds the operation of reading. Even an otherwise ordinary object, a hollowed envelope with a scribbled address, develops the aura of authenticity when viewed in the archival context. Its singularity and uniqueness, its status as relic, is reinforced by the ritual of care with which one approaches it. It offers in its very materiality, in the spectacle of the author's handwriting, the enticement of proximity, the promise of intimate understanding and indeed the lure of discovery. As I watched other researchers with their files scribbling notes in the purity of silence, it was easy to imagine in their place robed scribes in the fourteenth century for whom the possibility of discerning authorial intent was equally enticing. At the very least it was a lesson in visceral understanding, a chance to experience firsthand how the patrolling of access to objects and the mechanisms of hierarchy that undergird that access function to imbue objects with sacred power.[14]

It seemed fitting, then, to discover that unlike Derrida's papers, which have been documented and catalogued down to the individual letter, Kofman's, though sorted into files, remain uncatalogued. One thus has to know what one wants to see without knowing whether it even exists in the archive. It is a bit like reaching into a hat at a contest drawing. Whatever one retrieves must be named the winner.

I combed through the early manuscript versions of texts, trying to calculate whether there was anything significant to the edits. What did Kofman change and why? What could I learn from her reading notes? The earliest manuscript of *Rue Ordener*,

Rue Labat is a series of pasted-together fragments, as though the writing of it required first the work of cutting away words in order to see what was left behind.

I read the correspondence that followed the publication of each volume. For each book, she kept an elaborate list of addresses to which to send copies, a list of sixty to seventy, marked off with an x when the book was sent. Among notables such as Derrida, Nancy, Jankélévitch, Blanchot, are the names of her siblings. Each letter of receipt and commentary is carefully saved with its envelope. Jean-Luc Nancy, upon receipt of *Autobiogriffures*, notes that it is her seventh book. "Same as the number of your mother's children?" he queries. Kofman had herself a year earlier in *Comment s'en sortir?* pointed out the similarity between forms of intellectual and physical fecundity, the commonality between literary and physical acts of reproduction—their common purpose to "release man from the most fearful aporia of all: death."[15] Philosophy, she argues, tries to disown its Promethean quality, to denounce the wily contours of its ambitions. Kofman, while not relinquishing the desire for survival, also relentlessly exposed it as such. The archive, in its highly regimented efforts at preservation, cuts off the artifacts from life, trains one's eyes beyond the corpse, but offers in its stead, by means of the author's literary remains, the promise of discovery. Of what? The truth of what her work was *really* about? If this thing itself is beyond my reach, are the papers themselves only a fetish?

Among Kofman's files is one composed of her drawings, which includes a small pad of paper adorned with the Tour Eiffel, inscribed with the address of her local papeterie—38 Avenue Suffern, Paris, 15e—an enticing, if meaningless detail. Inside are a series of line drawings; one might be tempted to call them doodles, if they weren't the work of a thinker and artist keenly interested in the relationship between psychoanalysis and art.

The temptation with these drawings—mostly, though not exclusively, human figures with heads of disproportionate size—is to read them as a lens into Kofman's psyche. Some even appear to show the figure's intestines, drawn to prioritize the inside of the body over its form. One has a giant question mark in the center of the face. One looks like an angel, four legs and wings, all drawn to look fuzzy as though constructed out of static. In another, a large sexless figure towers over a smaller figure (a child?) with wings instead of arms, as though half bird. Most of the figures look as though they've been constructed almost from one line, but one that appears to have two heads is made only of dots, so that nothing connects. An array of theories emerge in my perusal. Is the tall form with the initial J on its back a portrait of Jacques Derrida? Is the sexless towering one Kofman's mother? Must I accept that they remain fundamentally inscrutable, except as a mirror into my own desire for truth, for insight, for originality, and indeed for immortality? Should I continue to seek out the "definitive" interpretation? Or is there a third way, a means of oscillating between inscrutability and interpretation?

It may be that it is difficult, even impossible, to resist in the book—whether scientific, religious, literary, or philosophical— its promise of truth, of meaning, of an antidote to the decaying body in all its materiality. It is this promise that binds together philosophy, literature, and religion—one to the other. Philosophy subordinates literature to its analytic truth claims, even as it relies on its figurations and mythical formulations to express its claims. Religion supplements philosophy with a divine guarantor; philosophy at the same time denigrates religion for its materiality, its fetishes. Literature mimics religion in its construct of the creator, but upends the promise of truth held out by the prospect of a divine creator. Each continuously plays a sleight of hand, proffering truth with one, and providing with the other a substitute, a fetish. Whether reading philosophical, literary, or religious texts, Kofman reveals this game at work, as well as the techniques of subterfuge that allow us to console ourselves with a placeholder by contrasting our prize, our almost-truth, with another's, what we declare to be the other's falsehood.

Kofman, despite her criticism of the philosophical tradition, understood herself as a philosopher, but she put this term in scare quotes, at one remove from the tradition, as if to communicate that she had no pretention of being the real thing but was only playing at it, like Little Hans with his toy.[16] I'd like to think that in all this she was modeling for us how to relate differently to the history of the philosophical tradition in its drive for an ever purer truth, by teaching or demonstrating how and why it makes more sense to be a fetishist after all.

READING AS A FETISHIST

To rehearse the history of the fetish is not only to tell the story of the social sciences, of colonialism, and of the pretext of objectivity that justifies the imposition of western categories and ideals on the cultures it encounters; it is to participate in the ritual of its recounting as a means to discover what it has to say about its practitioners, both in the encounter with others and as a lens turned back on ourselves. Kofman employed the term when it was already heavily saturated with uses and interpretations, perhaps unsustainably so. Nonetheless, recent years have seen an uncanny fascination with its multivalence and its stigma, as a lens into the history of our social scientific and humanistic disciplines. As William Pietz put it already in 1985, ten years after Kofman's reclamation of the term, "'Fetish' has always been a word of sinister pedigree. Discursively promiscuous and theoretically suggestive, it has always been a word with a past, forever becoming 'an embarrassment' to disciplines in the human sciences that seek to contain its sense."[17] Rosalind Morris, in one of a number of recent texts dedicated to its history, describes it "as one of relentless vacillation between dominant metaphor and disavowed designator, between valorized and vilified referent."[18]

The standard narrative traces the term to the second half of the fifteenth century, an artifact of the first voyages of European exploration. Nonetheless, even the etymology is contested, with

historians and theorists either conflating various possible etymologies, deriving the term from *fatum*, meaning divine utterance or fate, *facere*, meaning artificial or fabricated, or *fanum*,
meaning consecrated space. The word appears in Portuguese to
designate the charms or amulets used by the people of Guinea.[19]
It is then written about by the Calvinist Dutch merchants who
displace the Portuguese and promptly attribute to their Catholic
predecessors recognition of its nature, arising from a shared likeness between the pagan and Catholic use of material objects.[20]
It was thus not a term native to its practitioners but a means for
colonizers to describe and denigrate what were deemed to be
the religious practices of an indigenous people, particularly insofar as they falsely attributed causality to inanimate objects.[21]
Yet this description of how the objects functioned may itself have
been, in its own false attribution of causality and belief, a product of the colonizers' inability to understand Guineans except by
way of the colonizers' own logic, that is to say, by assuming that
Guinean natives were bad scientists, misled truth-seekers, naïve
believers.[22] From its beginning the term entrenched a universal
concept of religion that is simultaneously epistemological and
instrumental, defining the essence of religion in terms of truth-
seeking and the cultivation of divine favor. It is perhaps, then,
no surprise that from its first function as an improper name, the
fetish was generalized in 1760 into "fetishism" by the French En-
lightenment figure Charles de Brosses in one of the first works
of comparative religion, *Du culte de dieux fétiches*, in which it
becomes a diagnostic means of affiliating the practices of ancient times with those of present-day "primitive" people, thus
facilitating an evolutionary model of human development.[23]
De Brosses coins the term "fétichisme" in order to compare the
practices of contemporary Africans, Native Americans, and
Laplanders to the ancient cults of Phoenicians and Egyptians:
"So many similar facts of the same type establish with the utmost clarity that what is today the religion of African Negroes
and other barbarians was formerly that of ancient peoples."[24]

De Brosses's theory is an extension of Hume's analysis in *The Natural History of Religions* that religion originates from fear. Hume recognized that his tract was De Brosses's philosophical source and credited him with imbuing Hume's own theories with a further accumulation of facts.[25] It is thus fair to say that the notion of the fetish is coextensive with the development of modern philosophy of religion, of which Hume's *Natural History* remains as an early landmark, and that from its beginnings it is a term used to describe an affective response that results in a category error, the attribution to a foreign object of a false power that should properly be invested in what is great and true and original, i.e., the one true God.[26] The concept, which appears in De Brosses's work by means of what he considers to be an inductive argument, was deployed in order to fight off the residue of "figurism" or Neoplatonism still prevalent in the eighteenth century. Such antihistorical speculation, according to De Brosses, "attributed a knowledge of the most hidden causes of nature to ignorant and savage nations, and found intellectual ideas of the most abstract Metaphysics in the mass of trivial practices of a crowd of stupid and coarse men."[27] What began as an attempt to counter ahistoricism and Platonic metaphysics with an argument for empiricism and induction became a dehistoricized mainstay of the philosophy of religions, the concept broadening its scope with each subsequent deployment. Only thirty years after De Brosses's text, the charge of fetishism was instrumental to Immanuel Kant's *Religion within the Boundaries of Mere Reason*. Kant treats the concept as a synonym for sorcery, but broadens it to refer to any form of "counterfeit worship." He uses it thus to characterize ritual practices, including the observance of "statutory law," which he describes as operating through a false understanding of the nature of God, in seeking to influence Divine actions through amoral means.[28] Although Hegel, following De Brosses, relegates fetishism to the African religions, by describing it as symptomatic of a *slavish* disposition, he makes it a prototype for heteronomy. From here, its usage proliferates, appearing in Comte, Nietzsche, Freud, Marx, and those who take up their legacy in various forms.

From a particular historical encounter, a category error is generated, the narrative of which ironically demonstrates the perverse logic of colonialism: the conqueror finds in the encounter with those he exploits a "bad" or "childish" versions of its own mode of worship and thought. The move is then replicated when it becomes a philosophical tool for prescribing the relation between philosophical abstraction and its concrete manifestation in religious traditions, providing a means to differentiate modes of religious understanding that function symbolically—e.g., Christianity—from those predicated on a materialist "error."[29]

It is both the history of the term and its tendency to proliferate in usages, thus to become generalized, that allow it finally to be turned back on Christianity with Nietzsche, on capitalism in Marx, and finally to lose its ethnological function all together as it enters the Freudian lexicon, where the fetish is defined as a substitute for "the normal sexual object" that bears some relationship to what it replaces, usually some part of the body (such as a foot or hair) "which is in general very inappropriate for sexual purposes."[30] As Harmut Böhme has suggested, the history of the fetish is a story of modernity, in which a term used to describe the otherness of others became a means of recognizing the otherness retained within ourselves.[31]

For Kofman the fetish is both a term with a long history, reaching its modern apotheosis in Marx and Freud, and a species of the apotropaic function she locates across culture. From the Greek, ἀποτρόπαιον means "to turn away" and was often associated with the symbol of the Gorgon, which Athena wears on her breast plate in the *Iliad* and in many ancient Greek representations of the Goddess. For Kofman this symbol speaks to the ambivalence of the apotropaic and points to the source of fear, for, following Freud, she associates the head of the Gorgon with the maternal vagina, site of origin.[32] For Kofman, returning the history of the fetish to the lexicon of the apotropaic decenters

Freud's own account of the fetish as a response to castration anxiety. It helps to reveal that the castration complex itself might be serving an apotropaic function for Freud, allowing him to displace his own anxiety toward the more primal site onto an object—the fetish/phallus—that the man can at least demonstrate that he has. A primal fear of death, mystery, and the unrepresentable is recast as an anxiety of loss.

While fetish is a term inseparable from its colonial history, the apotropaic function suggests a common impetus across cultures to find strategies to escape from death in its most fearsome forms. For Kofman it is less a question of whether we do so and more a question of how.[33] One means by which we protect ourselves is by trying to distinguish the true from the false, good forms from bad, the pure from the impure, the philosopher from the sophist, the masculine from the feminine. Is it possible, her work continually asks, to occupy these distinctions otherwise? Are there means of deploying the apotropaic function of culture in which mischief and laughter are part of the game? Can we do so without attributing the lack to someone else? Without thus trying to secure for ourselves the position of master?

The fetish becomes a means to approach this question for Kofman through its Freudian deployment, that is to say, as a substitute object for the phantasm of the mother's penis, that also memorializes its loss. Because of its history, however, it can also serve her endeavor to interweave the philosophical and psychoanalytic registers. She ultimately conceives of it more broadly as that which veils, masks, or protects its user from the frightening and inaccessible real thing. The term itself shows up across her corpus, from the early 1970s forward. However, she more often employs the term apotropaeon or apotropaic in order to recall the reference to the maternal body. Against the history of the fetish as a term to denigrate the practice of the other and a tool with which to announce oneself as the true seeker of the real thing, Kofman asks whether the apotropaic function can be deployed against this dynamic and embraced for the very reason that it definitively is *not* the real thing.

Up to this point, it is only in gender theory that Kofman's work on the fetish has received much attention. In the 1980s and 1990s she briefly influenced American feminist literary theory, when theorists began seeking a basis for overcoming gender essentialism. However, those who found Kofman's notion of the fetish useful also tended to worry that she borrowed too much from an old lexicon. They claimed she was too dependent on the thinking of the great masters, on readings of Marx, Freud, and Derrida. They called for formulations that broke with the past and sought new ground.[34] In Kofman's corpus the concept resurfaces in multiple texts, becoming a means for her to intertwine the psychoanalytic and philosophical registers and through them to annunciate a critique of mastery in the history of philosophy. But even as this line of thinking runs through her work, her own embrace of the fetish involves a letting go of the thing itself, or at least a letting go of the claim to have been the one to have found it. She categorically does not announce herself as the originator of a new theory, nor does she credit herself as the original source for any insight. For the phallic logic of truth at the heart of metaphysics always proceeds by exactly such an announcement, by claiming to be the first to discover a truth, one which by virtue of its status *as* truth has nonetheless been there along.[35]

Through her own practice of always situating herself as something of a copy or copier of the "great masters," Kofman sets herself up as something of a fetishist, that is to say, she refuses to occupy the space of the center. In ventriloquizing her interlocutors, she reanimates the relationship between philosophy, religion, and literature in their competition for truth, but always by positioning herself in the derivative position.

2. PHILOSOPHIZING WITH A FETISH

Philosophy since Aristotle, Kofman argues in the opening section of *Freud and Fiction*, has operated through the assertion that preceding philosophers must be bested. The predecessor retains his value, but only insofar as he heralds and confirms the truth discovered and recognized by the thinker now declaring himself king of the hill. The point for Kofman is that this tendency toward mastery in the philosophical tradition can be comprehended through a psychoanalytic lens as the claim to possess the phallus and an expression of the fear of castration. It is an elaborate game played out as much in the history of thought as it is on the playground. If I have it—whatever you want to call it—the phallus, the ball, the truth—then you don't. In philosophy, the prize is the truth, to which fantasy or fiction is opposed and therefore denigrated. Literature is thus represented as philosophy's other, its inadequate (feminized) cousin—it is for this very reason that Kofman champions writing and literature, to reclaim what philosophy expels, sending the poets out of the city. If Plato is the first to subordinate literature to philosophy, Nietzsche is the first to break with this tradition and also the first to rehabilitate the Pre-Socratics, whom Aristotle denigrated. It is Aristotle, for Kofman, who is exemplary of the philosophical tradition and who stands at the origin of the tradition's rules of conduct, establishing "the inheritance of the whole of western philosophy."[36]

Just as Aristotle subordinates metaphor to concept, so he subordinates his predecessors to his authority: an exercise of mastery analogous to that which, in the *Politics*, he declares is natural for master to exercise over slave, father over child, male over female, Greek over barbarian. In this case we are dealing with more than an analogy:

> On the one hand the concept as literal "proper" sense as opposed to figurative sense is *kurion*, "the propriety of a name utilized in its dominant, master, capital sense": the master word that dominates other derivative or merely metaphorical senses. On the other hand, only the master, the father, the man, the Greek has the right to the word, to speech, to the logos.[37]

The violence of the political hierarchy that naturalizes the forms of power under which it operates is, she suggests here, inseparable from the philosophical apparatus that endorses it and encodes it with the aura of truth, it is thus also inseparable from the critique of the literary that sets the mechanism in motion. Meaning can only be established as proper if an improper counterpart is designated. What supports the hierarchy and thus the truth-telling of the philosopher is the prioritization of the proper. "All the rest is empty literature."[38]

Even for Aristotle, however, metaphor, despite his denigration of figurative language, is also always a necessary instrument, because only divinity "possesses knowledge in actuality. Only the divinity is the perfect philosopher and absolute master."[39] The human philosopher thus relies on figural language, requires metaphor and parable but at the same time must denigrate these forms in order to establish the thing itself as truth and himself as closer to it than the poets. He equally requires the engagement with others' ideas, but what *could* be a dialogue, and might even be represented as such, is far more often in fact a contest that manifests itself in the domination of his peers and predecessors, the rewriting of their insights to make them testify to the truth of his doctrine. *Their* access to partial truth buttresses his own claims to mastery.

Kofman includes this account of philosophy in her book *Quatre romans analytiques* (1974), in order to show that Freud's treatment of literature as "the infancy of psychoanalysis" is merely the repetition of a "fiction invented by western metaphysics as a whole."[40] While Kofman doesn't explicitly name this dynamic in philosophy in terms of the fetish, the relation she presents between philosophers and their predecessors and philosophy and its bad substitute, namely literature, mirrors the role that religion has played in the history of philosophy, where religion in its materiality is designated as a flawed but necessary supplement to philosophy's abstract expression. As a term for bad religion, fetishism thus designates the perversion of the relationship to the material, such that it is esteemed in and of itself rather than understood to be merely symbolic. Literary language, for the philosopher, functions as vehicle and provides the very means—through the notion of metaphor and analogy—for expressing the figural relationship itself. The difference between the two is this: while philosophy avowedly holds onto some version of true religion, as that which transcends its material expression to secure the philosopher's access to the truth, literature, even as its figures of speech are equally necessary to each and every claim to possess the truth, can be treated as a mere tool, only instrumental to the process and easily dispensed with.

As much as Kofman is concerned, from her earliest work, to articulate the relationship between literary language and philosophy, she is equally concerned with literature and art's relation to religion, or at least to the theological. In her first book, *L'enfance de l'art* (1970), one of her key questions is how the notion of the artist, whether painter or poet, correlates to the divine creator. Following Freud on art and literature, she considers how artistic production supplies a substitute, often for a neurotic fixation. "Art, religion, and philosophy are not neuroses, rather all are social solutions that spare the artist."[41] While this can be psychologically productive, religion and art might be understood to play parallel roles; both are "illusions which contrast with reality." In this sense art can uphold the ideology of the creator, as its substitute for the father, for God. "The artist kills God only to put himself in his place."[42] However, art and literature will also become the sites, the very means, by which to kill the ideology of the creator in ourselves, insofar as the literary text resists both the author's and the reader's attempts at mastery. Psychoanalysis can itself be a tool in this endeavor. It has the capacity to unseat this ideology, by showing that the artist's gift is not from "God or from 'kindly nature.' It is not innate but is rather the consequence of a double determinism (or a double chance): on the one hand, the play of psychic forces and a certain disposition toward a particular fate of the drives—sublimation; and on the other the chance experiences that the artist had to live out."[43]

At the same time, however, as Kofman shows in her readings of Freud reading art, psychoanalysis often ends up replicating the drive toward mastery by allowing analysis to become the master discipline, by treating the text or the visual object as something that can be easily decoded. Kofman, however, uses the tools of psychoanalysis to reveal this tendency and to show how the text resists.

In her reading of Freud's "The Uncanny," in "The Double Is/ and the Devil: The Uncanniness of the Sandman," Kofman dismantles Freud's conviction that the story is about the castration complex. As will also be the case in *The Enigma of Woman*, published six years later, Kofman suggests that the castration complex is a fetish for Freud, a substitute object, or a screen that blocks him from seeing in the story a more primary terror on display, and a more primary site of repression represented by the mother: "the repression of the presence of death with, and at the origin of, life itself," or the death drive.[44] But Kofman does not leave her analysis here, nor can she, since much of the aim of her reading has been to expose the dizzying consequence of E. T. A. Hoffman's layering of perspectives in his story "The Sandman." Far more important to her than correcting Freud's reading with her own is to expose the way Freud's analysis has subordinated literary representation to "a truth exterior and anterior to it," just as philosophy does with literature. Thus she must call her own reading into question as well, or at least consider the possibility that she too, like Freud and the protagonist of "The Sandman," Nathaniel, has fallen into his (the devil's) traps and lures, by mistaking the inanimate for the living:

> By carrying out an analysis that seeks only to complicate the Freudian schema, which remains faithful to it by replacing one ultimate signified with another, more universal one, I am con-

tinuing to confuse fictional and real people. Having subjected the work to my desire for intelligibility, I have then consumed it greedily, without leaving any remainder, proving my bad taste, indeed my animality.[45]

At stake in her claim that the death drive is behind and more fundamental than the castration complex is the suggestion that the relation of original and double becomes impossible to maintain, because the death drive is the vortex that not only scrambles our capacity to tell the difference but replaces the distinction between the imaginary and the real with "the problematics of a simulacrum without any originary model." This claim is not merely a product of the model of the unconscious that Freud himself has proffered; it is in the nature of fiction itself, which Hoffman, she suggests, has exploited in the story. "By multiplying the double, he not only complicates any reading of the text by interweaving and amassing themes, he also makes such thematic interweaving the very law itself of the text."[46]

If this too sounds like a masterful reading, one that claims to have gotten to the bottom, not only of Freud's mistake, but of Hoffman's strategies, leave it to Kofman to set even this interpretation into a state of flux. On the final page of her essay she suggests that with Hoffman's story, which is already preoccupied with the theme of literature, Freud is finally forced to recognize his own drive to mastery. But then she goes one step further and implicates herself in the process, as well as Hoffman and Freud, suggesting that desire itself, "her animality" as she calls it, drives every writer to one "vital defense: to travesty his text, to cover it over, to protect it behind a bundle of themes; or to ask endless questions about the 'fabrication of the text', which can also be a means of trying to master it."[47]

Hard to imagine that Kofman is not implicating herself here too, suggesting that the drive to mastery is *not* something that can be fully defeated. One can't claim to stand outside of it, or even to avoid its manifestation. One can, however, participate in its unveiling, ironically, by resisting the distinction between fabrication and exposure, or better yet, by scrambling the distinction, setting it into oscillation. While she does not use the term fetish here to talk about fiction, and while I cannot suggest that she was indeed thinking about the fetish, it is hard not to take note of the word "fabrication," from which the term fetish is derived. In using it here, there is already the suggestion that there are ways, and certainly literature might provide a means, to upset the hierarchy that accords a precedence to analytic truth, that truth which precedes the text.

A SHUTTLECOCK BETWEEN THEM

That "fetish" was a term that passed between Derrida and Kofman becomes clear when we consider the relation between her 1973 work *Camera Obscura of Ideology* and Derrida's 1972–1973 lecture course on religion and philosophy, for which the fetish was in fact a key reference point.[48] There is no claim for ideology without the religious motif, Derrida argues here, and the fetish becomes the necessary supplement to articulating the relationship between religion and philosophy—and the opposition between fetish and non-fetish—the space of truth. The term is key for Derrida for forging a connection between Kant and Freud, but he ultimately moves past it in the course by turning his attention to Hegel.

Less than a year after attending the course, Kofman dilates upon it in *Camera Obscura of Ideology*, which, she reports in the footnotes, she had first given as a presentation in the seminar. But Kofman's text is not a mere recapitulation of Derrida's argument. Derrida does not treat Nietzsche in the course, though he does begin working on him soon after—teaching "Oui, Nietzsche" the following year. Kofman, ignoring Kant altogether, traces the metaphor of the camera obscura, referring here both literally to the "dark chamber" and to the mechanism of a pinhole camera in the work of Marx, Freud, and Nietzsche.[49] Through a

series of efficient readings, Kofman treats the lure of the philosophical model of truth, which claims to be able to access or
represent truth, through the metaphor of vision. Her argument
proceeds through three thinkers who deploy the metaphor of
the camera obscura, all of whom also engaged with the figure
of the fetish. In this text the double meaning of camera obscura
plays against the double meaning of the fetish. While the main
text treats at great lengths the history of the metaphor of the
dark chamber/pinhole camera, the history of the fetish appears
only in the footnotes, where, borrowing from Baudrillard, she
describes the fetish as toggling between the religious and artistic spheres—referring to an object imbued with supernatural
powers, but coming from the Latin *factitius* and giving rise to
the Spanish *afeitar*, "to paint, to adorn, to embellish." Kofman
plays these two meanings and these two metaphors off one another. She describes in the text how both Marx and Freud get
caught up in the model of truth as representation through the
metaphor of the photographic image, even as both their theories
ultimately reject the philosophical model of vision that does not
recognize force as/and desire as always already transforming
the act of representation.

For Marx, Kofman points out, "Clear meaning does not pre-
exist ideological obscurity and there is no 'truth' without a labor
of transformation."[50] Yet when he describes the "real" relation
of reality to ideology—a term itself tied to the spectral through
its root in *eidos*—he succumbs to the metaphor of the camera
obscura, that is, to the idea of an inverted image, which needs
to be reversed for the truth to appear. The same can be said for
his conception of the commodity fetish, which distinguishes the
falsified "magical" relation attributed to objects as commodities
from what they "really" signify as products of labor. Insofar as
the fetish can signal a false notion of value, it can also, by virtue
of its falseness, point toward the true notion. For Kofman these
are two versions of the same metaphor, two varieties on the
trope of inversion, both dependent on the metaphysical schema

in which height, transcendence, and lucidity signify truth. To both of these models Kofman opposes a Nietzschean possibility.

Where Marx and Freud, despite both taking up these two metaphors for their own purposes, "are unable, in certain respects, to avoid being caught within the same field, even if certain shifts are effected: even if the stress is now placed, not on transparency, but on obscurity, not on objectivity, but on inversion," Nietzsche represents another way by virtue of the fact that he has "no nostalgia for clarity."[51] He passes through the stage of "hierarchical reversal" but opens up a new avenue through the very metaphors that have been instrumental to its maintenance: the camera obscura as dark chamber and the fetish as artistic fabrication.[52]

The notion of truth as transparency, which Marx and Freud had begun to unhinge, is dismantled in Nietzsche's verion of perspectivism, for which "no eye is without its point of view, and none is passive, even that of science."[53] The camera obscura of truth, for Nietzsche, is indeed a dark chamber impenetrable to sight, which renders the act of unveiling not only impossible, but indecent, for this version of the camera obscura also genders it, by associating it with mystery, with veiling, and thus with femininity. One can see the resonance here with Kofman's reading of the death drive in Freud, with her suggestion that the fear of castration is inseparable from a more primal fear, from the death drive at the origin of life. This site of darkness, whether understood in the psychoanalytic register as that site of death at the origin of life or in Nietzschean terms as the Dionysian abyss, cannot be rendered by representation, nor can it be possessed as phallus.[54] To presume the contrary is "the perspective of those who are unaware that, behind the veil, there is yet another veil. It is the symptomatic unawareness of the instincts' loss of virility," the manifestation of the "feverish fear of castration, for a penis and a stable world to cling to."[55]

Is there any remedy for this feverish fear, any successful means of coping? Enter the fetish. Freud's 1927 essay on fetishism argues that the fetish is the replacement for the penis, not just any penis but "a particular and quite special penis that has been extremely important in early childhood but has later been lost. That is to say, it should normally have been given up, but the fetish is precisely designed to prevent it from extinction." What is interesting in the essay is that the fetishist is not suffering from a pathology in the same way as a neurotic or a hysteric, for the fetishist is "quite satisfied with it," may even praise it as a kind of aid that "eases their erotic life." What it eases, according to Freud, is universal for the male sex: "Probably no male human being is spared the fright of castration at the sight of a female genital." Such a fright would seem in fact to make homosexuality or fetishism the obvious responses. It is something of a riddle, in fact, that so many men overcome it. "Why some become homosexual as a consequence of that impression, while others fend it off by creating a fetish, and the great majority surmount it, we are frankly not able to explain."[56] As Kofman points out in her reading of the text, Freud doesn't provide a viable explanation in his 1927 essay. "Far from being 'pathological,' either one under these conditions would be the *normal* destiny of the masculine libido." The only viable explanation, Kofman suggests, is penis envy, not the woman's actual desire for the penis, but the male displacement of his castration anxiety onto the woman. It is the attribution onto the woman of this desire that "provides man with reassurance against his castration anxiety."[57] If a man can believe that the woman envies the penis, then he will also believe that his envy stems from her lack of what he has. If she wants it back, he tells himself, then he must in fact possess it.

This is the same logic as "king of the hill": if I have it, the ball, the truth, the penis, then someone else does not. I need to stipulate an Other without the object in question in order to reassure myself that I am whole, immune from the mystery, darkness, and indeterminacy here represented by the mother's genitalia. By this line of thinking, heterosexuality is itself a defensive reaction to fear. The erection of the male organ, "man's display of his penis," is itself an apotropaic response, "as if to say, 'I am not afraid of you. I defy you. I have a penis.'"[58]

The fetish, on the contrary, represents a compromise position, leaving room for doubt as to the woman's castration, and thus to the possible castration of the man. It can serve an apotropaic function but without disguising its status as a stand-in for a lost object. It is ambiguous, for it announces itself as a substitute. As Freud himself puts it, the fetish functions like a memorial, marking an absence even as it provides a substitute for it.[59]

While Kofman's reading of Freud's essay on the fetish doesn't appear until 1980, in *The Enigma of Woman*, it is clear already in *Camera Obscura* that the Freudian fetish can be thought along with the Nietzschean conception of appearance. It can represent the possibility of illusion or indeterminacy that descends, like turtles, all the way down. The fetish can also provide a form of protection, if only through the prophylactic of laughter.

Citing the second preface to Nietzsche's *Gay Science*, she introduces here the figure of Baubo, quoting Nietzsche:

> "Is it true that God is present everywhere?" a little girl asks her mother; "I think that's indecent"—a hint for philosophers! One should have more respect for the bashfulness with which nature has hidden behind riddles and iridescent uncertainties. Perhaps truth is a woman who has reason for not letting us see her reasons? Perhaps her name is—to speak Greek—*Baubo*? . . . Oh those Greeks! They know how to live. What is required for that is to stop courageously at the surface, the fold, the skin, to adore appearance, to believe in forms, tones, words, in the whole Olympus of appearance. Those Greeks were superficial—*out of profundity*.[60]

It is bawdy Baubo, a mythological figure in the myth of Demeter, who brings the mother of Persephone out of mourning by lifting her skirts and letting Demeter see her belly. In *Camera Obscura* Kofman does not linger on this figure, but Baubo's presence here is crucial. She represents the possibility of laughter as the response to both the fear and desire for truth as that which is unveiled behind appearances. "To laugh at appearances rather than to deny them? Seek, you metaphysicians, to unveil the world and you will find still another veil, a painting on Baubo's stomach was the figure of a head, that of Iacchus."[61]

Kofman mimics Nietzsche's already ironized tone of exhortation here, speaking as his female counterpart, to introduce a figure already mythologically associated with Dionysius, as his female double. She slips then quickly from talking about Baubo to Dionysius, but he has already been introduced in the guise of Iacchus, a figure painted on Baubo's stomach, and thus closely identified with her genitals. As such, he/she represents an undecidablity between the sexes, and a new conception of both nakedness and the fetish. "Dionysius is naked," she writes, "without shame. He is naked because he is not ashamed of his own appearance, he has no need of metaphysical finery as so many fetishes." Dionysus would thus seem to mean the end of the fetish. Except that now the fetish has been reversed, following Nietzsche in *Twilight of the Idols*. It refers to the mistaken quest for the metaphysical truth itself, which is now portrayed as mere decoration on the nakedness of appearance. Dionysus's nakedness, she continues, with reference to *The Birth of Tragedy*, signifies the end of the very dualism between surface and depth, man and woman. His nudity is "that fetish that would put an end to all fetishisms."[62] Like the camera obscura in its double valence, the fetish too has been reclaimed for its double valence. If anything, Kofman has called into question the stability between the substitute and the real. This carries over to the trope of the camera obscura itself, which is now figured *as* a fetish in the Freudian sense: as photographing mechanism, as a "lightbox," it is not so much an instrument for seeing as that which protects the philosopher from seeing. It is, she writes, "that magical apparatus which serves to placate horror: it functions as *apotropaeon*."[63] As another term for the fetish, apotropaeon is particularly fitting for Kofman's usage here: it is that which turns the viewer away from what is unbearable; it functions as a screen, and indeed tropologically, that is to say, figuratively.

Nonetheless, given that this passage unfolds over a mere two pages of the work, it would be disingenuous to suggest that *Camera Obscura* provides, through a depiction of the fetish, a full-fledged alternative to the phallic mode of truth-seeking. But Kofman does at least give her reader the tools to recognize an opposition between the embrace of the world as mere appearance and a version of truth as right vision. She returns to the latter mode for the rest of the book, by ending with Descartes's account of vision and how the inverted image on the retina is righted. It requires an additional supplement. It must always be supported by a notion of the intellect as that which sees truly. But the intellect too requires a supplement, gaining the status of objectivity or transcendence only through divine support, "as rational intuition . . . received as light from God."[64] Is not the divine, then, also an apotropaeon? But insofar as it functions as such, the power of the divine is only secured when contrasted with a substitute. There is thus a fundamental instability between original and substitute that Kofman highlights by revealing how the divine itself is already supplementary in Descartes's account of vision.

The same year that Kofman published *Camera Obscura* she developed these few pages from the text into a larger essay given at the Institute of Psychoanalysis. It was then published, a couple of years later, in *Nuova Corrente* as "Baubo: Theological Perversion and Fetishism." Here she begins with fetishism—contrasting Nietzsche's view with Auguste Comte's and Freud's—and ends with Baubo.[65] The essay asks whether Nietzsche's notion of the fetish, which appears only rarely in his text, has some overlap with Freud's. The problem is that Nietzsche hardly uses the term. When he does, it is in a way analogous to that of De Brosses and others—to refer to a mistaken belief stemming from fear and the desire to assert some control over the cosmos. He does, however, reverse its charge by pinning it on the rational belief in causes, invented, according to Nietzsche, as a "comforting, liberating and relieving . . . form of explanation."[66] The point of Kofman's essay is less, however, to prove any consonance between Nietzsche and Freud than to show that one can use Freud's concept of the fetish to understand Nietzsche's relation to women. It might even seem that she is undertaking this task to relieve Nietzsche of the charge of misogyny. After having considered the sites in which Nietzsche describes truth as a woman, she concludes her essay with the claim that the severity of "the maxims and arrows Nietzsche directs toward women" should be read, thus, as a mark of "ambivalence," rather than of misogyny. Indeed such a reading might seem to fit the schema of many of Kofman's essays; as her commentators often suggest, her project is on one level a psychoanalysis of her philosophical subjects.[67] As true as that is of her method, she is also establishing through Nietzsche a logic of the fetish that contrasts it with the philosophical critique of the fetish stipulated on a claim to objective truth. In this sense Nietzsche's reversal of the fetish, pinning it on the belief in causes itself, already reverses the vector of the term.[68]

The question that drives the essay is not distant from the one Kofman asks of Marx. Can one perform a revaluation of values, a reversal, without remaining dependent on the form of hierarchy which undergirds that reversal, and thus remaining within a construction of value that depends on the concept of transcendence? Is Nietzsche merely reversing a Platonic hierarchical move that establishes transcendence by contrasting the vector of its gaze with something lowly? Not if the reversal itself exposes Platonism as already the function of a certain perspective. "Considered as perspectives of a certain form or life, truth is irrefutable. The mistake is the will to impose truth on other points of view."[69] This is in fact what Nietzsche's approach reveals, she suggests, but it can do so only by resisting a *singular* perspective.[70] Instead, Nietzsche "is always his own double." In the process of making this claim, Kofman begins to oppose the naïve version of the fetish, in which it can only appear as a substitute for the real thing—a consequence, in the Freudian idiom, of the fear of castration, which is also the fear of woman—with a possibility that does not do away with this opposition but puts it in motion, by means of a doubling and an oscillation of perspectives. Baubo and Dionysius are not even fully two distinct figures, but represent a doubling and an oscillation of the male and female perspective, a means thus for Kofman, ventriloquizing Nietzsche, of resisting the opposition between original and substitute. She concludes the essay by asking whether even Nietzsche's most potent denigrations of women are themselves the mark of ambivalence, of his love, in fact, for all who "had abandoned him when they might have served him as a lightning rod . . . or even an umbrella?"[71]

Nietzsche's umbrella famously served as *his* apotropaeon, that is to say, he never went out without it; it was his constant companion, his biographers report, a shield from the sun but also protection against the electricity in the clouds to which he was convinced he was particularly susceptible—something like a natural conductor.[72] It is also the centerpiece of Derrida's analysis of Nietzsche in *Eperons [Spurs]*. Kofman gave her own lecture, "Baubo," four years before Derrida published *Eperons* but did not include the comment about the umbrella until the later edition. When Kofman publishes the essay in English in 1988, she adds the comment about the umbrella and credits Derrida's own reading of the sentence "I have forgotten my umbrella," with brilliantly demonstrating its undecidability. She concludes the footnote with her own enigmatic statement, writing, "Derrida's umbrella thus protects us from all dogmatism."[73]

Kofman had been writing on Nietzsche before working with Derrida. Their relationship began, in fact, with a request for Derrida to read her first published essay on Nietzsche, "Metamorphose de la volonté de puissance du judaïsme au christianisme d'après 'L'antéchrist' de Nietzsche," a topic she would return to in one of her last books, reproducing the early essay in *Le Mepris des Juifs* (1994). But as she describes it in an interview, Derrida's seminars allowed her to "generalize the type of reading" she had done "in isolation on these two authors."[74] *Nietzsche and Metaphor*, first published as an essay in 1971 and then as a book in 1972, was certainly a product of that encounter. But there it is Kofman who reveals, if not the "undecidability" of Nietzsche's statements, then, perhaps, even more importantly, the way in which Nietzsche's notion of the concept as a forgotten or repressed metaphor creates a fundamental ambivalence for his own concepts. Derrida, meanwhile, published "White Mythology" in the same issue of *Poétique* in which the first version of Kofman's text appears. But Kofman's text, by focusing on metaphor in Nietzsche alone, suggests, if not directly, then at least by inference, that Derrida's own concept of undecidability, as well as his notion of deconstruction, is already Nietzschean. Of Nietzsche's use of aphorisms, for example, she writes:

> The aphoristic form is the actual writing of an artistic force positing and imposing forms which are as new and as numerous as there are readers to conquer and appropriate a text. A new reading/writing destroys the traditional categories of the book as a closed totality containing a definitive meaning, the author's; in such a way it deconstructs [*déconstuit*] the idea of author as master of the meaning of the work and immortalizing himself through it. The aphorism, by its discontinuous character, disseminates meaning and appeals to the pluralism of interpretations and their renewal; only movement is immortal.[75]

Not only does she use the term "déconstruire" for Nietzsche's process, she credits him with a form that thrives off of the function of dissemination in its capacity to transform the text, to undermine the status of author. Sounding a great deal like Derrida in some of his early formulations of his method, Kofman in a footnotes describes Nietzsche as participating in a form of repetition "which displaces, takes old constructions to pieces and recomposes them by connecting up what is different and separating what is similar: a new ludic construction."[76]

So what should we make of her enigmatic statement that "Derrida's umbrella . . . protects us from all dogmatism"? Is she now attributing to Derrida the concept of undecidability, which she had elsewhere credited to Nietzsche? Some years later, in 1982, she would use the term umbrella as a synonym for the apotropaeon. She would also suggest, following the joke, referenced in "Baubo," "that a wife is like an umbrella, one can always take a cab," that as a figure for "holding women in respect," Derrida's umbrella is also a form of mastery.[77] We could simply read it as an acknowledgment of Kofman's indebtedness to Derrida for helping her to define a method that allows her to expose the ambivalence in Nietzsche's statements. But Kofman's phrase about Derrida's umbrella, which we must ourselves accept as ambivalent, as protected *itself* from dogmatism, also harkens back to the fetish, to the apotropaic object. To say that Derrida's umbrella protects us is to suggest further that "Derrida's umbrella" is itself something of a fetish, an object to be used to protect "us," but also, perhaps, to protect him. But should we understand it now as a substitute, a memorial, a compromise? Should we also take it a step further and read it as an insight into the function that Derrida plays for Kofman? After having attributed the procedure of undecidability to Nietzsche, does attributing the insight of Nietzsche's undecidability to Derrida also protect her? Does it protect Kofman in the same way Nietzsche's umbrella protected Nietzsche? Or is this statement itself ironic? Is it a veiled accusation that Derrida has been using polysemy to shield himself, to play his own fort-and-da game, to provide his own "athletic support-belt?"[78]

THE END(S) OF MAN

In the last days of July 1980 at Cerisy, Sarah Kofman participated in the *décade* devoted to Derrida's work. In the essay she contributed, entitled "Ça Cloche," she continues the earlier conversation on the fetish that began with her presentation in Derrida's seminar. Derrida's *Glas* was published in 1974 and includes already some of the material from the 1972–1973 course. The fetish appears intermittently throughout this text, but Derrida's sustained meditation occupies only four pages of the Hegel column of the work's 262 pages, before the term jumps briefly to the Genet column. This section follows something of the history already developed in the course, includes a treatment of Marx and Kant, discusses De Brosses, and makes the claim from across this tradition that one can define the fetish by virtue of its status as substitute: "the fetish is opposed to the presence of the thing itself, to truth, signified truth for which the fetish is a substitutive signifier." The concept of the fetish is preserved by the promise of the thing itself. It is opposed to it and, according to this logic, there should be no fetish as long as the thing itself is present. One can conclude thus that its unremitting return is also a sign of what cannot come to presence. Analogously, the promiscuity of the term should be constrained by "the space of good sense," but "here is the headless head," Derrida writes, referring to the absent center, the first mover, the sovereign authority.

From here Derrida introduces Freud into the discussion and draws a distinction between a *strict* fetishism and a *general* fetishism, suggesting that it is through Freud's "completely subtle cases [*ganz raffinierten fallen*]" that such a possibility comes into view, which "rests *at once* on the denial and the affirmation" of castration.[79] The general fetishism is framed in terms of an oscillation that undermines the seeming stability between original and substitute: "the ligament between the contraries . . . its power of excess in relation to the opposition (true/nontrue, substitute/nonsubsitute, denial/affirmation and so on)."[80] When the term moves to the adjacent column, to the Genet column, it becomes explicitly literary. The sexual and the literary merge in Derrida's reading of Genet's *The Thief's Journal*; cross-dressing, postiche, and pastiche are each articulated as a form of travesty that knows itself to be a substitute and so calls into question the authenticity of the original. Derrida's slippage, too, from metaphor to metaphor in this column, each from a different mode of discourse—from stilite, to transvestite, to the organ with its "showpipes" and "valves,"—performs his notion of a generalized fetishism, a slippage from one discourse to the other and back again. In the other column he follows Hegel's analysis of Christianity and its dependence on sexual difference, which is, at the same time, being troubled on the left through the concept of the fetish.

Kofman's reading of *Glas* takes these pages as a key to Derrida's text. She titles her essay on Derrida's *Glas* "Ça cloche," as a play already on Derrida's title, with an emphasis on the "ça," which may, as a pronoun, refer to Derrida's text but is also a homonym with *Sa*, the term running through Derrida's text as an abbreviation of *Savoir absolu*—Hegel's absolute knowledge. But one is not primary and the other secondary, for *Sa* is already pointing back to *ça*, which is no mere pronoun but the French translation of Freud's Id. While *Glas* means "knell"—as in death knell—*cloche* translates to something like "rings awry." The image of the bell runs throughout both Derrida's and Kofman's text as an image for oscillation—the clapper clanging on two sides, which is exactly what Derrida contends the fetish produces—"the oscillation of the subject between two possibilities."[81] It is difficult not to see this oscillation as a description of the text of *Glas* itself, which forces its reader to move back and forth between its two columns of text, the literary Genet column and the philosophical Hegel column, upending any reader's desire to reconstitute a linear line of argument. Indeed, Kofman gives Derrida credit for having developed in *Glas* a generalized fetishism and describes the project as one of grafting "Freud's text onto the text of metaphysics."[82] It is this move, she suggests, that "makes it possible to unsettle the metaphysical categories," initiating "an oscillation between a dialectic and an entirely other logic."[83]

Yet at the same time she asks the crucial question, the question endemic to the fetishist, but one that also wonders aloud whether in playing the fetishist Derrida has not reasserted his own mastery: "to what ends?" The question recurs multiple times in her essay. How is Derrida getting himself off here? she asks. How is he taking credit for what has come before him, following in the long line of philosophers of which Aristotle is the exemplar? Would not it be the height of mastery "to erect two columns, to claim to always uphold a double discourse, to have one eye crossing the other so as to let nothing escape?"[84]

As Kofman develops this argument in *The Enigma of Woman* it is tied as well to Freud's theory of penis envy and its relation to the fetish. For the theory of penis envy is for Kofman its own "supplementary column" in Freud's oeuvre. It is the attribution to the female sex of the *desire* for the penis, an imaginary desire for an imaginary penis that the male sex must attribute to the female sex to assure his own heterosexual desire. Describing the solution of penis envy just after introducing the language of the supplementary column, Kofman writes:

> It is as if the father had castrated the woman and given the mother's phallus to the son, in the guise of a "supplementary column." Good for every purpose. Thanks to this columnar supplement, this duplication of his sexual power or of his genital organs, when confronted with woman's sex man should no longer be panic-stricken, as if "the Throne and Altar [were] in Danger."[85]

Kofman suggests here that on some level Freud knew that this supplementary column was a form of psychosis, or at the very least the manifestation of aggression in response to his own panic. For the 1927 essay on fetishism includes a digression in which he describes his interest in the fetish as resulting from a venture "along quite speculative lines," in which he had realized that neurosis results from a suppression of the Id, whereas psychosis involves "a detachment itself from a piece of reality" induced by the Id. "But soon after," he writes, "I had reason to regret that I had ventured so far." If Freud regrets this "speculative path," Kofman sees in his essay a brief glimmer of recognition that he has not himself remained in a state of oscillation between possibilities, because he cannot, it seems, restrain himself from a heroic mission down speculation's "dangerous path" toward penis envy. "Armed with the Oedipus complex . . . it is in fact the speculative path that he takes, the only possible one that will let his unreasonableness pass for reason, the only one that will bring to triumph as truth the idée fixe that obsesses him."[86]

Kofman does not directly accuse Freud of "psychosis," but she gives us the dots to connect. If deciding on an "idée fixe" is always either neurosis or psychosis, then Freud's "unreasonabless" that passes for reason, suggests a refusal of reality that we can only infer has a touch of psychosis.

The question then is when is a supplementary column an "athletic support belt," the image of compromise or undecidability, and when does it function as a mechanism of aggression, a master discourse to end all master discourses? The latter is the case when it becomes itself a generalizable logic, a speculative trajectory, or seems to, in a discourse that continually doubles back on itself. Derrida is implicated here if *Glas* can be read as developing out of Freud's text a theory of a "generalized fetishism." In *The Enigma of Woman* Kofman relegates this question to a footnote:

> Is it by chance, then, that Derrida speculates in *Glas* about a pseudospeculation on Freud's part . . . ? This analysis, first set in small print in one column, appears to me to be essential to the overall economy of *Glas*, of its generalized fetishism: it makes it possible to distinguish the erection on every page of a "supplementary column," supplementary to the fetish that is being parodied. It makes it possible to establish a relationship between the "fetish" and the *colossal*, from the outset always double.[87]

The choice of the verb "speculate" (*spécule*) is clearly no accident here, particularly as it is followed immediately by the charge of "pseudospeculation." Yet in asking this question Kofman is careful not to make assertions. She poses her strongest claims in questions and as suggestions. "Is it by chance?" she asks. "It makes it possible," she writes. She refuses for herself the winning move, in a strategy that she tells us she learned from Derrida. "When one speculates on the undecideable one can only lose," Derrida's *Glas* "makes abundantly clear."[88] It is at best an ambiguous charge. It is also perhaps an indication of what it might mean for Derrida's umbrella "to protect us from all dogmatism."

What remains unclear is whether Derrida loses by means of speculating, thus falling into the trap that he is trying to set, or whether speculating on the fetish must always entail losing, given the nature of the fetish, in which deciding always means neurosis or psychosis. In either case, Kofman puts herself at one remove from the question through her own commentary. At the very least, it is clear that she sees Derrida as introducing the concepts of writing and literature as a way of playing the game of the fetish without a chance of winning. "One never really comes but only oscillates from one posture, one postulation, to the other, one 'only plays at coming'; . . . one writes."[89] But can anyone really win at losing?

Kofman aligns fetishism with the play between the two columns as a means of making literature from philosophy of religion, even as she calls this strategy out as enabling a form of speculative recuperation. One way that Derrida thus loses is by virtue of the undecidability between these two options, by the fact that he can't ultimately control the interpretation of this discourse. Writing is the very means toward the crafting of a generalized fetishism from a "strict fetishism . . . , which desires (nothing but) the thing itself and the *Sa* of the thing." Derrida ends the philosophy of religion column of the text with the explicit suggestion that the making of literature is what remains for us from Hegel, Hegel after Nietzsche, "from the resemblance between Dionysius and Christ / Between the two (already) is elaborated in sum the origin of literature."[90]

It might seem, however, that it is Kofman, not Derrida, who is stabilizing the text by elevating the logic of the fetish in *Glas* to something like its master trope. Given the nature of the text, this might also seem like an accomplishment. It is for using this singular lens that Derrida faults her in the discussion at Cerisy following her presentation. "Can the passage of *Glas* on fetishism in Freud constitute the key to the text?" he asks.

> On the one hand there is not in *Glas* one but two textual analyses on fetishism, in the two columns, a duplicity that counts. On the other hand my effort was not to privilege any point of access [*point de passage*]. I resist thus a gesture that would constitute itself as a key to the text.[91]

Kofman then counters Derrida in a manner indicative of the dynamics of their relationship. "Generalized fetishism is not for me either a transcendental key," she responds. "But in rereading *Glas*, from that point of departure, many things became clearer. And it doesn't seem to me that one could do the same work beginning with Hegelian fetishism, except if, already, as you do, one reads Hegel through Freud."[92]

While this might at first look like a defensive response, it is also, read in light of Kofman's reading of Nietzsche's perspectivalism, a rebuke of Derrida. His assumption that Kofman was herself claiming to provide a transcendental key misses for Kofman what is essential to what it means after Nietzsche to read, to constitute an argument. It entails a perspective, a point of departure. As Kofman makes clear in all her texts, her lens is marked by her own drives, and indeed by her own trauma. She goes as far as appending to her texts accounts of her own auto-interrogation, reports of her own nightmares.[93] Derrida's resistance to Kofman's reading is indicative, then, of his own inability to forgo his position as master/author of the text, both because he insists on correcting her reading and because he presumes *as philosophical* the very stance that her work consistently calls into question. The exchange itself thus confirms the central question of her reading: How is Derrida continuing to get off in the text? How is he both denying and performing his own will to mastery? Even the proportionality of their responses indicates a divergence. Derrida follows Kofman's brief explanation, reproduced in full above, with a long excursus. He admits that it is by rereading Hegel through Freud that he is able to arrive at the notion of a "generalized fetishism," but then goes on to defend himself against Kofman's claim that he has simultaneously attributed "too much and too little" to Freud in developing this concept.[94] The debate between them is over whether Freud's notion of the fetish as replacement for the mother's penis, insofar as it is a fiction replacing a fiction, is enough to show that Freud, before Derrida, is already destabilizing phallogocentrism. Kofman, even as she criticizes Freud for producing penis envy as a male prophylactic and thus protecting himself from the insight produced by the notion of fetishism, sees the essay on fetishism as *already* an opening to a generalized fetishism, whereas Derrida suggests that it is only through *his* juxtaposition of Freud with the history of metaphysics that such a possibility appears.

It is the classic Kofman critique. Instead of claiming to see for herself, she claims that Derrida has not been faithful enough to the insights of *his* predecessors. She resists suggesting that she is in fact the one who sees the text's true meaning, its true dynamics, even as she speaks from the point of her experience. Her most potent critiques of Derrida involve the claim that he doesn't credit his predecessors enough. "Freud's text," she writes, does not ring awry exactly as Derrida says it does. In the end she will give neither herself nor Derrida the last word. Beyond oscillation there is "a step beyond," she writes, suggesting that the death knell of phallogocentricism leads one to Maurice Blanchot's neuter, "The happiness of saying yes, of endlessly affirming." Here too we can hear the tacit invocation of Nietzsche.[95]

Ending with a citation is, of course, also one of Derrida's hallmarks. And in many ways Kofman can be read as a rigorous practitioner of a reading practice remarkably similar to Derrida's own, a reading strategy without finality, or telos, "a blind tactics or empirical wandering," as Derrida refers to it in "Différance."[96] But if she faults Derrida for not giving enough credit to his predecessors, this is a fault it would be difficult to assign to Kofman. And this is the enormous risk she took in her own work. She submerges her insights in her texts, by crediting them always as having been already within the author about whom she is writing. At the same time, her method is to isolate and expose the difference between what an author says and what he does.[97]

KEEPING HIS WORD

Nowhere is this technique clearer than in *Smothered Words*. Published in 1987, it is Kofman's first text that explicitly dilates on her father's death at Auschwitz. This move might seem to bring her own experience out of the shadows, yet it is here that she takes up even more explicitly the technique of passive writing. In an interview with *Le Monde* in 1986, she refers to her method as one of "tenir parole," and describes it explicitly as a political act.[98] If for Nietzsche the human being is the promise-making animal, that is to say the one who can hold a word, this means also holding the words of others, letting them speak. In so doing, she writes, one also "prevents the power of killing, that is to say one delays, or holds back the return of Auschwitz."[99] Not surprisingly in *Smothered Words*, Kofman credits even this ethic to another, suggesting it is Robert Antelme's work that reveals this insight.

As a book, *Smothered Words* is her most dramatic work of displacement. It is truly a tissue of citations. It "behooves" her, she writes in the first chapter, "as a Jewish woman intellectual who has survived the Holocaust, to pay homage to Blanchot for the fragments on Auschwitz scattered throughout his texts."[100] Kofman credits Blanchot for having produced a "writing of the ashes, a writing that avoids all complicity with speculative knowledge."[101] The second half of the book is made up mostly of quotations from Antelme's *The Human Race*. She, a Jewish survivor of the Holocaust, filters her own reading of its significance through Antelme, a French hero of the resistance rescued by François Mitterand, and she defines the nature of Judaism through Blanchot, who stands at multiple removes both from this tradition and from the war.[102] This is not to say, though, that the text does no critical work. It was only when reading these two texts together, Kofman's and Blanchot's *The Writing of the Disaster*, that I was able to see for the first time that in Blanchot's strange work of fragments Auschwitz functions as a device. The event itself is put in the service of the speculative, for it appears as a species, an exemplar—indeed a privileged one—of the disaster, of that which is defined by its status as the exception to the category of experience. The work commences: "The disaster ruins everything, all the while leaving everything intact. It does not touch anyone in particular; 'I' am not threatened by it, but spared, left aside."[103] The references to the Holocaust, to the camps, to Auschwitz, appear late in Blanchot's work. It is not until page 47 that the words that become Kofman's epigram to *Smothered Words* appear: "The holocaust, the *absolute* event of history—which is a date in history—that utter burn where all history took fire . . . shattered without *giving* place to anything that can be affirmed."[104] Kofman rearranges the text, displacing it. To the claim that the disaster "does not touch anyone in particular," she gives a name—her father's: "Berek Kofman, born on October 10, 1900, in Sobin (Poland), taken to Drancy on July 16, 1942."[105]

There is not a word of criticism in the book, and yet, as Kofman herself says in the 1986 interview, this act of repetition in which her work participates, its practice of deconstruction, "drives toward a permanent disappropriation" both of herself and her subjects.[106] Although taking up only a few lines of the book, the details of her father's death at Auschwitz—buried alive for refusing to work on the Sabbath—not only disrupt Blanchot's account, they reorient it, giving it a locus of gravity in the most personal of losses, those from which Blanchot was precisely spared.

Kofman does not tell the story of what happened to her during the war until her last published volume, *Rue Ordener, Rue Labat*, a slim book, less than a hundred pages, as spare and searing as a blade. Since her death it has become the work for which she is best known. I have suppressed the narrative until now, both because it has overshadowed her reception as a philosopher and because she too waited until the end to tell her story.

The book is primarily concerned with the two years she was in hiding in Paris, but it opens with the loss of her father, a rabbi in the 18th arrondissement on Rue Duc, who was picked up on July 16, 1942. One of six children, Kofman was first sent to the countryside to hide with one of her sisters after her father's deportation, but her refusal to eat pork, her vomiting and tears, threatened to endanger both girls, and Sarah was sent back to Paris to live with her mother. With each successive roundup mother and child searched out a new hiding place in Paris. Eventually Kofman's mother sought the help of a gentile woman who had once admired the beauty of her blond children. Much of *Rue Ordener, Rue Labat* describes Sarah and her mother's experience living with Mémé, the gentile woman, who lives on Rue Labat. She takes them both in, but hides her mother in a back room and treats Sarah as her own, feeding her steak tartare, cuddling her in her own bed, dressing her up, and teaching her about music. When the war is over, Kofman tries to choose Mémé, describing her mother at an ad hoc court proceeding as physically abusive and showing the court marks from her mother's strap. Mémé wins custody, but her mother forcibly takes her back with the help of two men from their old neighborhood. Sarah discloses in the book that she was secretly grateful. Even after the war, her mother can hardly afford to feed and shelter her family. They live in cramped dwellings and receive paltry aid from the state. School is consistently the only place where Kofman describes feeling safe. Humor is her means of making friends. Eventually Kofman's mother sends her and her siblings to the Moulin de Moissac in the Tarn region, an establishment run by the Eclaireurs Israélites de France, where she receives a Jewish education and "learns a taste for all the 'joys' of scouting."[107] Eventually, in order to attend a lycée that teaches Greek, she is sent back to her mother, where she loses seven kilos and her taste for religion, taking up philosophy and studying finally at the École Normale Supérieure.

Kofman opens *Rue Ordener, Rue Labat* by setting up the book as both the destination at the end of her route, and that which she has avoided saying all these years:

> Of him all I have left is the fountain pen. I took it one day from my mother's purse, where she kept it along with some other souvenirs of my father. It is a kind of pen no longer made, the kind you have to fill with ink. I used it all through school. It 'failed me' before I could bring myself to give it up. I still have it, patched up with Scotch tape; it is right in front of me on my desk and makes me write, write.
>
> Maybe all my books have been the detours [*des voies de traverse obligées*] required to bring me to write about 'that' [*pour parvenir à raconter «ça»*].[108]

This passage has most often been read as *the* passage that invites a reading of her corpus through the prism of her life, but it also tells us something about what the act of writing meant to her. It is worth emphasizing that Kofman's father was a rabbi, to whom she suggests she felt the utmost fidelity. But she expresses that fidelity not by a devotion to her paternal tradition, but by embracing the broken remnant of what her father left her, by affirming that the writing that it compelled her to do is itself the legacy of her rabbinic father. One could say that the practice of literature is a poor substitute for faith, and perhaps Kofman's broken pen expresses that most clearly. As she writes in "Ça Cloche," "Fetishism makes it possible to unsettle the metaphysical categories," by virtue of being a poor substitute.[109] The broken pen thus would be exactly the point.

Not surprisingly, then, Kofman's relation to Judaism is consistently mediated. She never writes about the tradition directly but only its representation in the work of others, in Blanchot (*Smothered Words*), Nietzsche (*Le Mépris des Juifs*), Derrida ("Ça Cloche"), and Freud (*Pourquoi rit-on? [Why Do We Laugh?]*). Given that her own mode of writing is so consistently in the form of commentary, we can read this move, too, as a kind of displacement. Kofman might be said to have learned a Jewish form of writing from her father's broken pen, but she distances herself profoundly from his sources. Even those of her interlocuters who are Jewish persistently disavowed facets of their Jewish identity.[110] In Kofman's engagements with both Freud and Derrida she seeks to draw out the connections to Judaism in their work, and with Derrida it is a consistent feature of their correspondence. But the same can be also said for her readings of some of her non-Jewish authors. In her hands Nietzsche, whom the Nazis themselves appropriated as a philosophical source for their movement, becomes a model for her own version of ventriloquism and, in her penultimate work, something of a Jewish writer himself.

We can read this Judaizing move on Kofman's part as another facet of what she meant by "tenir parole." Nietzsche's own use of the phrase in *On the Genealogy of Morals* seems to suggest that insofar as our "promise-making capacity" is in opposition to the need for forgetfulness it impedes human health. But in Kofman's work, quite to the contrary, it becomes an ethic of reading, a way to recuperate a promising reading from a troubling text, to safeguard its word. It is a method she applies to Nietzsche himself, rescuing the thinker from the Heideggerian metaphysical reading, but also drawing out from his perspectivalism, a Janus-faced quality that Nietzsche, in Kofman's reading, associates with Judaism.[111] What emerges from her reading of *Ecce Homo* in *Explosions I* and *II* is a portrait of Nietzsche that disrupts the possibility that a subject can ever be defined by continuity. Instead she emphasizes the text's oscillation and contradictions. Nietzsche is both his mother and his father, Polish and German, Baubo and Dionysius. Finally, in *Le Mèpris des Juifs*, her last monograph before *Rue Ordener, Rue Labat*, she recuperates from his thought, if not a positive representation of Judaism, then the portrait of the Jew as a figure of uncanny strength and perseverance. "They have not yet said their last word," Kofman writes, paraphrasing Nietzshe in *Dawn*.[112] One might even say that she finds, in her reading of Nietzsche's statements on Judaism, one of Nietzsche's many faces. He admired, she suggests, how

> the intellectual suppleness of the Jew, his power of extreme adaptation, consequence of his wandering and his frightful trials, rendered him gradually able to mimetically (hysterically) play all roles, made him the exemplary comedian (the instinct for comedy became his dominant instinct). He not only became the artist and the jester *par excellence*, but above all, one capable of uniting all charms . . .[113]

It is not hard to imagine that Kofman saw in this portrait a vision not only of Nietzsche but also of herself. It suggests that her style of passive writing could itself be one way in which she expresses her Jewishness, her capacity to "mimetically play all roles," to be a jester and a ventriloquist at the same time. Many commentators have suggested it was the role of jester that she enjoyed most. Joking was clearly her favorite means of asserting a Jewish identity. This comes across most clearly in *Pourquoi rit-on?* which is primarily a commentary on Freud's *Jokes and*

Their Relation to the Unconscious, but also in Derrida's eulogy to Kofman, written over two years after her death. In what follows I consider both of these texts to see not only the role of humor in Kofman's thought but also how the texts illuminate the relationship between Derrida and Kofman. While this account will not upset the version of their story in which Kofman followed Derrida's lead, I will suggest in my final section that she nonetheless got the last word, if only by throwing her voice.

3. THE LAST LAUGH

TWO ENEMIES, A LOVE STORY?

Like Kofman's first book on Freud, *The Childhood of Art, Pourquoi rit-on?* considers Freud's relation to cultural production. In it, Kofman says that jokes are themselves "Janus-faced," exhibiting, in mocking, the double face of all things, the yes and the no, the sense and the nonsense. This insight she credits to Freud, but the question that motivates her reading is why Freud suppressed the Jewishness of the jokes that provide the basis for the work. In Kofman's unearthing of their Jewishness, and the lengths Freud went to in the book to elide it, jokes themselves become a way of being Jewish. Sure, a poor substitute, but again that seems itself to be part of the point. This is particularly poignant in the closing lines of the book.

Kofman closes with the following Jewish joke, told not by Freud but by his disciple Theodor Reik, who himself wrote a book on Jewish jokes:

> Finishing this book today, September 25, the day of Yom Kippur, I cannot resist peddling *finally* this Jewish joke told by Theodor Reik: "Two Jews, long-standing enemies, meet at the synagogue on the day of Great Atonement. One says to the other: 'I wish you what you wish me.' And the other replies, giving tit for tat: 'you're starting up again, already?'"
>
> By way of conclusion, let's let laughter have the last word.[114]

First, it is worth pointing out an important symmetry between the structure of what she does with this final joke and the opening to *Rue Ordener, Rue Labat*. We can read this final joke as another declaration of fidelity to her father by way of writing. Kofman is openly attesting to writing on the day of Yom Kippur. On the holiest day of the liturgical year, she is flaunting an activity forbidden by Jewish law. On Yom Kippur, she is finishing her book, but she is also telling a Jewish joke. One might contest that this is a poor substitute for prayer, but again this seems to be exactly the point.

The joke itself takes up a number of the themes of Kofman's work: It is a joke that is Janus-faced; like the fetish, it plays both sides. It can even be said to be about the "tenir parole," the keeping of another's word, and thus, as Kofman suggested, about politics.

But in suggesting as much, it is important to say that I am not the first to make this connection. Jacques Derrida makes it explicitly in his eulogy for Kofman in 1997. In fact, the joke is at the center of what he wants to say about her but also what he wants to say about politics. It is worth comparing Kofman's reading of Derrida in "Ça Cloche" to Derrida's reading of Kofman, which he leaves untitled, without a heading.

In Kofman's book the joke serves as a postscript following the text and a dotted line. Derrida makes it the centerpiece of his eulogy and leaves off the last line, taking for himself the final word. For Derrida the joke functions as an emblem of his friendship with Kofman. Derrida describes Sarah Kofman's life—he refers to her almost exclusively by her first name in the text—as a life of protestation and describes how their own friendship began with her protesting something he had "ventured in 'Plato's Pharmacy.'"[115] Interestingly he also provides a different origin story for the joke:

As I said, we must have told this Jewish joke to each other, and probably while eating. And we must have agreed that it was not only funny but memorable, unforgettable, precisely insofar as it treats this treatment of memory called forgiveness.[116]

It is no longer "Sarah's" joke in this telling, or Theodor Reik's, but one Derrida and Kofman told to each other. In certain ways this is fitting to the very genre of the joke, which Kofman describes in *Pourquoi rit-on?* as having a social origin. Jokes emerge not from one author but from a social context, having no single author, told over and again, changing in the telling, changing into-nation, tone, and meaning depending on their vehicle. Derrida does not, however, emphasize the social or plural origin in his retelling, but rather the theme of forgiveness. Kofman, as Derrida notes, does mention the role of forgiveness in the joke as a form—how it is experienced as a kind of pleasure granted by the superego: "the *forgiveness* that it in some sense grants, bringing humor close to the maniacal phase, since, thanks to these *'gifts,'* the diminished 'I' finds itself if not euphoric, at least lifted back up." But it is Derrida who italicizes the words "forgiveness" and "gifts" in his citation of Kofman as a means of introducing the themes on which he will dwell for the remainder of the essay. These are familiar themes for readers of Derrida, themes that he returned to throughout the 1990s. What follows in his text is an analysis of the joke about the two Jews that emphasizes many of these lines of thought—namely the impossibility of both these concepts—of the gift and of forgiveness: "The impossibility of forgiveness gives itself to be thought as, in truth, its only possi-bility. Why is forgiveness impossible. . . . Simply because what is to be forgiven must be and must remain unforgiveable."[117]

In 1997–1998 Derrida gave a seminar on the theme of perjury and the pardon, out of which he would develop a series of fruit-ful explorations in *Demeure* (1997), *Donner la mort* (1999), and *On Cosmopolitanism and Forgiveness* (2001), and it is certainly pos-sible that this joke is an important touchstone in Derrida's de-velopment of the theme. What is clear in the text is that Kofman, who, Derrida writes, "was put to the test of the impossibility of forgiveness, its radical impossibility," becomes an occasion for Derrida to develop this line of though. We could speculate endlessly on how and why Kofman's death represents the occasion for Derrida to zero in on this theme. Insofar as he does, his meditation on the "condition that forgiveness shares with the gift" seems to represent a lost connection, a reflection on mourning, defined by the fact that neither the apology nor forgiveness can any longer "hope to reach its destination." It is also the moment in which his text betrays her, as it veers from being a text about Sarah Kofman and her work to being one about Derrida's key concepts. In the end, though, it comes back to the joke in a way that perhaps reflects both thinkers equally:

> Here it is then the ultimate compassion.
>
> It is to tell the other, or to hear oneself tell the other, and to hear the other tell you, you see, you're doing it again, you do not want to forgive me, even on the day of Great Atonement, but me too, me neither, a 'me' neither, we are in agreement, we forgive ourselves for nothing, for that is impossible, so let's not forgive one another, all right? And then you burst into complicit, uncontrollable laughter, laughing like crazy, with a laughter gone crazy. For isn't this paradoxical agreement peace?[118]

At the end of *Smothered Words*, Kofman suggests that out of the Holocaust, out of Antelme's reflections, a new ethics could emerge that would establish a "new kind of 'we,'" a we that "is always undone, destabilized . . . a new 'humanism' one might say, if it were still acceptable to use this trite and idyllic word."[119] In a footnote she then defends her interest in retaining the word *humanism*: "Displacing and transforming it[,] I keep it because what other, new 'word' could have as much hold on the old humanism."[120] Here she is envisioning a new ethics or a "paradoxical peace agreement," that does not commence from shared understanding in the old sense—that is to say, from the kind of understanding in which two interlocutors declare, "We are of like mind, yes, we agree, we think alike"—but rather from a "tenir parole," to return to the term Kofman borrows from Nietzsche, in which the tending to another's words, even their repetition, can mean both their subversion and a kind of loyalty.

This, to my mind, is what is amazing about the joke—the way it holds together subversion and fidelity so closely that they become, if not indistinguishable, then at least intractably linked. From this confluence emerges the explosive phenomenon of laughter. Does this interpretation differ from Derrida's? Perhaps only by a hair's breadth. But it allows me to signal one of the fundamental differences between these two thinkers. Both took tremendous risks in the way they wrote, in allowing for their work to be taken and retooled, their intentions betrayed. But even in Derrida's own eulogy for Kofman, particularly when we compare it to Kofman's essay on Derrida, "Ça cloche," there is a difference between them. Derrida inhabits Kofman's text and then transfuses it with his own vocabulary and his own concepts. The joke she tells at the end of her book becomes a vehicle for Derrida to return to *his* themes. Kofman, by contrast, draws out of Derrida's text a theme already nascent there and develops it, crediting him all the while, even if in the process she exposes his disavowed drive to mastery.

AUTOBIOGRAPHICAL ANIMALS

In 1997, the same year that he published his untitled eulogy for Sarah Kofman, three years after her death, Derrida returned to Cerisy for the third *décade* on his work. This time he expressly chose the theme, titling the conference, 'The Autobiographical Animal," a counterpoint to the first *décade* on the theme "The Ends of Man," and commenced with the question of what it means to be seen by one's cat. Given that twenty-one years earlier Kofman had published *Autobiogriffures du Chat Mur d'Hoffman*, it is enticing to imagine that Derrida's discourse was inspired by her text, was even something of an homage to her.[121]

Both open by citing these lines from Montaigne's musing on his cat in "Apology for Raymond Sebond":

> How does he [man] know, by the force of his intelligence, the secret internal stirrings of animals? By what comparison between them and us does he infer the stupidity [*la bêtise*] that he attributes to them? When I play with my cat, who knows if I am not a pastime to her more than she is to me.

Like Kofman, Derrida takes as one of his text's themes the question of how the line between human and animal protects the human's sense of sovereignty, keeps him from confronting the power of his drives. In the first few pages Derrida even mentions the notion of Nietzsche's, from *On the Genealogy of Morals*, that the human is a promise-making animal. Soon after he invokes Kofman by name:

> I must immediately make it clear, the cat I am talking about is a real cat . . . it isn't the figure of a cat . . . nor is the cat that looks at, concerning me, and to which I seem—but don't count on it—to be dedicating a negative zootheology, Hoffman's or Kofman's cat Murr, although along with me it uses this occasion to salute the magnificent and inexhaustible book that Sarah Kofman devotes to it, namely *Autobiogriffures*, whose title resonates so well with that of this conference. That book keeps vigil over this conference and asks to be permanently quoted and reread [*Il veille sur elle et demanderait à être cite ou relu en permanence*].[122]

This reference is explicitly *not* a dedication to Kofman, for if the text is dedicated to anyone it is to Derrida's cat. Instead, Derrida says, he and his cat salute Kofman's book. Her book provides the text's first footnote in the French, a move that mirrors back Kofman's first footnote in *Autobiogriffures* to Derrida's *Of Grammatology*. At the same time, Derrida is differentiating Kofman's text from his own, her literary figure from his very real cat, his explicitly philosophical project from her literary one. From this point forward Kofman is not quoted, and if her book has been reread, Derrida makes no explicit sign of it in the text.

The remainder of Derrida's discourse is divided into three parts given over ten hours and addresses philosophy's failure since Descartes "to be seen by the animal."[123] As evidence of this failure, Derrida reads closely Descartes's *Meditations*, Kant's *Anthropology*, fragments from Levinas (particularly the essay "The Name of a Dog or Natural Rights," in *Difficult Freedom*), and Lacan. Then in the final, improvised session, he treats Heidegger's seminar from 1929–1930. One of the pervading themes of the work is that the strong differentiation of human from animal in the history of philosophy belies the very distinction that it marks out between the rationality of the human and the bestiality of the animal, insofar as this strong division is itself a battle "against the animal," in "a sacrificial war that is as old as Genesis." But in describing this war, in showing that his predecessors have all failed to consider what it is "to be seen by the animal," Derrida himself seems to be in a bit of a cockfight.

Although the session is improvised, it seems fitting that Heidegger, who had also critiqued the instrumentality of reason and the phenomenon of factory farming, is Derrida's final target. For Heidegger in 1929–1930 differentiates between the "deprived" animal and the human on the basis of the animal's failure, according to Heidegger, to be able to apprehend the world "as such [*en tant que*]."[124] Derrida calls into question the possibility of this "as such," this capacity to apprehend anything from the stairs, to a tool, to the sun *as such*, asking whether, even for a human, there can be a purity to this relation. He suggests finally that the failure of this distinction to hold breaks down the line between the human and the animal. In light of this failure, the whole framework of Heideggerian discourse is at stake: "'ontological difference,' the 'question of being," hangs in the balance.[125] Heidegger's project—but even more radically, the discipline of philosophy itself—would thus depend on the maintenance of a distinction that, Derrida is arguing, doesn't hold. He sides finally against Heidegger, with Nietzsche (and obliquely with Kofman?), writing:

> It is evident that the difference between Nietzsche and Heidegger is that Nietzsche would have said no; everything is in a perspective; the relation to a being, even the "truest," the most "objective," that which respects most the essence of what is such as it is, is caught in a movement that we'll call here that of the living, of life, and from this point of view, whatever the difference between animals, it remains an "animal" relation. Hence the strategy in question would consist in pluralizing and varying the "as such," and instead of simply giving speech back to the animal, or giving to the animal what the human deprives it of, as it were, in marking that the human is, in a way, similarly "deprived," by means of a privation that is not a privation, and that there is no pure and simple "as such."[126]

The conclusion thus harkens back to the theme of the conference, to the possibility that philosophy can only be that of "an autobiographical animal," speaking from the first person. In a revision of Descartes's formulation "I think therefore I am [*Cogito ergo sum*]," Derrida writes, "the animal that therefore I am/follow." This move returns us also to the original *décade*, to the possibility that multiplying, pluralizing, the ends of man is already to ask the question of the autobiographical animal.

If Kofman, three years dead, is obliquely invoked by this approach—her own work insistently dwelt on this very theme— why is her own work on the borderline between animal subjectivity and human subjectivity addressed only in passing? Does Derrida miss the opportunity to respond to her here?

It is odd what he says about her on the occasion of his return to Cerisy, after her death. Her book "keeps vigil" over the conference, and "asks to be permanently quoted and reread." The book asks, but Derrida does not answer. It is a pattern that was familiar to them both. The dissymmetry of their relationship, of their correspondence, attests to her unanswered demand. But is it also an opening, perhaps, to put these two works in conversation?

TO WRITE LIKE A CAT

If I am generous to Derrida, then I read his claim that Kofman's book "keeps vigil over this conference and asks to be permanently quoted and reread" as an invitation to follow, an opportunity to add even to the books in the B2430.K section of the library that are about Kofman, to continue the conversation when neither he nor she can any longer respond. Kofman's 1976 text is concerned with almost the same question as Derrida's 1997 text: How does the marker drawn between the human and the animal, by Descartes among others, protect the unity of the concept of the human being, "le nom de l'homme"? Kofman too is interested in showing how unstable this division is and how it props up the fiction of self-sovereignty. She is no less interested in the nature of the relation between autobiography and philosophy, a theme that pervades all of her work but especially her readings of Nietzsche's *Ecce Homo* in *Explosions I* and *II* (1992, 1993). And as we've seen throughout this essay, the relation between her own drives, her own trauma, her own animality and her philosophy is never far from the surface of any of her texts. But when she wrote in 1976 on the autobiographical animal, she did not write an autobiography, but about a fiction: E. T. A. Hoffman's *The Life and Opinions of the Tomcat Murr*.

Hoffman's novel is by all accounts a strange book. Published in 1818, quite late in his career, it alternates between two texts, Murr's coming-of-age story and the life of the composer Johannes Kreisler, a structure (or lack thereof) maintained by the conceit that the autodidact cat, who first taught himself to read and then began writing in secret, used another book, the biography of Kreisler, as his blotting pad. The printer then "accidently" printed both together, so that the final product switches back and forth between the two narratives, cutting from one to the other in what is presented to feel like random breaks. It is, one can say with some assurance, a book with its own oscillating structure, one that swings dizzily from one pole to the other.

In choosing to write about it in 1976, Kofman, no doubt, wanted to show both that the work of thinking about text as graft [*greffe*] preceded *Of Grammatology* (1967), and that the impact of an oscillating text as that which exposes as ruse authorial sovereignty, revealing "the headless head," preceded *Glas* (1974). Hoffman's book, Kofman writes, "comes to destroy the volume" by "breaking the traditional frames of reading." It is a "bastard biography which blurs the boundaries between humanity and animality . . . effacing the signature of the proper name and the unique author."[127] It is a book, too, about the potential of literature—even among the romantics—to "deconstruct the theological concept of the book, of the author, of the original genius, father of his work."

As Kofman puts it at the end of her first chapter:

> Double writing, at least, in *The Cat Murr*, the one contradicting, undoing, unstitching the other, in a less than simple manner: instead of the clawing [*la griffe*] of the cat destroying the book of man, rather on the contrary, it tries to write a book, without incident [*sans accroc*], that is more "human" than that written by the biographer of Kreisler, a true rhapsody made of bits and pieces. Double writing, double biography—at least.[128]

In Kofman's book it is not *she* who upsets the philosophical divisions between animal and human, revealing it as a fiction, nor is it Hoffman. Rather it is Hoffman writing as his own cat, Murr. The cat is already a machine of citations from Tiek, Cervantes, Shakespeare, and Schlegel, among others. The whole thing is then mediated by a fictional editor, who tries to make of the work something coherent, tries to expose all of Murr's plagiarism of other writers, and promises to restore missing pages of Kreisler's biography and, finally, to supply a forthcoming final volume that never appears. Thus, by the time we read *Autobio-griffures*, the grafting and ventriloquizing is at least four levels deep—five, for the readers of this text. It is the animal characters in the text that are able to reveal, from their perspectives, the way that human science,

> behind hollow and highflown [*creux et romflants*] words, such as "instinct," hides its ignorance. . . . Human science far from being knowledge is a system of quasi-paranoid projections, a product of resentment and jealousy that allows men to exercise mastery. Their reason, of which they are so proud, is a system of secondary rationalizations.[129]

But it is the multiplication of perspectives through fiction that allows the confrontation of the animal and the human perspective. Hoffman's book demands of its readers that they resort to the childlike position of listening to talking animals. At the same time, he uses the "mask of the beast" to expose the prejudice and ignorance of humans toward each other and toward animals. "If the dog and cat understand each other in so far as they denigrate the asinine human [*la bêtise humaine*], they do not any less espouse human prejudices." The cat calls the dog a monster, the dog calls the cat "a true Satan."[130] If we laugh at their asinine behavior, and it is difficult not to—for example, when Murr exclaims upon the beauty of "a lone dove cooing a mournful song" and then consumes it a moment later in what he describes to himself as a rapturous embrace—we laugh too at ourselves, at our duplicity, at the lengths we go to mask our appetites under the guise of art.[131]

Kofman describes Hoffman's book as already "the grafting of life onto literature," in its citational structure. The effect of which, she suggests, is "to efface the signature of the proper name." The cat Murr nonetheless models the "illusory narcissism" of "pseudo-geniuses," seeking the admiring love of a gray pussycat who praises his sonnets and clinging to his works in the forms that he has finished them, fearful of their "amputation" by editors. Meanwhile the text is scrambled amid Kreisler's biography and marked in places by the holes made by Murr's sharp claws [*les griffures*]. In attempting to emulate Jean Jacques Rousseau's *Confessions*, upon which Murr openly models his story, his text runs counter to his impulse to express himself and reveal his genius, by appearing itself as parasitic, and indeed finally as parody, a parody that exposes the animal desires, the violence, the mania, that the very act of writing is supposed to domesticate.

The contrasts between Derrida's and Kofman's texts, so clearly on the same themes, are sharp. Derrida's is a philosophical treatment of the theme of the animal, a reading and critique of the role the animal has played in the history of modern philosophy. It is at the same time an autobiography — straightforwardly both a meditation, his, perhaps the first to begin from the experience of being seen by a cat, naked, erect. It is also a resumé of his works, his exploration of how the theme of the animal, of sovereignty, of auto-immunity, had already surfaced in his corpus from "A Silkworm of One's Own" to "Faith and Knowledge," *Rogues*, and *Àdieu to Emmanuel Levinas*. He takes the text as an opportunity to consider his own corpus and gives it before an audience, at a conference honoring his work, on his birthday.

Kofman's, on the other hand, is a reading. It stays close to a single source and credits that text, through *its* plurivocity, *its* ventriloquism, *its* fictionalized portrayal of the very act of autobiography, with destabilizing the "theological concept of the book." Her text, thus, by virtue of repeating much of what is in Hoffman's book, is itself a tissue of citations. In one light, then, it might not seem to *do* much. It is a mere commentary, and it certainly doesn't claim to break any new ground. If anything, it reads Derrida's project back into Hoffman's. But what happens when Derrida's text on the autobiographical animal is read in light of Kofman's reading of Hoffman's? If Kofman's work is in fact seen as keeping vigil over the conference, if we answer the demand that her book be reread and quoted in relation to what Derrida's own work professes, then Derrida's own autobiographical discourse might seem to be guilty of the "illusory narcissism" that appears so manifestly in the confessions of Hoffman's cat. What could be more narcissistic then subjecting an audience to ten hours of yourself speaking as a way of celebrating your birthday?[132] What could be more narcissistic then taking the occasion to survey what you have already accomplished, where other great thinkers have failed? What could be more self-serving than asking in front of a crowd, "Mais moi, qui suis-je?"

Of course, as Derrida points out, this puts him at the end of a long line of philosophers, thinkers, and writers who have done the same:

> *Ecce animot*, that is the announcement of which I am (following) [*que je suis*] something like the trace, assuming the title of an autobiographical animal, in the form of a risky, fabulous, or chimerical response to the question "But as for me who am I (following)?" which I have wagered on treating as that of the autobiographical animal.[133]

Like Hoffman's tomcat, Derrida is asking the question of Rousseau's *Confessions*, and of Augustine's, but also of Nietzsche's *Ecce Homo*. In that sense he is also following them. Is he not also then following Hoffman's tomcat, and thus also Kofman's own text on Hoffman? He is grouping himself with a whole list of autobiographical animals, "that sort of man or woman who, as a matter of character, chooses to indulge in or can't resist indulging in autobiographical confidences." Kofman herself, of course, was, in the end, one of these as well, writing too of the desire for and the shame of the act.[134]

The same year that she published *Autobiogriffures*, she also published a brief essay entitled "'Ma vie' et la psychanalyse." "I always wanted to tell the story of my life," she begins. She then describes the undoing of that desire "to master" her life in analysis, which she calls "foolish and unfaithful," and its replacement with both a fear and a desire to spill her guts, to shit them out, to "establish an exchange that might transform *le 'caca' en or*."[135] When she finally did write *Rue Ordener, Rue Labat* she was consumed by an overwhelming depression, and her suicide followed within the year.

Given these parallels, what should we make of Derrida's seemingly triumphal *décade*, written the same year that he wrote his only essay on Kofman, her eulogy? In that eulogy, he writes that since her death

> I sometimes catch myself again making a scene before her, in order to catch up with her, and I smile at this sign of life, of the life in which I am no doubt still obscurely trying to keep her, that is, keep her alive. . . . As if I were making yet another scene before her in response to hers, just so as to make things last long enough, to say to her, you see, life goes on, it is still the same old story.[136]

Is it possible that Derrida's performance at Cerisy was, as he understood it, one of those scenes?

The final chapter of Kofman's *Autobiogriffures* is the only site in the text in which the theme of the apotropaeon is foregrounded. In these final few pages she writes about the portrait of Murr that Hoffman himself drew for the cover of the book and which still adorns current editions. In it Murr appears erect, in a stately robe, high among the surrounding steeples, with his quill in paw. The portrait, Koffman writes, in showing "the character as gentle and benevolent [*doux et bienveillant*], seems to eradicate his difference from man and would permit the identification of the reader, assuring the buyer of his pleasure."[137] At the same time, however, she argues, the portrait also produces a kind of doubling, an introduction of the other into the same. Isn't the theme of the lifeless double already a theme in Hoffman, signaling the theft of the soul?[138] On the one hand, she suggests, the portrait would seem to play the role of a "good *apotropaeon*." Like the penis in Freud's essay "The Head of the Medusa," it would function to confront the threat of the beast, and the beastly, declaring, "I have a penis, I am not afraid of you." But on the other—the very plurality of the text in its "more than doubling"—doesn't it destroy this reassuring portrait?[139] She closes the book thus, with an oscillation between the concept of the "good apotropaeon" and its destabilizing counterpart: "Writing, which freezes, like Medusa," or rather, which "captures [*entraîne*] man and cat in the derision of laughter, this 'shaking of the diaphragm,' which nature has refused the cat Murr, who, despite his seriousness, like man, still knows how to laugh."[140]

It is a feature of Kofman's books, as we've already seen, to let laughter have the last word, and she has done that literally here, closing the book on the word itself.[141] Is it too much to say that Derrida, too, has allowed for that possibility? If Kofman's book keeps vigil over the conference, it too functions like the gaze of Medusa, providing its double. It stands, at least by way of our reading, as witness over his scene.

I have heard people say that Kofman was in love with Derrida and that he found her to be something of nuisance. I've heard her described as one of his disciples, not even of the inner circle. Derrida's biographer Benoit Peeters relegated her to the status of "secondary importance to him . . . one of those who gravitated around" the great master.[142] I've heard too that she found his lack of response to *Rue Ordener, Rue Labat* crushing. Does it give him too much credit to suggest that he set up his performance to let her laughter have the last word? Perhaps.

In probing the connection and correspondence between Kofman and Derrida I aim to show that in many ways Kofman was the more faithful practitioner of the ethic she saw deconstruction as entailing. In the end maybe that means that her approach to the work of others, her method of reading, made her critical reception inevitable, created the empty space in the library under B2430.K. But even if by most standards this might seem like a failure, it is also, in its own way, liberating. Her work makes one want to imagine a world in which we learn to judge by criteria other than mastery, where success is not doled out to those who believe they possess the phallus, and confirm that belief by the besting of others, a world where instead we laugh at our own fallibility, even at the way our appetites betray us. It makes it possible to think of fidelity to the work of another, to reading and thinking with others, as a political gesture opposed to violence, as a "tenir parole," another way of embodying what it means to be a promise-making animal. Is it a poor substitute for prayer? Maybe that is exactly the point.

NOTES

This essay took various shapes in the course of its writing, and I am grateful for the invitations to present facets of it at Indiana University, Georgetown, Yale, Wesleyan and SUNY Buffalo. In addition to Constance Furey and Amy Hollywood, who were indeed my ideal interlocutors, I want to thank Terrence Johnson, Nancy Levene, Noreen Khawaja, Ulrich Plass, Steven Miller, and Sarabinh Levy-Brightman for their helpful comments, questions, and suggestions. As always, Ryan Coyne was my first reader and, as always, steadfastly generous and astute.

1. Jacques Derrida, *Religion and Philosophy*, fourth lecture, p. 16 (IMEC, 1972).

2. Ginette Michaud and Isabelle Ullern, *Sarah Kofman et Jacques Derrida: Croisements, écarts, differences* (Hermann: Paris, 2018), 212–14.

3. Sarah Kofman, *Comment s'en sortir?* (Paris: Galilée, 1983), 103–12.

4. The secondary literature on Kofman is largely dominated by attempts to understand her work in light of her life, to psycho-analyze her and diagnose her. See, for example, Sara Horowitz, "Sarah Kofman et l'ambiguïté des mères," in *Témoinages de l'après-Auschwitz dans la littérature juive-francaise d'aujourd'hui* (London: Brill, 2008); Joanne Faulkner, *Dead Letters to Nietzsche; or, The Necromantic Art of Reading Philosophy* (Athens: Ohio University Press, 2010), 114–48; Colin Davis, "Sarah Kofman and the Timebomb of Memory," in *Traces of War: Interpreting Ethics and Trauma in Twentieth-Century French Writing* (Liverpool: Liverpool University Press, 2018); Penelope Deutscher and Kelly Oliver, "Sarah Kofman's Skirts," in *Enigmas: Essays on Sarah Kofman*, ed. Penelope Deutscher and Kelly Oliver (Ithaca, NY: Cornell University Press, 1999); Frederica Clementi, *Holocaust Mothers and Daughters: Family, History, and Trauma* (Waltham, MA: Brandeis University Press, 2013), 149.

5. When Kofman treats the biblical character of Judith in *Quatre romans analytiques* (Paris: Galilée, 1974) it is in reference to and through Freud's *The Taboo of Virginity*. In *Smothered Words*, trans. Madeleine Dobie (Evanston, IL: Northwestern University Press, 1998), Judaism is broached via Blanchot's description. In *Pourquoi rit-on? Freud et le mot d'esprit* (Paris: Galilée, 1986), the Jewish joke is approached via Freud's *Jokes and Their Relation to the Unconscious*.

6. Kofman, as she reports in *Rue Ordener, Rue Labat* (Paris: Galilée, 1994), spent five years in Moissac at a school for Jewish children run by the Eclaireurs Israélite de France, at which study of Jewish texts was a major emphasis. In another project I have studied this movement and its emphasis on Jewish youth. A book is forthcoming, but see Hammerschlag, "Truth for Children," *Harvard Divinity Bulletin* (Fall/Winter 2018), 1–29.

7. In every presentation of this essay while in progress, someone from the audience made this connection. There are of course many traditions that operate through commentary. Whether Kofman understood her own work in this light isn't entirely clear. But it is one way to understand what she meant when she said that she wrote with her father's pen. *Rue Ordener, Rue Labat*, 9.

8. Orietta Ombrosi, "Sarah Kofman, una decostruzione al femminile dell'ebraismo," in *Ebraismo "al femminile": Percorsi diversi di intellettuali del Novecento* (Giuntina, 2017). Kofman's work is also often recognized as within the canon of French-Jewish writing. See *Daughters of Sarah: Anthology of Jewish Women Writing in French*, ed. Eva Martin Sartori and Madeleine Cottonet-Hage (Teaneck, NJ: Holmes and Meier, 2006), as well as *Shadows in the City of Light: Images of Paris in Postwar French Jewish Writing*, ed. Sara R. Horowitz, Amira Bojadzija-Dan, and Julia Creet (Albany: SUNY Press, 2020); Michele Bitton, *Présences féminines juives en France, XIXe- XXe siècles* (Paris: 2M, 2002); and my own anthology *Modern French Jewish Thought* (Waltham, MA: Brandeis University Press, 2018).

9. The Mishnaic tract *Pirke Avot* establishes a guide for authority and transmission.

10. Alain Peyrefitte, *Rue d'ulm: Chroniques de la vie normalienne* (Paris: Fayarde, 2014); Robert J. Smith, *The Ecole Normale Supérieure and the Third Republic* (Albany: SUNY Press, 1982). Descriptions of ENS often emphasize the independence of mind cultivated by the institution, but this goes hand in hand with certain cults of personalities and the establishment of political and intellectual alliances formed around instructors. Descriptions of life at the *kâghne* in its austerity and deprivation suggest a continuation of monastic asceticism.

11. Edward's Said's classic introduction to *The World, the Text and the Tradition* (Cambridge, MA: Harvard University Press, 1983), "Secular Criticism," makes this point most succinctly by naming as "theological" forms of criticism that adhere to Matthew Arnold's notion of culture as "the assertively achieved and *won* hegemony of an identifiable set of ideas . . . over all other ideas in society" (10). It is not surprising that Said himself looks to the French system as a source (3). Poststructuralism is often identified as a site of contestation to a model of continuity between religion and culture on this score; see Paul De Man, "Blocking the Road: A Response to Frank Kermode," in *Romanticism and Contemporary Criticism* (Baltimore, MD: Johns Hopkins Press, 1993). (Thanks to Sam Catlin for pointing

this essay out to me.) However, one only needs to read the secondary literature on the shelves of B2430 to see otherwise. One implicit question here is whether there is a way beyond the alternative between revering the master and killing him (or her).

12. Sarah Hammerschlag, *Broken Tablets: Levinas, Derrida and the Afterlives of Religion* (New York: Columbia University Press, 2016).

13. Kant speaks explicitly about the role of semblance in poetic fiction in "promoting the freedom of the mind," and describes the difference between illusion and fiction as taking place in the faculty of judgment in "Concerning Sensory Illusion and Poetic Fiction." Rosalind Morris helpfully ties this feature of Kant's thinking to his analysis of fetishism in *Religion within the Boundaries of Mere Reason*, ed. Allen Wood and George di Giovanni (Cambridge: Cambridge University Press, 2018), as common spaces of play, rehearsal, and the "performative stop gap," that for Kant are necessary to humans "en route to a fuller morality," but which in the analysis of his oeuvre are equally indispensable to him. I have also found much of value in contemporary revalorizations of the "fetish" in Bruno Latour and J. Lorand Matory, as they encourage an expansive notion of fabrication at odds with the strict divide between subject and object, and as they smudge the border between religious and other cultural practices, taking aim at a Kantian anthropology that Morris suggests even Kant can't fully maintain. It is quite interesting to consider how closely linked the Kantian "*als ob*" is to the verbal formulation of the fetish: "I know well, but all the same [*Je sais bien, mais quand meme*]." This is not the formulation privileged by Kofman, but is useful in thinking about the proximity between fiction and the fetish.

14. "Within the temple, the ordinary (which to any outside eye or ear remains wholly ordinary) becomes significant, becomes 'sacred,' simply by being there. A ritual object or action becomes sacred by having attention focused on it in a highly marked way." J. Z. Smith, *To Take Place* (Chicago: University of Chicago Press, 1987), 104.

15. Kofman, *Comment s'en sortir?*, 73; "Beyond Aporia," in *Post-*

structuralist Classics, ed. Andrew Benjamin (New York: Routledge, 2017), 31.

16. "Sarah Kofman," in *Shifting Scenes: Interviews on Women, Politics and Writing*, ed. Alice Jardine and Anne Menke (New York: Columbia University Press, 1991), 105.

17. William Pietz, "The Problem of the Fetish I," *Res: Anthropology and Aesthetics* 9 (Spring 1985): 5–17.

18. Rosalind Morris, "After de Brosses: Fetishism, Translation, Comparativism, Critique," in *The Returns of Fetishism: Charles de Brosses and the Afterlives of an Idea*, ed. Rosalind C. Morris and Daniel H. Leonard (Chicago: University of Chicago Press, 2017), 133–320. See also J. Lorand Matory, *Fetishism Revisited* (Durham, NC: Duke University Press, 2018); Alfonso Iacono, *The History and Theory of Fetishism*, trans. Vicktoria Tchernichova and Monica Boria (London: Palgrave Macmillan, 2016); Harmut Böhme, *Fetishism and Culture: A Different Theory of Modernity*, trans. Anna Galt (2006; Boston: DeGuyter, 2014).

19. De Brosses conflates these, describing "fetish" as a term that entails divine utterance and fate. Morris and Leonard, *Returns of Fetishism*, 336n13. William Pietz prioritizes *factitious*, suggesting that it originally meant manufactured; Pietz, "Problem of the Fetish I," 5. For more on the various etymologies, see Emily Apter, *Feminizing the Fetish* (Ithaca, NY: Cornell University Press, 1991), 4.

20. William Pietz, "Problem of the Fetish IIIa," *Res* 16 (Autumn 1988): 105–24, 109.

21. Like the term "religion" in that sense, as J. Z. Smith argues in "Religion, Religions, Religious," *Critical Terms for Religious Studies* (Chicago: University of Chicago Press, 1998), 269.

22. See Bruno Latour, *On the Cult of the Factish Gods* (Durham, NC: Duke University Press, 2010), 7.

23. For the intervening history between the sixteenth and eighteenth centuries, see Pietz, "Problem of the Fetish IIIa," and Iacono, *History and Theory*, 11–54.

24. Charles de Brosses, *Du Culte de Dieux fétiches ou Parallèle de l'ancienne Religion de l'Egypte avec la religion actuelle de la Nigritie*

(1970; Paris: Fayard, 1988), 182; De Brosses, "On the Worship of Fetish Gods," in Morris and Leonard, *Returns of Fetishism*, 45.

25. De Brosses only obliquely references Hume in the text, referring to him as a "famous foreign writer from whom I borrow part
of these reflections." De Brosses, *Du Culte de Dieux fétiches*, 111.

26. While De Brosses himself is considered a minor Enlight-
enment figure, *Du Culte de Dieux fétiches* has had an outsized—if
underacknowledged—influence on fields as diverse as anthropology, comparative literature, and political economy. As Daniel
Leonard points out in his introduction to the recent translation, the
work is pioneering in its approach to comparative ethnology. Morris and Leonard, *Returns of Fetishism*, 8.

27. Morris and Leonard, *Returns of Fetishism*, 44.

28. Kant, *Religion within the Boundaries of Mere Reason*, 172–73.

29. Matory, *Fetishism Revisited*, effectively turns this history
back on Marx and Freud by arguing that they, along with their predecessors, had missed the fact that Afro-Atlantic traders knew that
their gods were made, and thus already had and have a more sophisticated understanding of the social nature of value and agency.
He suggests that Marx and Freud thus suffer from the very sin
they impute to the primitive mind: they fail to recognize their own
theories as reflections of their social and cultural positions. There
is, then, a certain symmetry between Matory's and Kofman's readings of Marx and Freud, even though Matory lapses occasionally
into caricature, seeming at times to want to explain them away by
recourse to their biographies, while Kofman continues to position
herself as disciple, particularly to Freud.

30. Freud's first essay, "The Sexual Aberrations," in *Three Essays
on the Theory of Sexuality*, trans. James Strachey (New York: Basic
Books, 2000), 19–21.

31. Böhme, *Fetishism and Culture*. For more on the role of the
fetish in nineteenth- and twentieth-century European culture, see
Morris, "After De Brosses," 133–320; Apter, *Feminizing the Fetish*;
Laura Mulvey, *Fetishism and Curiosity* (Bloomington: Indiana University Press, 1996), 1–15; and Pietz, "Problem of the Fetish I."

32. Freud, "Fetishism" (1927), in *Miscellaneous Papers (1888–1938)*, vol. 5 of *Collected Papers* (London: Hogarth and Institute of Psycho-Analysis, 1924–1950), 198–204. See Sarah Kofman, *The Enigma of Woman* (Ithaca, NY: Cornell University Press, 1985), 85.

33. For another reading of the role of the fetish in Kofman's work, particularly in relation to Derrida, see Penelope Deutscher's essay "Oscillations: Sarah Kofman and Jacques Derrida on Fetishism," *In Gegenwart des Fetischs*, ed. Christine Blätter and Falko Schmeider (Berlin: Verlag Turia, 2014), 181–200.

34. See Elizabeth Berg, "The Third Woman," *Diacritics* 12, no. 2 (Summer 1982): 13; Naomi Schor, *Bad Objects* (Durham, NC: Duke University Press, 1995), 100; and Apter, *Feminizing the Fetish*, 110. Kofman resisted being associated with the strand of French feminism that become so prominent in the United States in the 1980s. She suggested that a move such as Luce Irigararay's to create "l'ecriture feminine" was in its very assertion of newness one that remains "fully within metaphysics." "Sarah Kofman," in Jardine and Menke, *Shifting Scenes*, 106. It is clear, as Berg points out, that in her opposition to Irigaray Kofman ends up subordinating her primary female interlocutor to her male ones. She holds a sustained argument with Irigaray, but relegates it to the footnotes of *Enigma of Woman*. Either Kofman is herself guilty of a kind of sexism on this score or her strategy of situating herself as commentator and disrupter of male discourse leads her to relegate the combat to the space under the bar. Interestingly, most of the footnoted references to Irigaray appear in the chapter entitled "The Battle of the Sexes." Kofman, *Enigma of Woman*, 12–15.

35. Kofman, *Quatre romans*, 20–21; published in English as *Freud and Fiction*, trans. Sarah Sykes (Cambridge: Polity Press, 1991), 9.

36. Kofman, *Quatre romans*, 21; Kofman, *Freud and Fiction*, 9.

37. Kofman footnotes Derrida's "White Mythology" heavily here, crediting him as her source for understanding the status of metaphor in Aristotle's work. Kofman, *Quatre romans*, 21; Kofman, *Freud and Fiction*, 10.

38. Kofman, *Quatre romans*, 23; Kofman, *Freud and Fiction*, 12.

39. Kofman, *Quatre romans*, 24; Kofman, *Freud and Fiction*, 13.

40. Kofman, *Quatre romans*, 18; Kofman, *Freud and Fiction*, 8.

41. Kofman, *L'enfance de l'art* (Paris: Galilée, 1970), 209; Kofman, *Childhood of Art*, trans. Winifred Woodhull (New York: Columbia University Press, 1988), 143.

42. Kofman, *L'enfance de l'art*, 212; Kofman, *Childhood of Art*, 146.

43. Kofman, *L'enfance de l'art*, 229; Kofman, *Childhood of Art*, 158–59.

44. Kofman, *Quatre romans*, 177; Kofman, *Freud and Fiction*, 158.

45. Kofman, *Quatre romans*, 177; Kofman, *Freud and Fiction*, 158–59.

46. Kofman, *Quatre romans*, 178; Kofman, *Freud and Fiction*, 160.

47. Kofman, *Quatre romans*, 181; Kofman, *Freud and Fiction*, 162.

48. Already in the course's first lecture he suggests that in Marx "religion is the very form of ideology." In the second lecture of the course he takes this a step further to show that in the history of the philosophy of religion, religion itself plays the role of fetish, and is named as such in Kant's treatment of priestcraft in *Religion within the Boundaries of Mere Reason*. Like the camera obscura in Marx, Derrida suggests "the fetish is not an accidental metaphor." Derrida, *Religion and Philosophy*, first lecture, pp. 4, 10 (IMEC, 1972).

49. Kofman references as well here the role of the metaphor in Rousseau, Da Vinci, and Descartes but maintains a primary focus on Marx, Freud, and Nietzsche. As Suzanne Gearhart points out, it is noteworthy that Kofman ignores Hegel in her treatment of the theme, particularly in her reading of *Glas*. Gearhart suggests that this subordination of Hegel to Freud is tied to Kofman's lack of attention to repression. Suzanne Gearhart, "The Remnants of Psychoanalysis after *Glas*," in *Hegel after Derrida*, ed. Stuart Burnett (London: Routledge, 1998), 147–70.

50. Sarah Kofman, *Camera Obscura de l'idéologie* (Paris: Galilée, 1973), 32; Kofman, *Camera Obscura of Ideology*, trans. Will Straw (Ithaca: Cornell University Press, 1998), 19. French pagination is followed by English in references below.

51. Kofman, *Camera Obscura*, 59; 40.

52. Kofman, *Camera Obscura*, 59; 41.

53. Kofman, *Camera Obscura*, 59; 41.

54. See Derrida, "Force and Signification," in *Writing and Difference*, trans. Alan Bass (Chicago: University of Chicago Press, 1978), 3–30, for another rendering of this dynamic.

55. Derrida, "Force and Signification," 43.

56. Freud, "Fetishism," 200.

57. Sarah Kofman, *L'énigme de la femme* (Paris: Galilée, 1980), 101; Kofman, *Enigma of Woman*, 85.

58. Kofman, *L'énigme de la femme*, 101; Kofman, *Enigma of Woman*, 85, quoting Freud, "Medusa's Head," in *Standard Edition*, vol. 18, trans. J. Strachy (London: Hogarth, 1922), 273.

59. Freud, "Fetishism," 199.

60. Nietzsche, "Preface for the Second Edition," in *The Gay Science*, trans. Walter Kaufman (New York: Random House, 1974), 38. Quoted in Kofman, *Camera Obscura*, 64; 43–44.

61. Kofman, *Camera Obscura*, 64; 44.

62. Kofman, *Camera Obscura*, 65; 45.

63. Kofman, *Camera Obscura*, 69; 47–48.

64. Kofman, *Camera Obscura*, 75; 52.

65. Although she doesn't discuss Comte's theory at any length here, there is something to his account of fetishism as immediate and more rational in its epistemological modesty than German Idealism, that resonates with her account of the Freudian fetish as compromise.

66. Kofman, "Baubo," in *Nietzsche's New Seas*, ed. Michael Allen Gillespie and Tracy B. Strong (Chicago: University of Chicago Press, 1988), 176, quoting Nietzsche, *Twilight of the Idols* (6.3.87).

67. See Penelope Deutscher, "Complicated Fidelity: Kofman's Freud (Reading *The Childhood of Art* with *The Enigma of Woman*," in Deutscher and Oliver, *Enigmas*, 159–73. As Deutscher points out, this does not imply a single lens; rather, "the curiosity of Kofman's work is how she manages to deploy a heterogeneous Freudianism . . . she mimics multiple Freuds" (172).

68. It is a move of Nietzsche's that will be repeated by J. Lorand Matory and Bruno Latour over a century later.

69. Kofman, "Baubo," 186.

70. As she puts it in *Nietzsche and Metaphor*, "Diversifying metaphors . . . suggests that none is proper or more 'proper' than any other, that the 'proper' is simply the appropriation of the 'world' by a certain perspective which imposes its law on it." Sarah Kofman, *Nietzsche et la metaphore* (Paris, Galilée, 1983), 122; Kofman, *Nietzsche and Metaphor*, trans. Duncan Large (London: Athlone Press, 1993), 103.

71. Kofman, "Baubo," 199.

72. See Leslie Chamberlain, *Nietzsche in Turin* (New York: Picador, 1996), 130, and Sue Prideaux, *I Am Dynamite: A Life of Nietzsche* (New York: Tim Duggan Books, 2018), 183.

73. Kofman, "Baubo," 202.

74. "Sarah Kofman," in Jardine and Menke, *Shifting Scenes*, 108.

75. Kofman, *Nietzsche et la metaphore*, 168; Kofman, *Nietzsche and Metaphor*, 116.

76. See Derrida, "Ellipsis," in *Writing and Difference*, 294–300, and Kofman, *Nietzsche and Metaphor*, 186n23.

77. See Sarah Kofman, "Kant and Respect for Women," *Social Research* 49, no. 2 (Summer 1982): 385–86. For more on this theme in Kofman as it relates to her reading of Kant, see Natalie Alexander, "Rending Kant's Umbrella," in *Enigmas: Essays on Sarah Kofman* (Ithaca, NY: Cornell University Press, 1999), 143–58.

78. Freud, "Fetishism," 202.

79. Rosalind Morris, in her discussion of Derrida's *Glas*, suggests that Derrida's formulation of the double-bind for which the fetish is established here as a figure is itself a departure from "the conventional psychoanalytic understanding of the fetish as a response to the crisis of having or not having 'it.'" Morris, "After De Brosses," 271. In *Glas* Derrida says that there is "enough" in Freud "to reconstruct starting from its generalization a 'concept' of the fetish that no longer lets itself be constrained in the space of truth." Derrida, *Glas*, trans. John P. Leavey and Richard Rand (Lincoln: University of Nebraska Press, 1986), 209. One of the key points of disagreement between Derrida and Kofman is whether Derrida's "departure," to use Morris's term, is already within Freud's own

concept by virtue of the fact that the substitution of the fetish is already a substitution for a fantasy object.

80. Derrida, *Glas*, 211.

81. Derrida, *Glas*, 211.

82. Sarah Kofman, "Ça Cloche," in *Les Fins de l'homme: A Partir du travail de Jacques Derrida* (Paris: Galilée, 1981), 99; Kofman, "Ca Cloche," in *Selected Writings* (Stanford, CA: Stanford University Press, 2007), 82. French pagination is followed by English in references below.

83. Kofman, "Ça Cloche," 100; 83.

84. Kofman, "Ça Cloche," 105; 88.

85. Kofman, *L'énigme de la femme*, 105; Kofman, *Enigma of Woman*, 89, quoting Freud, "Fetishism," 199.

86. Kofman, *L'énigme de la femme*, 113; Kofman, *Enigma of Woman*, 97.

87. Kofman, *L'énigme de la femme*, 104; Kofman, *Enigma of Woman*, 87.

88. Kofman, *L'énigme de la femme*, 104; Kofman, *Enigma of Woman*, 87.

89. Kofman, "Ça Cloche,"105; 88.

90. Derrida, *Glas*, 262.

91. *Les Fins de l'homme*, 113; translation mine.

92. *Les Fins de l'homme*, 113.

93. See in particular the second part of Kofman, *Comment s'en sortir?*

94. *Les Fins de l'homme*, 113.

95. Blanchot, *The Last Man*, trans. Lydia Davis (New York: Columbia University Press, 1987) 4; *Les Fins de l'homme*, 112. Quoted in Kofman, *Selected Writings*, 96.

96. Derrida, *Margins of Philosophy*, trans. Alan Bass (Chicago: University of Chicago Press, 1982) 7.

97. See Kofman's comments on this point in Jardine and Menke, *Shifting Scenes*, 108.

98. "Interview with Sarah Kofman," *Le Monde*, April 27–28, 1986. An entire book could be written on the role that Nietz-

sche plays as an object of displacement, particularly by means of Kofman's readings in *Explosion I: De l'Ecce Homo de Nietzsche* (Paris: Galilée, 1982), *Explosion II: Les enfants de Nietzsche* (Paris: Galilée, 1993), and *Le mépris des Juifs: Nietzsche, les Juifs, l'antisémitisme* (Paris: Galilée, 1994). It is important to note, too, that she killed herself on the 150th anniversary of his birth. I will merely touch on it here.

99. "Interview with Sarah Kofman" (1986).

100. Sarah Kofman, *Paroles suffoquées* (Paris, Galilée, 1987), 14; Kofman, *Smothered Words*, 7–8.

101. Kofman, *Paroles suffoquées*, 14; Kofman, *Smothered Words*, 9.

102. See Maurice Blanchot, *The Instant of My Death*/Jacques Derrida, *Demeure*, trans. Elizabeth Rottenberg (Stanford, CA: Stanford University Press, 2000). During the war Blanchot published *Thomas l'obscure*, *Aminidab*, *Faux Pas*, and numerous essays in periodicals, collected after the war in *La Part du feu* and elsewhere.

103. Maurice Blanchot, *Writing the Disaster*, trans. Ann Smock (Lincoln: University of Nebraska Press, 1986), 1.

104. Blanchot, *Writing the Disaster*, 47.

105. Kofman, *Paroles suffoquées*, 16; *Smothered Words*, 10.

106. "Interview with Sarah Kofman" (1986).

107. Kofman, *Rue Ordener, Rue Labat*, 94; 82.

108. Kofman, *Rue Ordener, Rue Labat*, 3, 9.

109. Kofman, *Selected Writings*, 83.

110. See Derrida's *Archive Fever: A Freudian Impression*, trans. Eric Prenowitz (Chicago: University of Chicago Press, 1995), as well as my analysis of this facet of Derrida's own relation to Judaism in *Broken Tablets* and in Sarah Hammerschlag, *The Figural Jew* (Chicago: University of Chicago Press, 2010).

111. In another of her direct attacks on Heidegger, Kofman describes him as attempting to protect Nietzsche from Nazi appropriation at the same moment he was distancing himself from the movement, and in the process losing him, giving him only a single name and a single thought, "that of the will to power." Kofman, *Explosion I*, 66.

112. Friedrich Nietzsche, *Morgenröte*, KSA 3 (Berlin: De Gruyter, 1967), aphorism 205, 180–18.

113. Kofman, *Le Mepris des Juifs*, 45. There is far too much to say about the topic of Nietzsche and Judaism here, but I plan to address it in a forthcoming essay.

114. Kofman, *Pourquoi rit-on?* 198.

115. Derrida, in Kofman, *Selected Writings*, 22.

116. Derrida, in Kofman, *Selected Writings*, 27.

117. This section is not included in the version published in *Work of Mourning*. It appears in subsequent publications of the essay in *Les cahiers du Grif* 3 (1997): 131–65, and then as the introduction to Kofman, *Selected Writings*, 29.

118. Kofman, *Selected Writings*, 30.

119. Kofman, *Paroles suffoquées*, 73; *Smothered Words*, 62. Kofman equally emphasizes the possibility of this I-We in the end of "Ça Cloche."

120. Kofman, *Paroles suffoquées*, 89–90; *Smothered Words*, 82.

121. Kofman uses the Montaigne quote as an epigraph to her text; Derrida cites it within the first few pages of his opening talk. Montaigne, *Essais* (Paris: Gallimard, 1950), 2:498; Montaigne, *The Complete Works of Montaigne*, trans. Donald M. Frame (Stanford, CA: Stanford University Press, 1957), 331.

122. Jacques Derrida, *L'animal que donc je suis* (Paris: Gallilée, 2006), 23; Derrida, *The Animal That Therefore I Am*, trans. David Wills (New York: Fordham, 2008), 7.

123. "'I inflicted a twelve-hour lecture on them!' he wrote, with some pride to his friend Catherine Malabou," Benoît Peeters reports. Benoît Peeters, *Derrida: A Biography*, trans. Andrew Brown (Cambridge: Polity Press, 2013), 484. Other sources suggest the lecture was closer to ten hours.

124. Derrida, *L'animal*, 214; Derrida, *The Animal*, 158.

125. Derrida, *L'animal*, 219; Derrida, *The Animal*, 160.

126. Derrida, *L'animal*, 219; Derrida, *The Animal*, 160.

127. Sarah Kofman, *Autobiogriffures: Du Chat Murr d'Hoffman* (Paris: Galilée, 1984), 75.

128. Kofman, *Autobiogriffures*, 18.

129. Kofman, *Autobiogriffures*, 23–29.

130. Kofman, *Autobiogriffures*, 32.

131. E. T. A. Hoffman, *The Life and Opinions of the Tomcat Murr*, trans. Anthea Bell and Jeremy Adler (New York: Penguin, 1999), 21–22; Kofman, *Autobiogriffures*, 91.

132. Or twelve hours; see note 127.

133. Derrida, *L'animal*, 73; Derrida, *The Animal*, 48.

134. Kofman, *Sarah Kofman*, 172; *Selected Writings*, 250.

135. Kofman, *Sarah Kofman*, 172; *Selected Writings*, 250.

136. Kofman, *Sarah Kofman*, 135; *Selected Writings*, 4.

137. Kofman, *Autobiogriffures*, 149.

138. See Kofman, "The Double Is/and the Devil," in *Freud and Fiction*, and, in Hoffman, *Tomcat Murr*, the discussion of the painter Ettlinger, as well as Kofman's *Vautour Rouge* (Paris: Aubier-Flamarrion, 1975).

139. Kofman, *Autobiogriffures*, 151.

140. Kofman, *Autobiogriffures*, 151.

141. Kofman, *Pourquoi rit-on?* 198.

142. Michaud and Ullern, *Sarah Kofman et Jacques Derrida*, 67. In his biography of Derrida, Peeters describes Kofman as "fragile, childish, terribly thin skinned," someone whom Derrida made a point even of avoiding.

DYSTOPIA, UTOPIA, *ATOPIA*

Amy Hollywood

The enthusiast suppresses her tears, crushes her opening thoughts, and—all is changed.

MARY SHELLEY, *Journal*, Feb 7, 1822 Marked by
Herman Melville in his copy of *Shelley Memorials*
(Used as an epigraph by Susan Howe for the first section, "TURNING,"
of her two-part book *The Nonconformist's Memorial*)

I like to be stationary.

BARTLEBY
(Epigraph of the second section, "CONVERSION,"
of *The Nonconformist's Memorial*)

INTRODUCTION: AN APOCALYPTIC DILEMMA

A few years ago, not long after Donald Trump became the forty-fifth president of the United States, the historian Jill Lepore wrote a review essay castigating a recent spate of dystopic novels written and published in the United States for succumbing to political despair.[1] She joined other presumably moderate voices in suggesting that the United States has trouble avoiding apocalyptic modes of thought, and she worried that concerns about the deep rifts in the US and global political landscape, about the effects of climate change and the reality of species extinction, and about what seems to some of us to be a state of constant, interminable war, were merely further instances of the anti-intellectualism and theologically unhinged legacy of our Puritan fathers.[2] (I should note that Lepore doesn't blame the Puritans, but it remains a popular trope. I admire much in the writings and legacy of the Puritans of the Massachusetts Bay Colony, moreover, who were decidedly not anti-intellectual and no more theologically unhinged than their contemporaries, but they were not—are not—my fathers.)

The problem with these critiques, often coming from historians, is how ahistorical they are. States do fall, societies crumble, and civilizations have been wiped from the face of the earth—some entirely, others in any form that would be recognizable to their ancestors. The very Puritans often blamed for a tendency toward the apocalyptic in US culture began the process of destroying the indigenous people of New England. English settlers' fears of their own apocalyptic destruction brought about that of the people whose lands they stole.[3] And of course, the waters are rising and species are becoming extinct at alarming rates. We may be able to stem the tide, and it is more than likely that the human race will survive for the foreseeable future. There is a certain kind of "pornotroping," a gleeful unsettling eroticism, in many of the stories of oddly reshaped human remnants surviving after the plagues or nuclear wars or large-scale environmental disasters that appear in much contemporary literature.[4] The world in tatters, either the one we live in now or a projected future, perhaps ought not to be the site of pleasure.[5] Yet it remains the case that life already looks dystopic to many and that fundamental, deleterious changes are occurring, and at ever increasing speed. The dystopic can be deeply realist—in Flint, Michigan, or Atlanta, Georgia, in Syria or Myanmar, and in other places too numerous to name. Across the globe at the moment of this writing, the catastrophe is now. Moreover, dystopias generally are not only tales of despair, for even as they tell of what their authors and the communities from which they come most fear, they also imaginatively suggest how we might best live through and with or against it. We don't all fear the same things, either, and that too seems vitally important.[6]

Here I want to step back in time and look first at the way two very different people responded to emerging conflicts in Europe and around the world in the first half of the twentieth century. It is an admittedly odd move to bring together the German jurist and political philosopher Carl Schmitt and the American ex-patriot poet H.D., but I do so for two reasons. First, they each engage in thought experiments that might be taken as dystopic, but just as easily as utopic—and hence, their work undoes the sharp contrast on which these generic distinctions are made. Second, both bring into play issues central to the work of the contemporary US poet Susan Howe, with which I will close. Howe's poetry and essays, particularly in *The Nonconformist's Memorial*, lead me to posit the usefulness of the idea of atopia, a thinking of the past, present, and future in which the alpha privative points to a more radical kind of "no place" than that first posited by Thomas More's utopia.[7] At the center of my argument is the idea that literature—and other works of the imagination—may be the necessary non-place, or place without the limitations of place, for thinking pasts and futures that are literally uninhabitable. As much as I may try, I can't actually live in a book. Yet it is vital for human life that we have the capacity—psychically, imaginatively, intellectually, and affectively—to dwell within these spaces without the limitations of space, even if only temporarily. The ability to occupy imaginative constructs enables us to envision more just political futures—although this is not all that it does.

CARL SCHMITT AND UTOPIC WHITE SOVEREIGNTY

Carl Schmitt was not particularly interested in the imagination, and yet he used his to dangerous ends. In the 1920s, the jurist wrote a series of works in political philosophy; the most famous among them, *Political Theology: Four Chapters on the Concept of Sovereignty*, is often taken to be the central text for the project of political theology.[8] Schmitt brings together a chorus of voices, from Thomas Hobbes to Juan Donoso Cortés, to suggest that in the face of a crisis in Western liberal constitutional democracy the sovereign requires resuscitation, and with him (he seems always to be a him, figurally if not literally), the decision. The sovereign is, by definition for Schmitt, the one who is able to determine when a "state of exception" from the normative operation of the law is required. The thing most to be feared is chaos, a chaos resulting, for Schmitt, not from lawlessness but from indecision. Liberal constitutionalism's endless talk, Schmitt fears, neuters the state and thereby renders it impossible for it to institute order. Yet behind the sovereign, always and often unspoken, lies military force, for it is ultimately fear of his superior capacity for violence, usually in the form of control over a standing army, that renders the sovereign sovereign. All of the complex developments of symbolic power that mark early modernity in Europe—developments traced so ably in recent scholarship on the period—rest ultimately on the capacity for physical violence, even as they are also attempts to render that violence unnecessary.[9] The most charitable readings of Schmitt argue that he hoped, in 1922 at least, that if people could be persuaded to *believe* in the sovereign and assent to his decision, descent into war might be avoided. Yet one man's utopia—a world in which the sovereign's access to symbolic power and, veiled behind it, military force would be sufficient to invest him with the power to create order out of disorder—is another's dystopia.

Of course, in the 1930s, Schmitt was an apologist for the use of military force to insure sovereignty, laying bare the violence underlying his account of jurisprudence and the accepted moments of exception from the law. The link to dystopia becomes clear in a tellingly literary allusion, for during and after his active participation in the Nazi party, Schmitt repeatedly refers to one of the strangest of Herman Melville's works, the novella *Benito Cereno*, in connection with that involvement.[10] The title character is the captain of a ship that has been taken over by its formerly enslaved cargo. After a murderous mutiny apparently masterminded by the Senegalese Babo, Benito Cereno is kept alive to steer the ship to a port in which the Africans will not be enslaved.

The story, however, is told from the perspective of the captain of an American vessel, Amasa Delano, who happens on the slave ship in a deserted cove off an uninhabited island. (Amasa, a master?—the historical record on which Melville bases his story yields a telling pun.)[11] Everything we see of Cereno's ship through the first three-quarters of the tale we see through the eyes of Delano, who is presented as cheerful, optimistic, and decidedly dim—Melville's view of the United States in the years leading up to the Civil War is clear. (Melville writes, then, in the context of another, earlier moment of crisis for democratic institutions, hence perhaps Schmitt's interest in the story.) Delano is completely taken in by Cereno's performance of sovereignty over his ship, a performance we later learn was directed and watched closely by Babo under the guise of slavish servility.[12] Fully outfitted in flawlessly clean velvet and lace, Cereno presents himself as so powerful—and his human cargo as so compliant to his commands—that they are able to work on the ship unfettered alongside of white sailors.[13] The ship, in the eyes of Delano, despite the thirst, hunger, and illness of its crew and human cargo, is a kind of utopia of sovereignty, one in which Cereno rules supreme and Babo stands continually and eagerly at his side, ready to do his bidding. The reader is left wondering how, in the face of the misery of the ship and those on board it, Cereno can be so well and cleanly dressed, a question that seems not to occur to Delano, pointing to his intense desire to believe in the white captain's sovereignty—or his inability to imagine anyone else's, or at any rate, that of a Black man.

Cereno tells a story of disease, storms, and calms that have decimated his crew and left all remaining on board in dire need of water and food. Delano, despite occasional worries that Cereno is plotting his death, promises assistance. Toward nightfall, Delano enters a sealing boat manned by his own sailors in order to return to his ship. Cereno then dives from the side of his own vessel into the sealing boat and Delano still believes that Cereno intends to kill him. Only when Babo reveals himself armed and ready to kill Cereno does Delano finally understand that the real sovereign of the ship is not Cereno but Babo and his confederates. Yet of course, in the terms of the story, and of Schmitt's recounting of the story, Babo cannot be sovereign, although no explanation is given of *why* this is the case. Melville's story ends with trial documents in which Cereno tells of the slaves' revolt, for which they are ultimately sentenced to death. Babo, once subject to the law, does not speak, an act of recognition that within the terms set by white men, he, as a Black man, can never be granted the privilege of sovereignty. His subjection to the law suggests, moreover, that every claim to sovereignty, which in principle for Schmitt demands the suspension of the law, is in some ways always also bound by it.

For Schmitt, of course, Cereno is the hero, however unlikely, of the story. Already in the 1930s, Schmitt writes, he and others in Germany saw their fate in that of Benito Cereno: "Benito Cereno, the hero [!!] of Herman Melville's story, was elevated in Germany to the level of a symbol for the situation of persons of intelligence caught in a mass system."[14] Tracy B. Strong's reading of Schmitt's identification with Cereno is almost as disturbing as the identification itself. Taking on fully Cereno's claim that the revolt and mutiny were instances of pure evil to which he was forced to succumb in order to keep greater evil from occurring—his intent, he claims, is to save the lives of as many of the whites on board as possible and he only jumps into Delano's boat because he knows Babo intends to capture Delano's ship that night—Strong finds Schmitt's appeal to the story "complexly revelatory":

> The captain of the ship might be thought of as the model of what we mean by a "sovereign." Yet here we have a story about a man obliged to accept the pose of being in control while actually going along with evil because his safety required it. At the very end of Melville's story, after Babo and the other slaves have been captured, a shroud falls from the bowsprit of Cereno's erstwhile ship to reveal the skeleton of the slave owner murdered by the revolted slaves, and over it the inscription, "Follow your leader." *Benito*

Cereno is about, among other things, what being a sovereign or captain is, how one is to recognize one, and the mistakes that can be made when one doesn't.[15]

Just as Captain Delano thought so little of the Africans on board the ship that he couldn't entertain the possibility that they might be sovereign over it, so Strong—and presumably Schmitt—cannot imagine that their revolt might be justified, an act of sovereign decision through which a people manifest themselves, an active response to the "state of exception" that is slavery itself.

As I said, one person's dystopia—a murder ship with a skeleton for a masthead—might be another's utopia or, at the very least, a realist unveiling of the truth of the violence represented by the very existence of the slave ship itself. The slaves' utopic desire is to bring the ship to a port in which they will not be enslaved. What they want, more precisely, is for Cereno to take them back to Senegal, a trip he claims is beyond his ability.[16] Schmitt's fantasy of a sovereignty that requires no authorization by the law is given the lie by the very tale he uses in an attempt to legitimate his Nazism, for it is the law that ultimately refuses to acknowledge Babo as a subject and thereby seals his fate. It is the law that insists Delano and the "the slave owner murdered by the revolted slaves," to use Strong's curious formulation, are the ship's true sovereigns. Supported by the law, the state's violence is rewritten as justified force, and only with its legitimating set of assumptions about who and who is not capable of sovereign subjectivity can it stand opposed to the putatively savage violence of the Black slave in revolt.

H.D.'S DYSTOPIC UTOPIA

H.D., poet, novelist, and a visionary of quite a different sort, spent the 1930s and 1940s going into psychoanalysis and writing. She didn't go to just anyone, but to the father of psychoanalysis himself, Sigmund Freud. Having lived through World

War I, convinced that there would be another, she went to Freud to help her think about how psychically to survive it. The force of the sovereign decision, the violence unleashed when multiple political actors name their enemies, refuse to back down in the face of the threat of violence, and armed warfare results, is the background against which she writes her three-book poem *Trilogy* (1944–1946). Her agreements and disagreements with Freud—on women and religion, she explains in *Tribute to Freud*, they would never agree—shape its content.[17]

H.D.'s poem is realist, dystopic, utopic.[18] Its opening lines, "An incident here and there / and rails gone (for guns) / from your (and my) old town square," place it firmly within the ruins of Blitz-cratered London. Yet the first poem of *The Walls Do Not Fall* (1944) rests on a contradiction and undoes any fixed temporality for the sequence. Placing the reader immediately within ruins, the poem seems at odds with the title of the book in which it appears:

there, as here, ruin opens
the tomb, the temple; enter,
there as here, there are no doors:

the shrine lies open to the sky,
the rain falls, here, there
sand drifts; eternity endures:

rain everywhere, yet as the fallen roof
leaves the sealed room
open to the air,

so through our desolation,
thoughts stir, inspiration stalks us
through gloom:[19]

"There as here" suggests both the presence of war-torn London and some other time or times—and places. The open tomb evokes Christ risen, the language of temples and shrines suggests an ancient pagan world, yet over the entire passage hovers the destruction brought about by German bombs falling on London, buildings roofless, crumbling walls, all open to the air. And yet, despite the destruction, the title of the poem tells us, the walls do not fall.

Whether the inspiration that keeps the walls up leads one to the past or to the future remains an open question throughout *Trilogy*. H.D. draws on biblical figures (Mary Magdalene, Mary of Bethany, the Virgin Mary, the three Wise Men who came to Christ shortly after his birth, hosts of named angels) and ancient mythology (Isis, Astarte, Venus), yet also insists that the future does not rely on a return to past gods or goddesses. She draws on every resource available to her, yet at the same time raises questions about how this interpretative and creative assimilation works and about its significance. The speaker of the poem claims that the dream of her childhood is the Holy Ghost and at the same time "that way of inspiration / is always open, // and open to everyone." Inspiration enables anyone and everyone to act "as go-between, interpreter":

> it explains symbols of the past
> in to-day's imagery,
>
> it merges the distant future
> with most distant antiquity,
>
> states economically
> in a simple dream-equation
>
> the most profound philosophy,
> discloses the alchemist's secret
>
> and follows the Mage
> in the desert. (*Walls*, 29)

Yet even as she recognizes the necessity of mining the past and bringing it into the future, she admits the triteness of the move:

> This search for historical parallels,
> Research into psychic affinities,
>
> has been done to death before,
> will be done again;
>
> no comment can alter spiritual realities
> (you say) or again,
>
> what new light can you possibly
> throw upon them? (*Walls*, 51)

To the skeptic's questions, the poem insists on the particularity of each repetition—and hence its value:

> my mind (yours),
> your way of thought (mine),
>
> each has its peculiar intricate map,
> threads weave over and under
>
> the jungle-growth
> of biological aptitudes
>
> inherited tendencies,
> the intellectual effort
>
> of the whole race,
> its tide and ebb. (*Walls*, 51)

All of this might be read as an outdated, romantic conception of the folk, some quasi-biologistic, Lamarckian insistence that each people reads the past, present, and future through its own

inherited bloodlines. There is a danger of both atavism and esotericism in H.D., the worst kind of modernist and what will
become New Age confusions, in which an incoherent jumble of
classical and biblical sources, all meant to name the same eter-
nal realities, are united in some vaguely conceived universal
conscious or unconscious.

Yet H.D. is more interesting than this, more canny and more
critical. We are all human, perhaps,

> but my mind (yours)
> has its peculiar ego-centric
>
> personal approach
> to the eternal realities,
>
> and differs from every other
> in minute particulars,
>
> as the vein-paths on any leaf
> differ from those of every other leaf
>
> in the forest, as every snow-flake
> has its particular star, coral or prism shape. (*Walls*, 51–52)

These particular minds, even as they stand powerless before the
wonder of the walls that do not fall ("*I do not know why*"), go forth
without a known rule or procedure:

> *we are voyagers, discoverers*
> *of the not-known,*
>
> *the unrecorded;*
> *we have no map;*
>
> *possibly we will reach haven,*
> *heaven.* (*Walls*, 59)

There is, for H.D., no going back, although the past reimagined may help the poet survive the present and move into the future. The following two books of *Trilogy*, *Tribute to the Angels* (1945) and *The Flowering of the Rod* (1946) richly and enigmatically lay out the poet's vision and the possibility it offers of "haven, / heaven."

Two aspects of H.D.'s vision are important for me here: the poet's vision is of a woman, a very human and yet somehow also divine woman, holding a book that is, and this is the second vital point, empty. If *The Walls Do Not Fall* provides a context and poetics for the narrator's visionary response to war and political chaos, *Tribute to the Angels* and *The Flowering of the Rod* give it flesh, even as in both H.D. refuses to offer a determinative account of either the vision or the future it might bring forth. In *Tribute to the Angels*, even as the vision is conjured, the poet refuses to name it, "for there is no name for it." The poet's patron demands that she name it, but she insists, "there is no name"; "he said, / 'invent it'" (*Tribute*, 76). But again the speaker demurs: "I can not invent it."

H.D. goes on both to name and unname it, in the same short, sometimes colloquially clear, other times spectrally opaque lines she uses throughout *Trilogy*:

> I can not invent it,
> I said it was agate,
>
> I said, it lived, it gave—
> Fragrance—was near enough
>
> to explain that quality
> for which there is no name;
>
> I do not want to name it,
> I want to watch its faint
>
> heart-beat, pulse-beat
> as it quivers, I do not want

to talk about it,
I want to minimize thought,

concentrate on it
till I shrink,

dematerialize
and am drawn into it. (*Tribute,* 77)

This is not simply an acknowledgment that what she has seen cannot ever be adequately named—the thinnest kind of apophasis, the simple statement of ineffability—but a refusal of the act of naming itself, of talk that leaves her outside of and other than what she sees and smells and hears.

And yet despite this refusal, H.D. continues to move back and forth between the old and the new, the esoteric and the plain, the Christian and the pagan, across the senses and beyond them to a place in which the poet can "shrink // dematerialize" and be drawn into what she encounters. "This is no rune nor riddle," she insists, "it is happening everywhere" (*Tribute,* 84). It is both a "new sensation" "not granted to everyone // not to everyone everywhere" and as readily available as "an old tree / such as we see everywhere" (*Tribute,* 85).

. . . and some barrel staves
and some bricks

and an edge of the wall
uncovered and the naked ugliness

and then . . . music? O, what I meant
by music, was—

music set up ladders,
it makes us invisible,

it sets us apart,
it lets us escape;

but from the visible
there is no escape;

there is no escape from the spear
that pierces the heart. (*Flowering*, 85–86)

The poet lives in a dystopic world, a visible world in which "there
is no escape from the spear / that pierces the heart"—H.D.'s
Moravian roots are showing here, in this deeply Christocentric
image[20]—yet in and through that world, the naked wall of a
building shorn of its front and roof, a vision and a music lift her
up to that which is invisible, to the utopic sight and smell and
sound of a woman holding an open blank book.

The following sections of *Tribute to the Angels* give the woman
names drawn from Christianity and ancient Greek and Egyp-
tian and Roman religions—she is Isis and Astarte, Venus and
Aphrodite, but most prominently she is Mary, Our Lady, and
"Holy Wisdom, / *Santa Sophia*, the SS of the *Sanctus Spiritus*, // so
by facile reasoning, logically / the incarnate symbol of the Holy
Ghost" (*Tribute*, 101). Yet she does not bear a child but a book,
and she is not the Queen of Heaven "frozen above the centre
door / of a Gothic cathedral" (*Tribute*, 102). The poet both hears
and names the suggestions of her unnamed interlocutor, she ac-
cepts them and adds to them, yet she also rejects them, often in
the same breath, as inadequate to her vision.

O yes—you understand, I say,
this is all most satisfactory,

but she wasn't hieratic, she wasn't frozen,
she wasn't very tall;

she is the Vestal
from the days of Numa,

she carries over the cult
of the *Bono Dea*,

she carries a book but it is not
the tome of the ancient wisdom,

the pages, I imagine, are the blank pages
of the unwritten volume of the new (*Tribute*, 103)

She is Psyche, but outside of her cocoon; a Sybil, but not shut up in
a cave. The old names are necessary even as they are inadequate.
    The woman and her book offer the only way out of the realm
of the dead and dying in which the poet finds herself.

But nearer than Guardian Angel
or good Daemon,

she is the counter-coin-side
of primitive terror;

she is not-fear, she is not-war,
but she is no symbolic figure

of peace, charity, chastity, goodness,
faith, hope reward;

she is not Justice with eyes
blindfolded like Love's (*Tribute*, 104)

Refusing the hypostasizing reifications of the ancient gods and
goddesses, H.D. insists on the particularity and humanity of the
woman she sees.

Most importantly, perhaps, the woman does not bear Christ, nor is she his harbinger.

> I grant you the dove's symbolic purity,
> I grant you her face was innocent
>
> and immaculate and her veils
> like the Lamb's Bride,
>
> but the Lamb was not with her,
> either as Bridegroom or Child;
>
> her attention is undivided,
> we are her bridegroom and lamb (*Tribute*, 104)

"We are her bridegroom and lamb." "We," H.D. insists, are the other to whom the woman attends, for whose future she waits. The book she carries, if it tells the old story, tells it in a different way, one in which what matters is the present and the future; even in looking to the past, H.D. attends not to Christ but to those who were with him. She refuses the language of sacrifice and atonement, finding in parts of the Christian story the refusal of the violence on which that story seemingly depends.

> her book is our book; written
> or unwritten, its pages will reveal
>
> a tale of Fishermen,
> a tale of a jar or jars,
>
> the same—different—the same attributes,
> different yet the same as before. (*Tribute*, 105)

"A tale of a jar or jars" leads into *The Flowering of the Rod*, in which H.D. reimagines the story of Kaspar, one of the three Wise Men who came bringing gifts to the infant Jesus, and the woman who anointed Christ's feet.

In *The Flowering of the Rod*, like the other poems in *Trilogy*, H.D. is not concerned with keeping the various historical, biblical, and mythological stories straight, and she takes a lovely and loving delight in that freedom. Emphasizing the otherness and abjection of those to whom the unnamed Christ revealed himself, H.D. insists that they are both particular and, in some fundamental way, unknown.

> So the first—it is written,
> will be the twisted or tortured individuals,
>
> out of line, out of step with world so-called progress;
> the first to receive the promise was a thief;
>
> the first actually to witness His life-after-death,
> was an unbalanced, neurotic woman,
>
> who was naturally reviled for having left home
> and not caring for house-work . . . or was that Mary of
>   Bethany?
>
> in any case—as to this other Mary
> and what she did, everyone knows,
>
> but it is not on record
> exactly where and how she found the alabaster jar
>   (*Flowering*, 129)

So many Marys and unnamed women who might be associated with them ("O, there are Marys a-plenty, / (though I am Mara, bitter) I shall be Mary-myrrh"; *Flowering*, 135). H.D. wants to imagine where she got the jar. And while the woman who anointed Christ's feet was said to have done so with nard and the wise man Kaspar traditionally gives the infant Jesus frank-incense, H.D. fills the jar with myrrh, the bitter resin used by the ancient Egyptians to mummify corpses, by the ancient Is-raelites to anoint their kings, and by Nicodemus and Joseph of Arimathea to wrap Christ's dead body (John 19:39).

Inventing a new myth—told as rumor, gossip, word of mouth—in which Mary receives the jar of myrrh with which she will anoint Jesus's feet from Kaspar, "an Arab, / a stranger in the market-place" "(or so some say)" (*Flowering*, 130), this same Kaspar understands that the story—his story—is also always and primarily Mary's story. He sees something in her and gives a precious, unopened jar of myrrh to her without charge and without question. In one of the longer poems in the sequence, H.D. probes and troubles what Kaspar knows and how he knows it, even as she acknowledges that we will never know for sure:

> And no one will ever know
> whether the picture he saw clearly
>
> as in a mirror was pre-determined
> by his discipline and study
>
> of old lore and by his innate capacity
> for transcribing and translating
>
> the difficult secret symbols,
> no one will ever know how it happened
>
> that in a second or a second and a half a second,
> he saw further, saw deeper, apprehended more
>
> than anyone before or after him;
> no one will ever know
>
> whether it was a sort of spiritual optical-illusion,
> or whether he looked down the deep deep-well

of the so-far unknown
depth of pre-history;

no one will ever know
if it could be proved mathematically

by demonstrated lines,
as an angle of light

reflected from a strand of a woman's hair,
reflected again or refracted

a certain other angle—
or perhaps it was a matter of vibration

that matched or caught an allied
or exactly opposite vibration

and created a sort of vacuum,
or rather a *point* in time—

he called it a fleck or flaw in a gem
of the crown that he saw

(or thought he saw) as in a mirror;
no one would ever know exactly

how it happened,
least of all Kaspar. (*Flowering*, 165–66)

All of this unknowing of the how, but what Kaspar knew was that
this young woman, come to him seeking myrrh, was herself the
answer to every question.

Perhaps she herself did not know. (Perhaps it is necessary
that she not know.) Perhaps she believed that the aroma emanat-
ing from her was the myrrh Kaspar had given her, or the child,

simultaneously a grown man, she did not hold in her arms. In the closing lines of *Trilogy*, Kaspar both knows and doesn't know:

> But she spoke so he looked at her,
> she was shy and simple and young;
>
> she said, Sir, it is a most beautiful fragrance,
> as of all flowering things together;
>
> but Kaspar knew the seal of the jar was unbroken.
> he did not know whether she knew
>
> the fragrance came from the bundle of myrrh
> she held in her arms. (*Flowering*, 173)

Kaspar knows and he does not know; he does not know whether the woman knows; it does not matter, in some vital way, if either he or she knows. In that unknowing, the woman is herself the hope for a future, the possibility posed by an unwritten-in book, the unassuming refusal of war and violence and bloodshed. The work of the poet, H.D. suggests, is to create the space in which this woman can be imagined and in which she can be recognized. Partly through learning, perhaps, but also through opening oneself to chance, to seeing "a fleck or flaw in a gem / of the crown that he saw // (or thought he saw) as in a mirror." Kaspar figures the poet, then, and his recognition of what he sees, hears, smells, feels—and what lies forever beyond him.

A CONCLUSION BEFORE THE REFUSAL TO CONCLUDE

We seem—we are—worlds away from Carl Schmitt's purported *Realpolitik*, yet his account of sovereignty seems no more or less phantasmatic to me than does H.D.'s vision of a woman looking to the future among the ruins. Certainly, the sovereign to whom

Schmitt attached himself did not control chaos, but instead unleashed it on those considered to be the enemy, whether within
or external to the state. Schmitt's appeal to *Benito Cereno* misses
its central challenge, for in the novella, Melville shows the difficulty, perhaps even the impossibility, of knowing who the sovereign is, and he suggests that the sovereign can only ever be
the perpetrator of violence (whether as the slaver or the slave in
revolt). This is a form of unknowing Schmitt himself roundly
rejects; hence his misreading of Melville's story, for Schmitt,
like Delano and like the US court in which Babo and those who
revolted with him are tried, assumes without question that only
the white man can be sovereign.

Schmitt argues, moveover, that the sovereign must be thor-
oughly known and knowable, as must be his decrees. In naming the "state of exception," then, the sovereign is given power
to do what he will, but there is no mystery to be fathomed
here. Insofar as the sovereign is secular, it is precisely in that,
unlike the God of Christianity, the sovereign can and must be
known, his power transparent, his will clear—even as he is
also capable of, justified in, deception. Babo, when he deceives
in order to exercise power, Schmitt deems evil. Yet any revolt
against the sovereignty of another, a sovereignty over one's own
body that is backed by the law as well as the violence the law
has at its disposal, must involve deception. The paradoxical—
perhaps better, flatly contradictory—result is that only those
recognized as subjects by the law can be transparent in their
abrogation of it—only they are conceded the legitimacy to
deceive *with clarity*. This is the dilemma Melville so tellingly
reveals.

Unlike many contemporary theorists interested in political
theology, sovereignty, the state of exception, and their possible
convergence with the negations of apophatic theology, Schmitt
is not interested in mystery. Yet as much as Schmitt desires
the apparent transparency of the decision, the basis on which
the decision is made cannot be rendered openly.[21] In Melville's

story, white supremacy hides itself under the mundanity of the thinkable, and something like this seems always to be the case, rendering Schmitt's political claims utterly incoherent. (Their philosophical incoherence does not, however, mean that they are wrong. His account of how power works may be accurate, although the argument cannot be made philosophically, but only historically or sociologically. Moreover, if he is right, that offers little political or ethical comfort and provides no normative justification.)

Perhaps most importantly for my purposes here, an unknowable human sovereign is just as, even more, frightening than a knowable one. (Although again, I do not think that the sovereign as described by Schmitt can ever truly be transparent in the ways in which Schmitt claims.) To bring negative theology together with political theology understood in the Schmittian sense yields a totalitarian nightmare. Negative theology is not simply a display of epistemic humility.[22] It is not about undoing the sovereign or putting limits on human conceptions of power. On the contrary, the interplay between cataphatic and apophatic theology, the naming and unnaming of God, as articulated within Neoplatonic and Christian thought, works in exactly the opposite manner; the unsaying of the divine names of the one or of god do not deny those predicates to the divine, but instead undo the limitations that circumscribe them for human understanding. As articulated in terms of a god or a source of reality understood to be transcendent—and also paradoxically absolutely immanent—to the human realm, a note of humility is struck; as finite beings, humans can never know the one or god in its undelimited, infinite power, goodness, and simplicity. Yet nothing human—whether it be a sovereign leader, political structure, or institution—can ever be the object of apophasis properly understood.

Pure decision with no knowledge of that on which it rests, other than the brute violence with which it can enact its will, is a perfect dystopia. For all of its inadequacies, as I write this in the fall of 2020, the things standing between the United States and unmitigated disaster are the endless chatter of constitutional democracy and, more importantly, the courts, the press, grassroots resistance movements, and other small- and large-scale organizations that are helping to keep people alive, safe, and resilient in myriad ways; only through these institutions and organizations can we resist the movement toward unilateral power, whether held by a single person or larger entity. (We are on the brink of losing even that.) Yet the ideal of transparency on which most models of deliberative democracy depend are themselves both phantasmatic—we never know ourselves or others with this transparency—and dangerous—those not transparent to the state become its enemies.

The late twentieth and early twenty-first centuries have uncovered the inadequacy of this putatively stark choice between sovereignty and democracy, exposing the underlying hold of capitalism on politics worldwide. In perhaps hitherto unprecedented ways, moreover, one might argue that everything we do and say is saturated by political economics.[23] This fact renders political discourses that ignore capitalism and its infiltration of every aspect of human (and nonhuman) life always inadequate to their object. To understand our situation requires constant, careful, critique—and exposure, exposure of the political-economic realities that undergird sociality. Although for very different reasons than those proclaimed by Schmitt, I think that valorizing unknowing or mystery in these conditions is profoundly dangerous.

Yet at the same time, I continue to hope that some things are in excess of, irreducible and persistently resistant to, the political-economic sphere and its determinative power. I have written in the past that regardless of any (and every) utopian political project, humans, as long as we are human, will always die. The way we die is fundamentally shaped by politics—by differences of class, race, gender, ability, religion, and the kinds of political-economic polities in which we live—but death cannot be reduced to those conditions. In the face of death, there is too much we will never know. Death is mysterious, but H.D. reminds us that just as or more mysterious are the acts of imagination that enable us to live in the face of our own death, that of others, that of entire societies and peoples. This is the form of unknowing nurtured by poetry and by religion, both of which, I argue, might stand as unlikely allies with the call for political critique and theoretical acumen recently returning to the humanities after a decade or two of what some have characterized as defeatist quietism.

The forms of political and economic critique required by the present moment—as well as the hope that some aspect of life might exceed, or minimally not be fully saturated by, the political—push beyond the distinction between dystopia and utopia, yet without relinquishing the hope that there might be an *outside* to the condition in which we find ourselves now. This is also the non-space—the cusp between the political-economic and what might be irreducible to it—in which the power of apophasis might best be deployed. I realize that the atopia of my title is redundant, given that utopia itself means "no place." But I want to introduce the term because of its philologically unsound echoing of anarchy, antinomianism, and apophasis and because of its opening onto the question of the alpha-privative. "Atopia" signals the place that is both a place and the undoing of the limitations of place, not a "no place" but "a place unconstrained by the limits of place." The great poet of atopia, for me, is Susan Howe, with whose work I'll end this essay. I will suggest that for Howe atopia exists in books, manuscripts, and artworks on the printed page. (There are certainly many other atopias, but these are Howe's.) Here, often, chaos reigns. My question, to myself, politically, affectively, aesthetically, is why this is an atopia in which, at least as it exists on the page where alone it can be rendered, I want to live. It is not a question I can answer here, or perhaps anywhere.

SUSAN HOWE'S ANTINOMIAN ATOPIA: THE REFUSAL
OF CONCLUSIONS

The problem of sovereignty and the figure of Mary curiously converge in Susan Howe's *The Nonconformist's Memorial*, a poem notably influenced by H.D.'s *Trilogy*.[24] The book is divided into two parts, "TURNING" and "CONVERSION," each of which is itself divided into two parts. "TURNING" includes the title sequence, "The Nonconformist's Memorial," which pivots around the Puritan dissenter Ann Hutchinson and the biblical figures of John and Mary Magdalene, and a shorter sequence, "Silence Wager Stories." "CONVERSION" includes "A Bibliography of the King's Book or, Eikon Basilike" and "Melville's Marginalia."[25] ("A Bibliography" was also published earlier in a small press edition.)[26] These sections include both prose and poetry and both center on books, books about books that Howe comes across, as if by chance, in libraries. *The Nonconformist's Memorial* is far too long and complex to present or analyze in detail here, but I want to point to the ways in which it performs the undecidability and chaos of both sovereignty and nonconformity in a specifically literary form.

Schmitt argues that sovereignty and anarchy are mirror images of each other, with the former resting on the inherent wickedness of humanity and the latter on its inherent goodness. He insists that in the face of human evil, only the sovereign can bring order, whereas the anarchist's misplaced belief in human goodness can only bring about chaos. Presumably, the anarchist would see it the other way: anarchy would beget a well-ordered state of living together, while sovereignty is a reign of terror in which human wickedness is nurtured and unleashed. Yet as always, Schmitt's dualist cast of mind gets in the way of his imagining other possibilities. In many ways, Howe's work in *The Nonconformist's Memorial* aligns with Schmitt's assumptions in its concern with sovereignty and anarchy, yet by enacting the impossibility of the sovereign decision, whether it be that of the king or his nonconforming subjects, her pages point to ways out of the constricting terms deployed by her sources.

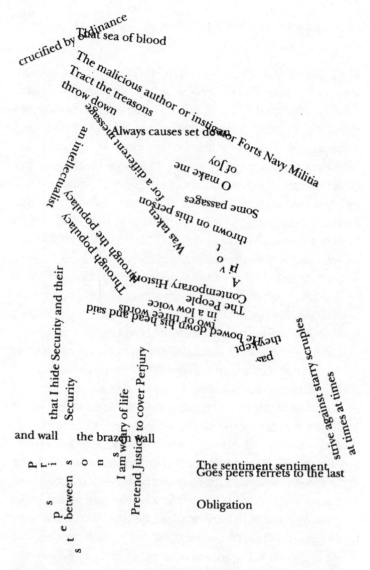

FIGURES 3.1-3.2. From Susan Howe, *The Nonconformist's Memorial* (New York: New Directions, 1993), pages 56 and 57. Courtesy of New Directions.

s
t
e
p
s

P
r
i
n

between

Security

that I hide Security and their

and wall

the brazen wall

I am weary of life

Pretend Justice to cover Perjury

Obligation

The sentiment sentiment
Goes peers ferrets to the last

strive against starry scruples
at times at times

pas-
they kept
He bowed down his head and said
two or three words
in a low voice
The People
Contemporary History

A
pi v
o
t

Was taken

thrown on this person for a different message

Through populacy
through the populacy

an intellectualist

Some passages

O make me
of Joy

crucified by
Fors Navy Militia
The malicious author or insti
Tract the reasons
or causes set down
Always causes set down
throw down

Trijnance
vast sea of blood

Turning constantly to the historical record and the gaps within it, fascinated, like H.D., with what we cannot know, but more insistent than H.D. in her attempts to be clear about what we do know and to leave open the gaps where we don't, Howe, in *The Nonconformist's Memorial*, often uses the short, regular lines we find throughout H.D.'s *Trilogy*. But in place of the colloquial ease of much of H.D.'s poem, Howe's lines are opaque even as she eschews the esoteric. I will cite in full the first poem of "The Nonconformist's Memorial," which appears with one other before the poem's numbered opening; in it one can see and hear the relationship between its form and texture and that of H.D.

Contempt of the world
and contentedness

Lilies at this season

other similitudes
Felicities of life

Preaching constantly
in woods and obscure

dissenting storms
A variety of trials

Revelations had had
and could remember

far away historic fact

Flesh become wheat

which is a nothingness
The 1 John *Prologue*

Original had no title
Ingrafted onto body

dark night stops suddenly
It is the last time

Run then run run

Often wild ones nest in woods
Every rational being[27]

The lilies and the wheat evoke *Trilogy*, as do the short regular
lines. Yet the diction is fragmented, the distance of the past
rendered visceral—"far away historic fact"—by the ruptures
between lines and couplets. The Christian story is here, and the
Eucharist, but also a particular moment in that story, that of the
nonconformists of the poem's title.

This sequence and the book as a whole deal with the nonconforming Puritans of England and New England, but also with
one specific nonconformist, a woman who refused to conform
with the other Puritans of the Massachusetts Bay Colony and as
a result was banished from it. Howe does not write the names:

The act of Uniformity

ejected her

and informers at her heels

Citations remain abbreviated

Often a shortcut

stands for a Chapter (*Memorial*, 5)

The English Act of Uniformity that led Ann Hutchinson, her favorite preacher, John Cotton, and her preacher brother-in-law, John Wheelwright, to take their families from England to New England, does not lose its hold in the new world. Instead Hutchinson is forced from the Bay Colony, with "informers at her heels" ready to report back to the magistrates and ministers of Boston and Cambridge the "good news" that Hutchinson gave birth to a monstrous child and, later, that she and her family were killed by Native peoples. For John Winthrop and other early chroniclers of New England, these facts serve as proof that Hutchinson's visions and sense of surety in salvation were demonic.[28]

After these preambles—two epigraphs and the two page-long poems just cited—Howe immediately connects the banished, running nonconformist with the unnamed woman who bathed Jesus's feet with precious oils. The poem is difficult to reproduce, for every other line is upside down. The recto page from top to bottom reads

1.

nether John and John harbinger

In Peter she is nameless

headstrong anarchy thoughts

She was coming to anoint him (*Memorial*, 6)[29]

But there are lines between the three main verses of the poem, tightly pressed against them on the page. Flip the book over and you read:

As if all history were a progress

A single thread of narrative

Actual world nothing ideal (*Memorial*, 6)

A world turned upside down, the actual world.[30] The same poem, reversed, appears on the following page, with two additional lines: "The nets were not torn / The Gospel did not grasp" (*Memorial*, 7). Like the "jar or jars" of H.D.'s *Trilogy*, Howe's untorn nets point to that which is not contained within the Gospel; the open-endedness of the stories it tells leave space for new words and new futures, as well as different imaginings of the past.

This unnamed woman, a "love-impelled figure," is associated throughout Howe's sequence of poems with Mary Magdalene and most specifically with the moment in the Gospel of John in which Mary sees Christ risen in the garden and he tells her, "Touch me not" (John 20:17; the entire passage from which this line comes serves as the second of two epigraphs to the poem [John 20:15–18]).

> She ran forward to touch him
> Alabaster and confess
>
> Don't cling to me
> Pivot
>
> Literally the unmoving point around which a body
> Literally stop touching me
> turns
>
> *We* plural are the speaker (*Memorial*, 11)

Howe's lines almost overlap, teeter on the edge of illegibility. They cling to each other and to the page. "How could Love not be loved" (*Memorial*, 13), Howe asks. The interplay of movement and stillness repeats that of the epigraphs to the book's two sections. Like Mary Shelley's enthusiast, Mary Magdalene is called on to suppress her desire, yet with that, "all is changed." Bartleby, who likes to be "stationary," becomes a figure for the unmoving center around which a body turns. (TURNING and CONVERSION run, then, throughout Howe's book.)

Howe knows the philological discussions around the lines in John's gospel; she knows that the line can be read not simply as "don't touch me," but more forcefully as "don't cling to me," "get off of me." She cares about these debates, but she does not pretend to resolve them or desire to make sense of them.[31] The poem seems, at times, explicitly to reject H.D.'s claims to imaginative recreation and its opening onto the possibility of new futures. Of the woman told not to touch, Howe writes:

> No community can accompany her
> No imagination can dream
>
> Improbable disciple passages
> Exegetes explain the conflict
>
> Some manuscripts and versions
>
> Her sadness (*Memorial*, 15)

Yet the poem goes on to use H.D.'s language, of "snow and white as wool" (*Memorial*, 17) bearing "witness" (*Memorial*, 17) to yet another "Parallelism" (*Memorial*, 18).

Although Howe points to the women who go unnamed throughout the Gospels—and in her own poem, the unnamed Ann Hutchinson—she provides one name persistently displaced by H.D.

> Scene Calvary the open destitute
>
> Under the burden of it
>
> seeking to get to it
>
> Quiet peace

I will use the bare name

Christ

Hallucinated to infinity

as minister of the sea

Walking on the sea and feeding (*Memorial*, 19)

Less tormented by Christianity because more distant from it, Howe names Christ, like Mary Magdalene, like Ann Hutchinson as Howe imagines her, a human alone, impelled by love but rejecting its touch.

For Howe, as for the "Believing unbelieving reader / there is now no rest" (*Memorial*, 29), just as there was no rest for Ann Hutchinson, despite her confessions to the ministers of the Massachusetts Bay Colony (and just as there was no rest for the magistrates and ministers of the Colony themselves). Ann Hutchinson is sent into exile. The "I" of Howe's poem wanders in exile—but all Protestant dissenters, she reminds us, "walk along this road" (*Memorial*, 31). Howe tries to hear and to be clear ("Reader I do not wish to hide / in you to hide from you"), but she cannot ("There I cannot find there / I cannot hear your wandering prayer / of quiet"; *Memorial*, 30–31). Moved "Recollectedly into biblical / fierce grace," Howe does not pretend to have it or to understand it.

Dense in parameter space

the obscure negative way

Any trajectory is dense

outside the threshold

Turn again and lean against

Moving away into depths

of the sea

Her Love once said in her mind

Enlightenedly to do (*Memorial*, 33)

God speaks to Ann Hutchinson; he does not speak to the poet. Instead she listens, ever so closely, to the words of Ann Hutchinson and other named and unnamed biblical and nonconforming figures, making poetry out of the place of her—or is it just my—confusion?

I don't pretend to be able to interpret or explicate Howe's work, but I do think that it is important to show the ways in which she performs the endless complexity of the very claim to nonconformity—and with it, that to sovereignty. For the nonconformist asserts, precisely, sovereignty—and so cannot tolerate the nonconformity and the sovereignty of another. The third part of *The Nonconformist's Memorial* renders the political aspects of the question explicit. In a prose opening to the sequence "MAKING THE GHOST WALK ABOUT AGAIN AND AGAIN," Howe describes *The Eikon Basilike, The Pourtraicture of His Sacred Majestie in his Solitude and Sufferings*.[32] Published on the day of Charles I's execution by nonconformist revolutionaries and widely distributed despite the work of the censors to keep it away from the public, the *Eikon Basilike* purports to have been written by the king. It contains essays, poems, prayers, and emblems all meant to justify the Royalist cause.

John Milton's defense of regicide in *The Tenure of Kings and Magistrates* and in *Eikonoklastes* attempts to displace this portrait of Charles I as a political—and so Howe writes, secular—Christ, martyred at the hands of his executioners. Milton does so by arguing, among other things, that Charles was not properly Christian. Evidence for the claim lay in the fact that the *Eikon* includes a poem, "'A prayer in time of Captivity,' said to have been delivered to Bishop Juxon, by Charles on the scaffold" (*Memorial*, 48–49):

> The prayer, a close paraphrase from "no serious Book, but the vain amatorious Poem of Sir Philip Sidney's *Arcadia*," was the prayer of a pagan woman to an all-seeing heathen Deity.
>
> A captive Shepherdess has entered through a gap in ideology. "Pammela in the Countess Arcadia," confronts the inauthentic literary work with its beginnings in a breach.
>
> Fictive Pamela's religious supplications were a major issue in the ensuing authorship controversy. (*Memorial*, 49)

Here lies precisely the gap in ideology H.D. mines, purposively, in *Trilogy*. Howe's work negates, subsumes, and repeats H.D.'s gesture.

As it turns out, Howe tells us, the *Eikon Basilike* is a forgery. Or perhaps better, following Howe,

> The *Eikon Basilike* is a puzzle. It may be a collection of recollections written by a ghostly king; it may be a forged collection of meditations gathered by a ghostwriter who was a Presbyterian, a bishop, a plagiarizer, a forger. (*Memorial*, 49)

"But" Howe claims, "it is *A Bibliography of the King's Book; or, Eikon Basilike*, by Edward Almack, that interests me. My son found it at one of the sales Sterling Memorial Library sometimes holds to get rid of useless books" (*Memorial*, 49). Susan Howe loves nothing more than a useless book. Or better, a book about books, one rendered apparently obsolete by more recent research but to Howe, a poetic historian of the mistakes and conjectures made by historians, one of signal value for demonstrating the anarchy—an often beautiful and inspiring chaos—into which researches on the *Eikon Basilike* lead.

Howe takes these books, these books about books, and she cuts them up. She scatters lines and phrases, her own and those of the cut-up books, across the page, in an anarchic undoing of all the rules for what a book—or a poem—should look like. Yet at the heart of the most complex of these pages, with phrases at all angles, upside down, sideways, and cutting across each other in an almost unreadable blur, lie the words, "The People / Contemporary History" and "O make me / of Joy" (*Memorial*, 57). The atopic non-space of joy is, I contend, the poem itself. A place that is not a place and that is more than a place, but which is also the unlimited place in which we can imagine history, the multiple, contending, contradictions of a past that constantly revises itself, that can always be imagined otherwise. Sidney's Pamela, praying to a heathen god, like H.D., "She is the blank page / writing ghost writing" (*Memorial*, 68), but always in sight of the knowledge that "No men / as expected / *ever* will be / Saviors" (*Memorial*, 65). The hope for saviors is itself, Howe suggests, part of the problem that gives rise to the tormented history out of and to which she writes.

For the hero of Howe's book, if there can be said to be a hero, which strictly speaking there is not, lies somewhere in the place between Ann Hutchinson and Herman Melville, between Mary Magdalene and Bartleby, between Bartleby and the Irish poet, translator, essayist, copyist, clerk, and possible revolutionary James Clarence Mangan. (Europeans, though, always Europeans. It is certainly possible, even necessary, to criticize Howe for her European-centered imaginary, although one might more generously read her as asking why white America, with its eyes always toward Europe even as it claims to found a "new world," is "such a violent nation." Why, as she puts it, "do we have such contempt for powerlessness?"[33] Howe's "we" could be taken to include only white America. Yet might this contempt

for powerlessness be a virus that spreads, infecting others outside that seemingly hegemonic "we"? That is one of the many
questions Howe's work forces us to ask. It should also be noted
that the figure of the Native American haunts Howe's poetry,
as does that of the Native Irish in relation to English colonizers. She does not purport, cannot, I think, claim, to speak for
them. Her revisionary questions are both necessary, and never
enough. Babo will—must—speak, and white Americans, all
Americans, must listen.)

Mangan may or may not have been the model for Melville's
Bartleby, as Howe fantasizes. She tells us that Melville's *Marginalia*, another book about books that becomes the object of
her obsessive attention, shows that Melville knew Mangan's
work—perhaps too late for him to have been Bartleby, but then
again, perhaps not. On Howe's page Mangan and Bartleby come
together. For the possible Irish revolutionary—the biographical
record on Mangan is dim—who likely died of starvation during
the great famine, is one of the stationary centers around which
The Nonconformist's Memorial turns. Not Christ, but Mangan.[34]
Not sovereign, but scribbling, then starving. The still center
around which democracy attempts to decreate and recreate
itself—and yet first, before anything else, the people need to eat.

*
**

Or is the center *David Copperfield*'s Mr. Dick, who continually
tried to write his own history only to have the beheaded Charles I
appear over and over again on his neatly written pages. Long
passages from *David Copperfield* appear in "A Bibliography of the
King's Book," passages about Mr. Dick and the kites he makes
from his manuscripts, pages on which the regicide continually
intrudes. "He showed me that it was covered by manuscript, very
closely and laboriously written; but so plainly, that as I looked
along the lines, I thought I saw some allusions to King Charles
the First's head again, in one or two places" (*Memorial*, 81). Mr.
Dick and David and his schoolfellows play, joyously, with these

kites. And when Mr. Dick's dear friend and supporter, David's aunt Miss Betsy Trotwood, loses the bulk of her capital because of the nefarious dealings of the servile savant Uriah Heep, Mr. Dick becomes, like Mangan, like Bartleby, a copyist.

*
**

These are the pivoting stationary marginal centers—multiple, always, and so elliptical—around which the poem turns, around and out of which new literary, social, political, economic imaginaries might be formed and reformed. Literature—dystopic, utopic, atopic—is not enough, but it is both necessary and more than necessary, that more than enough without which we will never know what will might can suffice, that more than suffices, refusing the logic of sufficiency entirely, as all good alpha privatives necessarily do.

NOTES

This essay was prompted by three invitations and three questions, each of which shape its contours. The first was the invitation from Constance Furey to participate in this volume and to think about faith, fidelity, and devotion as modes of relation to others and as styles of reading. The second was from David Newheiser, an invitation to think about the relationship between negative theology and political theology. A third came from Niklaus Largier and Alex Dubilet and was specifically about utopia. The topics converged around years of reading of H.D., Susan Howe, and the literature on their work. My debts to this scholarship are often invisible and hard to retrace, although I will attempt to point to the primary influences. Most important, perhaps, was time spent with the Susan Howe papers at the Archive for New Poetry, housed at the Mandeville Special Collections Library at the University of California, San Diego. There it become clear how important teaching H.D.'s *Trilogy* was to Howe at the time she was working on *The Nonconformist's Memorial*.

I am grateful for these invitations and to audiences at the University of California, Berkeley, the Australian Catholic University (in Rome), New York University, Princeton University, and Yale University for their patience and questions. A special acknowledgment must be made to Rowan Williams, Hent de Vries, Noreen Khawaja, Caleb Smith, Adam Stern, Constance Furey, and Sarah Hammerschlag for extremely careful readings of the paper in its various stages. During the time of conceiving and writing this paper I was also working with Constance, Sarah, and others, under the enthusiastic leadership of Eleanor Craig and Kris Trujillo, on what became a special journal issue: Eleanor Craig, Amy Hollywood, Niklaus Largier, and Kris Trujillo, eds., "The Poetics of Prayer and Devotion to Literature," *Representations* 153 (2021). I am extremely grateful to Eleanor and Kris, especially, for their commitment to that project and for their persistence good will and friendship. Many thanks to the librarians at the Mandeville. To Susan Howe—thank you for not telling me I am wrong, for offering words of encouragement, and for providing an ever vibrant model of reading, thought, sound, and sight. And a forever gift to R.L., who first gave me H.D. to read more than thirty-five years ago.

1. Jill Lepore, "A Golden Age for Dystopian Fiction," *New Yorker*, June 5 and 12, 2017.

2. See Betsy Hartmann, *The America Syndrome: Apocalypse, War, and Our Call to Greatness* (New York: Seven Stories Press, 2017), and Lisa Vox, *Existential Threats: American Apocalyptic Beliefs in the Technological Age* (Philadelphia: University of Pennsylvania Press, 2017). There is a large and vibrant literature on utopian and dystopian literature, at the center of which stands Fredric Jameson's work on utopia. A longer version of this argument would need to grapple with Jameson and the debates around him. Yet for my purposes, contemporary political deployments of the terms are more salient than the sophistications of literary criticism. See Fredric Jameson, *Archaeologies of the Future: The Desire Called Utopia and Other Science Fictions* (New York: Verso, 2005). Also important for my thinking has been Constance M. Furey, "Utopia of Desire: The Real and Ideal

in Aemilia Lanyer's *Salve Deus Rex Judaeorum*," *Journal of Medieval and Early Modern Studies* 26, no. 3 (2006): 561–84, and Constance M. Furey, "Utopian History," *Theory & Method in the Study of Religion* 20, no. 4 (2008): 385–98.

3. Lepore has written about these wars and so knows the dangers apocalyptic thinking can bring about; hence I imagine her concerns in the *New Yorker* piece. But I am torn, as for the Wampanoag, Nipmunk, Pocumtuck, and Narragansett, the prophesied end of the world as they knew it *was* the end of the world as they knew it, although not the wholesale destruction of them as peoples, as is too often assumed. See Jill Lepore, *The Name of War: King Philip's War and the Origins of American Identity* (New York: Vintage, 1998), and Lisa Brooks, *Our Beloved Kin: A New History of King Philip's War* (New Haven, CT: Yale University Press, 2019).

4. "Pornotroping" is Hortense Spillars's term for the ways in which the bodies of African Americans are repeatedly stripped of their humanity in explicitly sexualized ways within American culture. See Hortense Spillars, "Mama's Baby, Papa's Maybe: An American Grammar Book," in *Black, White, and in Color: Essays on American Literature and Culture* (Chicago: University of Chicago Press, 2003).

5. For a brilliant exploitation, and undermining, of these apocalyptic desires, see the TV show *The Leftovers*.

6. Omar El Akkad's *American War* describes a second US Civil War taking place in the 2070s, but really at stake is an imaginative investigation of what the war currently taking place in the Middle East might look like if it were visited on American citizens on US land. In the face of repeated drone strikes, racial divisions in the deep south are rendered moot, almost unworthy of being named—or named only in passing to demonstrate that they are no longer pertinent. Although the novel is brilliantly written, I am dubious about this imaginative scenario. Even more problematic is El Akkad's decision to make its central figure a six-foot-three-inch-tall queer woman of African American and Mexican American descent, a literally towering figure who becomes the ultimate tool of those

who want the war never to end. Conversely, Ben H. Winter's *Underground Airlines* imagines an early twenty-first century in which the enslavement of people of African descent was never made illegal in four southern states and rigid apartheid-like distinctions between Blacks and others reign even among the free. These radically different visions of a dystopic future tell us a great deal, I think, about the present.

7. A pertinent passage from Thomas More's unfinished *The History of King Richard the Third* appears at a key moment in *The Nonconformist's Memorial*, making the link between sovereignty, regicide, and utopia.

8. There is, of course, an entirely different tradition of political theology, with a very different political orientation, for whom the key figure is the German Catholic theologian Johannes Baptist Metz. Whereas Schmitt argues that the concepts he deploys are secularized theological notions, Metz asks how an explicitly Christian theology can attend to concrete political situations of suffering and injustice. His work, particularly in its rapprochement between Christian theology and Marxism, is central for that of Jürgen Moltman and Dorothee Sölle, and for the emergence of liberation theology in South America. See, especially, Johannes Baptist Metz, *A Passion for God: The Mystical-Political Dimension of Christianity*, trans. J. Matthew Ashley (New York: Paulist Press, 1998).

9. A vital question is whether violence is rendered unnecessary through the development of symbolic power or displaced on to violence against those defined as other to "Western European man." I cannot make the argument here, of course, but it seems clear to me that both things occur at the same time. For the development of symbolic power as a way to displace internecine strife, the most salient and powerful work remains that of Stephen Greenblatt, and he also comes to see the operations of displacement in effect on colonized others. Susan Howe was reading Greenblatt and Sir Walter Raleigh as she worked on *The Nonconformist's Memorial*. Most important for Howe, from what I can find in the archive, are Stephen J. Greenblatt, *Sir Walter Raleigh: The Renaissance Man and*

His Roles (New Haven, CT: Yale University Press, 1973), and Stephen Greenblatt, *Renaissance Self-Fashioning: From More to Shakespeare* (Chicago: University of Chicago Press, 1980). See also Stephen Greenblatt, *Marvelous Possessions: The Wonder of the New World* (Chicago: University of Chicago Press, 1991). For a brilliant argument about the continuing role of violence internal to elite early modern culture, see Cynthia Marshall, *The Shattering of the Self: Violence, Subjectivity, and Early Modern Texts* (Baltimore, MD: Johns Hopkins University Press, 2002).

10. Adam Stern expertly lays out the ambiguous role the figure of Don Quixote plays in Schmitt's work, demonstrating that Schmitt can never fully maintain the purported sobriety demanded by his theory of sovereignty. Instead, the decision to make a decision must be brought about in a state of denial of what is—in Schmitt's view during the Weimar period, the endless chatter of liberals. Hence Schmitt's complex relationship to Romanticism and in particular to Quixote, who, despite not seeing things as they are, is praised for his decisive activity. (The Romantics, according to Schmitt, are damned because what he views as their subjectivism necessarily leads to passivity.) Yet as Stern shows, one can be, arguably must be, an enthusiast, in Schmitt's world, even as he seems to call for sobriety. See Adam Stern, "Political Quixoticism," *Journal of Religion* 95, no. 2 (2015): 213–41.

Others have written about Schmitt's engagement with Melville, most recently, Werner Sollers, "'Better to Die by Them Than for Them': Carl Schmitt Reads 'Benito Cereno,'" *Critical Inquiry* 46, no. 2 (2020): 401–20, which contains much useful historical information.

11. My thinks to Caleb Smith for reminding me that the pun is history's, not Melville's.

12. Is the name Babo significant here and does it bear any relationship to the Baubo so important for Nietzsche and Kofman? See Sarah Hammerschlag's essay in this volume.

13. I am leaving aside for the moment powerful arguments that humanity is precisely what is denied to the slave, stripped from

them in the Middle Passage itself. There is a large literature, but see Saidiya V. Hartman, *Scenes of Subjection: Terror, Slavery, and Self-Making in Nineteenth-Century America* (Oxford: Oxford University Press, 1997); Frank B. Wilderson III, *Red, White, and Black: Cinema and the Structures of U.S. Antagonisms* (Durham, NC: Duke University Press, 2010); Frank B. Wilderson III, *Afropessimism* (New York: Liveright, 2020); and Calvin L. Warren, *Ontological Terror: Blackness, Nihilism, and Emancipation* (Durham, NC: Duke University Press, 2018).

14. Carl Schmitt, "Remarks in response to a talk by Karl Mannheim (1945–46)," in *Ex Captivate Salus: Experiences des années 1945–47. Textes et commentaires*, ed. A Doremus (Paris: Vrin, 2003), 133; cited by Tracy B. Strong in his foreword to the English edition of *Political Theology*. See Carl Schmitt, *Political Theology: Four Chapters on the Concept of Sovereignty*, trans. George Schwab (Chicago: University of Chicago Press, 1985), viii.

15. This is from Strong's introduction to Schmitt, *Political Theology*, x. Also worthy of note is the very odd phrase "revolted slaves," surely an attempt to avoid the phrase "revolting slaves," but in its very formulation calling up that sense of abject distaste.

16. It is as if, according to the logic recounted by Hartman and others, once the Middle Passage has taken place, there is no possibility of return. See Hartman, *Scenes of Subjection*, and Saidiya Hartman, *Lose Your Mother: A Journey along the Atlantic Slave Route* (New York: Farrer, Straus, and Giroux, 2008).

17. My reading of H.D., psychoanalysis, and religion has been profoundly shaped by the intense period of scholarly interest in H.D. during the 1980s. Most important for me is Susan Stanford Friedman, *Psyche Reborn: The Emergence of H.D.* (Bloomington: Indiana University Press, 1981), which first drew out in careful detail H.D.'s relationship to psychoanalysis and to esoteric and occult religious traditions. Friedman reads H.D. as a universalist in a way I will challenge here, but her work remains vital to an understanding of H.D. Friedman makes extensive use of the archival material at Yale's Beineke Rare Book and Manuscript Library and also of the

pieces then available of Robert Duncan's work on H.D., now wonderfully available in its entirety. See Robert Duncan, *The H.D. Book*, ed. Michael Boughn and Victor Coleman (Berkeley: University of California Press, 2011).

Rachel Blau Duplessis, in her study of H.D., credits L. S. Dembo's H.D. issue of *Contemporary Literature*, published in 1969, with jump starting scholarship on the poet. Norman Holmes Pearson's careful collecting of the manuscript sources and gift to Yale University of the H.D. papers were also crucial to the rediscovery and assessment of H.D.'s long and varied career. For some of the most important work from the 1980s, in addition to Friedman's study, see Janice S. Robinson, *H.D.: The Life and Work of an American Poet* (Boston: Houghton Mifflin, 1982); Barbara Guest, *Herself Defined: The Poet H.D. and Her World* (New York: Quill, 1984); Rachel Blau Duplessis, *H.D.: The Career of That Struggle* (Bloomington: University of Indiana Press, 1986); Susan Stanford Friedman and Rachel Blau Duplessis, eds., *Signets: Reading H.D.* (Madison: University of Wisconsin Press, 1990); and Susan Stanford Friedman, *Penelope's Web: Gender, Modernity, H.D.'s Fiction* (Cambridge: Cambridge University Press, 1990). For a useful bibliography of H.D.'s work and the scholarship on it up to 1990, see Michael Boughn, *H.D.: A Bibliography, 1905–1990* (Charlottesville: University of Virginia Press, 1993). For more recent work and bibliographies, see Nephie J. Christodoulides and Paulina Mackay, eds., *The Cambridge Companion to H.D.* (Cambridge: Cambridge University Press, 2011); Annette Debo and Lara Vetter, eds., *Approaches to Teaching H.D.'s Poetry and Prose* (New York: MLA Press, 2011); Lara Vetter, *A Curious Peril: H.D.'s Late Modernist Prose* (Gainsville: University Press of Florida, 2017); and Elizabeth Anderson, *H.D. and Modernist Religious Imagination: Mysticism and Writing* (London: Bloomsbury, 2013).

The H.D. International Society website is full of useful information and also offers evidence to support my sense that scholarly interest in H.D. has waxed and waned since the 1980s, with high points in that decade and in the 2000s. The *H.D. Newsletter* was active from 1987 to 1991 and *H.D.'s Web*, an e-newsletter, from 2007 to 2011. This might have more to do with the vagaries of online platforms, however, than with interest in H.D. See https://hdis .chass.ncsu.edu/. There is also significant interest in H.D.'s work in Europe, particularly in France. For thoughtful reflections on H.D.'s place in the canon, see Miranda B. Hickman, "'Uncanonically seated': H.D. and Literary Canons," in *Cambridge Companion to H.D.*, 9–22.

18. There is a large body of literature dealing with *Trilogy*, most of it thinking about the poem in relation to the war. Moreover, every major study of H.D. has something to say about the poem. I have been influenced by readings of the poem by Friedman, Duplessis, and Guest, in the works cited above, although my reading is less systematic than any of these. See also Elizabeth Anderson, "Burnt and Blossoming: Material Mysticism in *Trilogy* and *Four Quartets*," *Christianity and Literature* 62, no. 1 (2012): 121–42, and Antoine Cazé, "*Helen in Egypt* et *Trilogy*: Les écritures de guerre de H.D.," *Études anglaises* 67, no. 1 (2014): 66–80.

There is also an ongoing fascination with H.D.'s putatively occult sources and mythmaking in *Trilogy* and related works. See, for example, the republication of *The Majic Ring*, formerly published pseudonymously, and the introduction by Demetres Tryphonopoulos, *The Majic Ring by H.D.* (Gainsville: University Press of Florida, 2009). On *The Majic Ring*, see also Helen Sword, "H.D.'s *Majic Ring*," *Tulsa Studies in Women's Literature* 14, no. 2 (1995): 347–62. See also Scott Freer, *Modernist Mythopoeia: The Twilight of the Gods* (New York: Palgrave, 2015); Matte Robinson, *The Astral H.D.: Occult and Religious Sources for H.D.'s Poetry and Prose* (London: Bloomsbury, 2016).

19. H.D., *The Walls Do Not Fall*, in *Trilogy* (New York: New Directions, 1973), 3. The volume also contains *Tribute to the Angels* and *The Flowering of the Rod*. Hereafter, I cite the poems parenthetically as *Walls*, *Tribute*, and *Flowering*.

20. For the centrality of images of Christ's side wound and heart within Moravian theology, see Aaron Spencer Fogelman, *Jesus Is Female: Moravians and Radical Religion in Early America* (Phila-

delphia: University of Pennsylvania Press, 2008), and Craig D. Atwood, *Community of the Cross: Moravian Piety in Colonial Bethlehem* (College Station: Penn State University Press, 2012). There is much about this background in H.D.'s prose work. For a biographical account, see Robinson, *H.D.: Life and Work*, 3–9. For careful reflection on how to read the prose and its relationship to autobiography, see Nephie J. Christodoulides, "Facts and Fictions," in *Cambridge Companion to H.D.*, 23–36.

21. This is a point made tellingly, and repeatedly, by Jacques Derrida, although it is often missed in readings of his work on sovereignty, power, and violence. See especially Jacques Derrida, *Rogues: Two Essays on Reason*, trans. Pascale-Anne Brault and Michael Naas (Chicago: University of Chicago Press, 2005).

22. I am grateful to Hent de Vries for asking a crucial question that helped me clarify this point. The kind of minimal theology De Vries sees in Theodor Adorno, or the epistemic humility demanded by Immanuel Kant, are quite different, in my view, from apophatic or negative theology as they are articulated within the Christian tradition. It seems to me a mistake to call this kind of epistemic humility negative theology. Minimal theology is much more suited to the task. See Hent de Vries, *Minimal Theologies: Critiques of Secular Reason in Adorno and Levinas*, trans. Geoffrey Hale (Baltimore, MD: Johns Hopkins University Press, 2005).

23. For salutary reminders of this point and discussions of its implications for the humanities, see the entire issue of *Social Text* 34, no. 2 (2016), but especially, Nico Baumbach, Damon R. Young, and Genevieve Yue, "Introduction: For a Political Critique of Culture." Also relevant is the large body of work devoted to neoliberalism.

24. Although Susan Howe writes a great deal about the literature of the United States, she does not write explicitly about H.D. anywhere that I can find. She did teach *Trilogy* regularly during the 1980s when she was at SUNY-Buffalo, however, and a key couplet from *Trilogy* appears as an epigraph to *Singularities* (Hanover, NH: Wesleyan University Press, 1990), published just before *The Non-*

conformist's Memorial (and written at the same time as many of the
poems contained in the latter volume). The epigraph is: "under her
drift of veils / and she carried a book."

As with H.D., I have been reading and rereading Howe's work,
and the emergent—now well established—criticism of that work,
since the late 1980s. It is difficult for me always to know where
various insights embedded in my reading come from, but I can
say that I have been enormously helped by the following studies,
even when I don't fully agree. For important full-length studies of
Howe's work, see Lew Daly, *Swallowing the Scroll: Late in a Prophetic
Tradition with the Poetry of Susan Howe and John Taggart* (Buffalo,
NY: M Press, 1994); Rachel Tzvia Back, *Led by Language: The Poetry
and Poetics of Susan Howe* (Tuscaloosa: University of Alabama
Press, 2002); Stephen Collis, *Through Words of Others: Susan Howe
and Anarcho-Scholasticism* (Victoria, BC: English Literary Studies, 2006); Elisabeth W. Joyce, *"The Small Space of a Pause": Susan
Howe's Poetry and the Spaces Between* (Lewisburg, PA: Bucknell University Press, 2010); Will Montgomery, *The Poetry of Susan Howe:
History, Theology, Authority* (New York: Palgrave Macmillan, 2010);
and W. Scott Howard, *Archive and Artifact: Susan Howe's Factual Telepathy* (Northfield, MA: Talisman, 2019). Also on Howe and H.D.,
see Kathleen Crown, "Documentary Memory and Textual Agency:
H.D. and Susan Howe," *How2* 1, no. 3 (2000), accessed June 28,
2020, https://www.asu.edu/pipercwcenter/how2journal/archive
/online_archive/v1_3_2000/current/readings/crown.html.

I have also been inspired by the modes of reading articulated in
Kathleen Fraser, *Translating the Unspeakable: Poetry and the Innovative Necessity* (Tuscaloosa: University of Alabama Press, 2000),
and Juliana Spahr, *Everybody's Autonomy: Connective Reading and
Collective Identity* (Tuscaloosa: University of Alabama Press, 2001).
My greatest debts, though, are likely to Howe's own critical and
other prose writings. See Susan Howe, *My Emily Dickinson* (Berkeley: North Atlantic Books, 1985); Susan Howe, *The Birth-mark: Unsettling the Wilderness in American Literary History* (Hanover, NH:
Wesleyan University Press, 1993); Susan Howe, *Spontaneous Particu-*

lars: *The Telepathy of Archives* (New York: New Directions, 2014); and Susan Howe, *The Quarry* (New York: New Directions, 2015).

25. The title of the first sequence and of the book is taken from Edmund Calamy's *The Nonconformist's Memorial; Being an Account of the Lives, Sufferings, and Printed Works of the Two Thousand Ministers Ejected from the Church of England, chiefly by the Act of Uniformity, Aug. 24, 1666*, first published in England in 1702. The text's title is self-explanatory, its history very complex.

For a handful of the many studies devoted to Howe's *The Nonconformist's Memorial*, see Susan Schultz, "Exaggerated History," *Postmodern Culture* 4, no. 2 (1994); Peter Nicholls, "Unsettling the Wilderness: Susan Howe and American History," *Contemporary Literature* 37, no. 4 (1996): 586–601; Elisabeth A. Frost, "'Unsettling' America: Susan Howe and the Antinomian Tradition," in *The Feminist Avant-Garde in American Poetry* (Iowa City: University of Iowa Press, 2003), 105–35 (Frost makes the link to H.D.'s *Trilogy*); G. Matthew Jenkins, "The Nearness of Poetry: Susan Howe's *The Nonconformist's Memorial*," in *Poetic Obligation: Ethics in Experimental American Poetry after 1945* (Iowa City: University of Iowa Press, 2008), 159–81; Norman Finkelstein, "Susan Howe: History as Séance," in *On Mount Vision: Forms of the Sacred in Contemporary Poetry* (Iowa City: University of Iowa Press, 2010), 114–37.

Of the many insightful interviews with Howe, of particular pertinence for this text is "An Interview with Susan Howe by Lynn Keller," in *Innovative Women Poets: An Anthology of Contemporary Poetry and Interviews*, ed. Elisabeth A. Frost and Cynthia Hogue (Iowa City: University of Iowa Press, 2006). And for a fascinating account of teaching with the text, see G. Mathew Jenkins, "'My Susan Howe' or 'Howe to Teach,'" in *Poetry and Pedagogy: The Challenge of the Contemporary*, ed. Joan Retallack and Juliana Spahr (New York: Palgrave Macmillan, 2006), 213–23.

26. For insightful comments on the ways in which Howe's poetry and poetic prose moves between different editions, and an extremely helpful bibliography, see Howard, *Archive and Artifact*.

27. Susan Howe, *The Nonconformist's Memorial* (New York: New Directions, 1993), 4. Hereafter cited parenthetically as *Memorial*.

28. For the primary texts around Ann Hutchinson, see David
D. Hall, ed., *The Antinomian Controversy, 1636–39: A Documentary
History* (Durham, NC: Duke University Press, 1990), and the second
edition, which includes a preface, published in 1992. See also two
studies of particular importance for Howe, Amy Schrager Lang,
*Prophetic Woman: Ann Hutchinson and the Problem of Dissent in the
Literature of New England* (Berkeley: University of California Press,
1987), and Patricia Caldwell, *The Puritan Conversion Narrative: The
Beginnings of American Expression* (Cambridge: Cambridge University Press, 1983).

29. Although the spacing of the first two, page-length poems
can be reproduced in citation, this becomes more and more difficult as we move into the book. I have given an approximate sense
here, although as I wrote above, the page looks quite different
and includes other marks. Many people have written insightfully
about Howe's use of the page and her beginnings as a visual artist.
W. Scott Howard argues, I think correctly, that these visual effects
intensify in the late 1980s, at the same time Howe turns her attention most fully to the history of the United States and the violence
on which it rests. See Howard, *Archive and Artifact*, 8–30. See also
Ming-Quian Ma, "Articulating the Inarticulate: *Singularities* and
the Countermethod in Susan Howe," in *American Women Poets in the
Twenty-First Century*, ed. Claudia Rankine and Juliana Spahr (Hanover, NH: Wesleyan University Press, 2002), 329–52.

30. Of course, the whole history of English Revolution lies here,
in the name of a popular seventeenth-century ballad, made the
title of Marxist historian Christopher Hill's history of the period.
See Christopher Hill, *The World Turned Upside Down: Radical Ideas
during the English Revolution* (New York: Penguin, 1984).

31. Is this akin, in some way, to Sidney's and Luther's emphasis
on the vivacity of the Psalms as opposed to debates about their right
interpretation? Although Howe, I think, would argue—as would
I—that interpretation is always also already happening. How do
we best describe, then, the difference? On this issue, see Constance
Furey's essay in this volume.

32. On this sequence, see Jessica Wilkinson, "Resurrecting

Absence: Susan Howe's *A Bibliography of the King's Book or, Eikon Basilike* and the Historically Unspoken," *Cultural Studies Review* 14, no. 1 (2008): 161–78.

33. "Poets aren't reliable. But poetry may be. I don't think you can divorce poetry from history and culture. The photographs of children during the war in Europe, when I was a small child and the Holocaust was in progress—not only the Holocaust but the deaths of millions of people in Europe and Asia—prevented me from ever being able to believe history is only a series of justifications or that tragedy and savagery can be theorized away. I've recently been editing the question-from-the-audience section of a book . . . that consists of lectures some of us gave for a course Charles Bernstein gave at the New School last year. Someone in the audience said, 'Is anything real? I personally don't know if anything is real.' In the text, in a printed bracket, there is the word *laughter*. During the real event, the audience must have laughed, and I was too preoccupied at the time to notice. When I saw *laughter* in the brackets, it made me angry. There is real suffering on this little planet. I mean we can discuss whether the Hittites believed in chronology and history before Herodotus, and in Bensonhurst, Brooklyn, this month, a young African American man was murdered by a gang of Italian American teenagers. Where did the poison of racial hatred in America begin? Will it ever end? Why are we such a violent nation? Why do we have such contempt for powerlessness? I feel compelled in my work to go back, not to the Hittites but to the invasion or settling, or whatever current practice calls it, of *this* place. I am trying to understand what went wrong when the first Europeans stepped on shore here. They came here for some reason, something pushed them. What pushed them? Isn't it bitterly ironic that many of them were fleeing the devastation caused by enclosure laws in Britain, and the first thing they did here was put up fences? Racism is by no means unique to America. There are things that must never be forgotten. It's not a laughing matter." This is from an interview with Edward Foster, first printed in the journal *Talisman* and republished in Howe, *Birth-mark*, 163–64.

34. On "Melville's Marginalia," the final section of *The Noncon-formist's Memorial*, see Megan Williams, "How Not to Erase(her): A Poetics of Posteriority in Susan Howe's *Melville's Marginalia*," *Contemporary Literature* 38, no. 1 (1997): 106–32, and Jessica Wilkinson, "'Out of Bounds of the Bound Margin': Susan Howe Meets Mangan in *Melville's Marginalia*," *Criticism* 53, no. 2 (2011): 265–94.

AFTERWARDS

An image appears in each of our essays, that of a woman, standing in the midst of library stacks, scanning the shelves. For Furey and Hammerschlag, the woman reflects their own relationships to their subjects. Furey asks what it is to read devotionally a canonical author, such as Luther, with all the commentary his work has elicited, all the possibilities it has opened, but also all the violence for which it is responsible. Hammerschlag, to the contrary, reckons with a gap, a void on the shelves where Sarah Kofman's books do not appear, because they are not grouped under her name but scattered elsewhere, with works on the authors about whom she writes. Hollywood describes Susan Howe's poetry and prose as centering on books, "books about books," encountered "as if by chance, in libraries" and sometimes discarded from them, then cut up and reconstituted into new forms. These three different images of women in the library represent the progression of the volume, which begins by reflecting on the ways we read and receive the canon, then asks how we read those who were excluded from it, but who were themselves devoted to these received traditions. Can we learn from their devotion, see it even as a form of subversion? Finally, in her engagement with Howe, Hollywood introduces the possibility that reading, even those books discarded by the library, might provide the opportunity for imagining a new non-place that is the future.

Coming to the end of the process of writing this book similarly provides a chance both for retrospection and prospection, a chance to consider what has occurred in the meantime and to imagine the future. Each of these essays reflects on the ways in which the act of reading dramatizes the tension between these two temporal modes. We conclude this book as the year 2020 itself comes to a close, as the outcome of one of the most critical elections in US history is finalized and the first inoculations for a virus that is still ravaging the world distributed. The exercise of writing in a year marked by overlapping crises sharpens our sense of how perspective is temporally indexed. We often require the distance of time—great swaths of time—in order to be able to witness and name the moments when history's pages turn, but this year it feels as though we are perched on its deckled edge. The rush of the turn provides only a second of stillness, like that moment at the crest of a wave when we anticipate the violence of the break but cannot even begin to make sense of what will be washed out to sea and what will remain.

It is enticing to think at the end of 2020 that the worst is behind us, indeed, that we can even put the past behind us. All three of these essays insist that the practice of devoted reading teaches us something quite different. For us, the conjunction of religion and literature reveals the complexity and intricacy of our entwined relations to others—past, present, future, historical, and fictional—and thus enables the imagining of new forms of sociality that better take these ties into account. We could never have known when we began this book how closely the public health crisis that brought about so much death, destruction, and disruption in 2020 would mirror our claims. Seeking to contain a pandemic, epidemiologists ask us to isolate, alone or in small groups, familial or otherwise, because we are all, as a species and beyond our species, so intimately connected. The forms of sociality essential to human life and flourishing are, cruelly, the air through which the virus spreads, sickens, and kills. That the physical substrate for survival is undertaken by essential workers, often poorly paid, often nonwhite, whose health has not been protected in the United States in the ways the situation demands, is a tragedy compounding the tragedy through which we are living.

The three of us, able to work from home, turned to our libraries (although the actual university library was often inaccessible), to our books, and to each other (in words and meetings enabled by new technologies) in order to overcome our isolation. We recognize that the library is at best an ambivalent symbol. It is a repository of privilege, a place of order and quiet, whose access is too often policed in order to maintain the distinctions that perpetuate the unequal meting out of pain. And yet, it is also a repository of records, the archive of human attempts to classify, understand, and respond to a world that is anything but just. Libraries are brimming with accounts of war, famine, and mass atrocity. They contain shelves of thought that justify human aggression, as well as narratives of suffering and protest, representations of the quotidian and the otherworldly. Innumerable stories are told only obliquely, interstitially in the books and records on its shelves, and others—more than we can ever know—do not appear at all. Yet standing among what *is* there creates connections across time and place. To try to think with and through both those present and absent is a form of engagement that must also always be a reckoning and an imagining of possible futures.

Reading is, on one account, anything but heroic. As the three of us have met from the shelter of our own homes over the past twelve months to discuss our essays about reading and to map out this book, we have felt that intensely. At the same time, the very experience of isolation has been the most telling indicator of human interconnection. The virus reveals vividly (and viciously) the way in which one small human action ricochets through the lives of more people than we can ever know. It exposes the lie of a political theory that constitutes humans as discrete bundles of choices and personal freedoms. We see our project as one with political implications, precisely because each of us believes that our interconnectivity must be foregrounded in conceptions of human subjectivity, in relation both to the past and to the present. We believe, moreover, that what we read and how we read shape assumptions about what is essential, dispensable, and changeable. Reading is a form of interconnectedness that can itself be transformative. It can amplify and sometimes alter our vision of reality, focus our attention on how we relate to one another, and, indeed, bring new modes of sociality into being.

In our essays and through our conversation we have tried to articulate, and to model, the ways in which we think reading, reading devotedly and engaging others with fidelity, shifts the foundational assumptions for political engagement. Instead of grounding our accounts of the political subject in freedom, rights, and independence, we begin with relationality, fragility, and opacity. In the face of large-scale devastation, our textual interventions and those about which we write might be inconsequential. Indeed, the larger crises of our time require structural transformations that far exceed the individual. Yet as the coronavirus shows, each of us is imbricated in the larger worlds of which we are a part. No fundamental change can occur without the transformation of our very forms of sociality, transformations that require imagination and the modes of engagement necessary to nurture and elicit it. Each of our essays focuses on incidents of reading that both participate in and bear witness to human atrocity: the European wars of religion, the transatlantic slave trade, Auschwitz. In these encounters, literary, poetic, and exegetical, we reflect on the smallness of human life in its ineradicable connection to the existence of other beings, on the relative unimportance of any single act of interpretation, and yet its capacity to spark unforeseen, sometimes even momentous, consequences, on the noise even the quiet act of reading can make.